D1210033

Writing Realism

Writing Realism

Howells, James, and Norris
in the Mass Market

by Daniel H. Borus

The University of North Carolina Press
Chapel Hill   London

Library of Congress Cataloging-in-Publication Data

Borus, Daniel H.
  Writing realism : Howells, James, and Norris in the mass market /
by Daniel H. Borus.
      p.   cm.
    Bibliography: p.
    Includes index.

    ISBN 0-8078-1869-0 (alk. paper)
    1. American fiction—20th century—History and criticism.
2. American fiction—19th century—History and criticism.
3. Realism in literature. 4. Howells, William Dean, 1837–1920—
Criticism and interpretation. 5. James, Henry, 1843–1916—
Criticism and interpretation. 6. Norris, Frank, 1870–1902—
Criticism and interpretation. I. Title.
PS374.R37B67   1989   89-31157
813'.5'0912—dc19   CIP

Design by Julianne Mertz Whitling

The paper in this book meets the guidelines for permanence and
durability of the Committee on Production Guidelines for Book
Longevity of the Council on Library Resources

Printed in the United States of America
93   92   91   90   89   5   4   3   2   1

for Ben Borus, 1919–1989

Contents

Acknowledgments

It is one of the contentions of this book that no one truly writes in isolation. What is true for the realists is also true for me. In varying degrees, all scholarship is a collaborative effort. Although the following people are in no way responsible for the failures and idiosyncracies of analysis of the study, they were instrumental in its completion.

I have benefited and learned from discussions with Howard Brick. His trenchant and perceptive readings and suggestions for modification have made the text far better than it would have been without his intervention.

Joseph Kett and Dorothy Ross shared willingly their immense store of knowledge about the late nineteenth century and provided an encouragement that is rare. They saved me from errors of fact and emphasis. Although they certainly did not agree with all my conclusions, they were exemplary in their support. Robert Cross and Harold Kolb gave the work a close reading and rescued me from numerous infelicities of writing.

The idea that germinated the study originated in Theodore Mason's seminar on American realism. Mason's thorough survey of the dominant texts of the school helped illuminate the ambivalent nature of American realism and prompted speculation on its historical roots.

Gillian Brown gave the work a thorough reading and shared her notions of genre and textual analysis.

Emory Elliott read the work at a late stage and directed me to some of the more recent works in the New Historicist criticism. His National Endowment for the Humanities seminar on History and the American Novel helped clarify certain crucial points.

Other readings and helpful comments came from Edward Ayers, Thomas Fick, Barbara Hochman, Randall Kindelberger, Ann J. Lane, Bruce Ragsdale, David Rosen, Michael Steinberg, James West, and Christopher Wilson.

The staffs of The Clifton Waller Barrett Collection of the Alderman Library of the University of Virginia, the manuscripts division of Butler Library of Columbia University, Firestone Library of Princeton University, Houghton Library of Harvard University, the Berg Collection of the New York Public Library, and the New-York Historical Society were unfailingly courteous and responsive.

Whatever travails realist authors had in their dealings with their publishers, my relations with the University of North Carolina Press have been exemplary and friendly. Without the aid of the staff, this book would never have seen completion. Lewis Bateman and Iris Tillman Hill believed in and supported the book. Sandra Eisdorfer expertly managed the many steps of the production that transformed the manuscript into a commodity, albeit of a scholarly sort. Laura Oaks employed her astute critical eye to refine the text in ways for which I am most grateful.

Special thanks are due to my parents, Ben and Rita Borus, who, while not always sure why their son was taking so long to complete the study, understood its importance.

Writing Realism

CHAPTER ONE

History, Literature, and the American Realists

Ever since its emergence in the United States in the 1870s and 1880s literary realism, the subject of this study, has attracted critical scrutiny. The first attempts at explication and analysis came from the realists themselves. Forced by detractors to justify their practice, realists, many of whom were practicing critics, outlined the basic principles that constituted their chosen genre. In the process they laid out in considerable detail the formal properties of the novel that they valued and gave sophisticated readings of their key texts. When the academy embraced realism in the middle of the twentieth century and enshrined a number of its works in the canon, the number of critical studies of realism proliferated. In subsequent years each generation of commentators has put forth some interpretation of the literary explosion of the last third of the nineteenth century.[1]

The centrality of realism to literary studies might well prompt a reader to inquire why another book on the subject is needed. To justify itself another work must do more than either ratify previous findings or invert earlier work while addressing the same questions and staying within the same boundaries that have been marked out for the last one hundred years of criticism. We know much of *what* realism was (and is), but we know less about *why* realism was. It is this last problem that this book takes as its fundamental point of departure. This study is not a literary taxonomy in which common elements are discovered and texts are assigned places within or outside realism, or a reinterpretation of major works, or grand historical speculation in which some facile correspondence between the spirit of the age of industrialism and the nature of the texts is postulated and then proven. Rather it poses a deceptively simple question: why did a significant number of serious novelists choose to write realist texts in the late nineteenth century? Put another way, why was the privileged literary form of the late nineteenth-century United States one that proclaimed as its aims accurate notation and natural expression? This is as much a historical question as a literary one, and this book explores the ways in which history presented certain choices to novelists and novelists responded to those choices.

Literary realism would at first glance seem to be on the periphery of present-day historical studies. During the 1970s and 1980s historians have treaded softly in the realm of literature. Recent textbooks barely mention the rise of realism. In *The Great Republic*, to cite one recent effort, John DeForest's *Miss Ravenel's Conversion from Secession to Loyalty* rates mention for its attempt to settle the intellectual disputes that led to the Civil War, not for its pioneering attempts at realism. William Dean Howells is accorded less space and then only for his assumption of the editorship of the *Atlantic*. Henry James is noted for his self-imposed exile, and Frank Norris receives no mention at all.[2] Literature studies have fallen into the netherworld of a specialty-laden discipline. Where once the major works of United States fiction would have been at the heart of cultural studies, most historians have opted for an outlook that concentrates on the symbols and rituals of American life. At the 1977 Wingspread Conference on New Directions in American Intellectual History, cultural anthropology, rather than literature, emerged as the primary buttress to intellectual history. Howells rated a mention only to the extent that he entered a discourse network; how this network contributed to the character of realism was only a tangential issue.[3] Henry James was cited as a negative reference point, a reminder of the days of intellectual history in which great writers were assumed to represent the whole of American thought.

A number of factors account for this shift in focus. The social history of the 1960s is one such force. In its concern for mass phenomena and exacting measurement, social history has by implication suggested that "high" culture was a minority pursuit, limited only to a fairly unrepresentative elite. Furthermore the exasperating array of literary critical theories has made criticism impenetrable for the nonspecialist. Structuralism, deconstruction, hermeneutics, phenomenology, and semiotics have made work with literary texts far more difficult and have left historians far less assured about their statements. Equally unsettling have been the constant revision of the canon and the challenge to the very idea of a canon itself. Within the realm of historical studies themselves, the American Studies school of myth and symbols carried with it an assumption of a unified American mind that many historians today find untenable.[4]

While these reservations point out the danger of unwarranted generalization, it does not follow that a study of realism holds such limited value for the intellectual historian. Historians study ideas to understand how men and women conceived of their times and their place in them.[5] The value of intellectual history lies in its ability to map shifts in currents of thought and to reveal the connections between diverse individual thinkers, including links unrecognized by historical actors. The strength of intellectual history is its demonstration of both the possibilities and limitations contained in the postulates and conceptions that governed past thought. The specialty addresses not only what was thought and how it was thought but what was capable of being thought. If thought is first and foremost a confrontation with the possibilities of the historical moment through the medium of ideas, then even the most withdrawn and elusive thinker, struggling in apparent anonymity, commands our attention, for he or she ultimately is no more able to transcend history than the most popular one. There may indeed be times in which such a thinker reveals more starkly the conflicts and possibilities of an age than his or her more conventional counterparts.

The novel, it must be admitted, poses special problems for the historian of ideas. Unlike sociology, philosophy, and other endeavors more readily usable by the intellectual historian, the novel does not proceed by openly making a claim about the nature of history or society. It is not, strictly speaking, a system of ideas supported by a mode of argumentation and evidence. Its practitioners are rarely systematic thinkers in the manner of a John Dewey or a William James. Indeed, the novel is not, at least on its surface, about ideas at all. Rather it deals in its eighteenth- and nineteenth-century forms with narrative. The story and its characters, not the analysis, no matter how much it informs an author's treatment, dominate a novel. Unlike other forms of intellectual production that aim for the construction of general laws and principles, the novel has as its object the specific and individual. This central characteristic gives to the novel its own logic. It is one of the reasons that we can identify a novel as fiction and not an economic treatise or even journalism. To complicate matters further, at times the logic of narration endows novels with a second voice, one that is separate from the actual narrator. Novels often seem to know more than their authors, and it is often a mistake, as a number of commentators have remarked, to identify the narrator with the author.[6]

The paradoxical position of the novel in intellectual history—that the form is both the most accessible to the general reader and problematically related to the concerns and methods of the historian—can be addressed by regarding fiction as a particular form of language whose various rules of composition place it in a discourse about history and society. Like other thinkers, the novelist may not be (and in the case of fictionists, is usually not) aware of the implications of the use of the rules adapted to meet the desired end. The stress on the rules of discourse is an important one because, whereas the novel is a social vision, it is not an unmediated one. The form of composition simultaneously alters the vision and confers meaning itself. Consequently the intellectual historian must take an interior view of fiction in order to excavate the ideas contained within the formal aspects and to chart fully the terrain in which the novel was written and to which it responds.[7]

It is, in my opinion, not quite correct to regard literary realism as if it were solely an expression of the class position of its practitioners. Dismissing realism as "middle class" expression or "high culture" is a limited and self-defeating tactic. Such formulations are not so much false as incomplete. To be sure, realist writers belonged to that amorphous entity, the urban middle class. That class, however, did not exist as an impervious and complete whole. It drew its identity as much from what it denied as what it affirmed. A conception of the middle class could hardly have existed without the "negative references" of immigrant workers, black migrants, and restless agrarians. It was with these and other groups that the urban middle classes struggled, concurred, and lived. In the course of creating a cultural life realists invariably incorporated, in however disfigured a form, experiences other than their own. Hence their ideology did not derive purely from their origins and allegiances. One of the tasks that realists set for themselves was the construction of a common culture in which all classes could partake. This culture would serve, as we shall see, to reforge bonds that national growth had rent. However mistaken their belief that their novels spoke to and for all Americans, it is unquestionably true that realists took to empirical observation with unprecedented enthusiasm because they felt that through such activities they could transcend the divisions and fragmentations that had accompanied capitalist development. Such a project invariably brought with it the modifications that accompany the experience of history.

Just as the class origins of the realists did not prevent attempts to reach beyond the limits of class, so too did realism assume an importance beyond the numbers who directly consumed it. Historians, it is true, are more comfortable with recorded instances of direct influence and happier with proof of actual readership. Such an approach puts undue stress on conscious understanding of intent and influence. To rely solely on acknowledged influences is to suggest that an age speaks for and explains itself. Realism was just as much a way of seeing as a set of texts, and those ways of seeing permeated the entire culture through indirect borrowings, common material, and social expectations. Mass culture may not have completely copied realism, but it shared certain preoccupations of representation and subject matter. The value of realism may just be that it gave comprehensive but by no means complete expression to a set of challenges of the late nineteenth century. Frank Norris was not so incorrect when he argued that the novel was the expression of the modern age because it dealt with the preoccupations of the age. Those preoccupations were felt even by those who never heard of Frank Norris or William Dean Howells.

Though most students of literature would generally agree that history and literature are intertwined (New Critics and some deconstructionists are here firm dissenters), the nature of the connection remains elusive. There are, I think, three ways in which the relationship has been considered. In the first of these, perhaps the most unsatisfactory for both historians and literary critics, the literary text is seen as a direct reflection of the history in which it was written. Historical events and conditions are viewed as measures against which the text can be measured for fidelity. Books are read for their ability to confirm what other historical sources have indicated, and authors are judged by their ability to evaluate these conditions.

This first historical approach to realism was that of Vernon Louis Parrington.[8] As he saw the matter, the strength of realism was its ability to tap the changes that industrialization and the rise of scientific thought effected. Although Parrington regarded realism as the first literary tradition to protest the excesses of the age, he felt that it did not go far enough. Naturalism, realism's successor, was in Parrington's view the genre most committed to literary resistance to the new industrial order. William Dean Howells, he believed, evaded the "deeper and more tragic realities that reach to the heart of life." Howells failed to "probe the depths of emotional experience. Neither the life of the spirit nor the passions of the flesh is the stuff from which he weaves his stories. The lack—and allowing for all his solid excellence [which Parrington chose, mistakenly, to call Marxian] it remains grave—sprang in part from his own timid nature that recoiled from the gross and the unpleasant, and in part from the environment in which he perfected his technique."[9]

Parrington's method makes the ability of literature to reproduce the major characteristics of its moment their central criterion of evaluation of literary contribution. Literature is most valuable when it acts convincingly as reportage and serves as a type of campaign document for various political parties of intellectuals, views most congenial to a historian in search of historical facts.[10] Lost in the concern to reduce literature to its *overt* political content is much that both novelists and critics of all stripes find as essential; narrative styles and use of language are two major concerns that are given short shrift. For Parrington, not surprisingly, "literary" claims were restrictive and obfuscatory. Howells, for instance, failed to penetrate to the "real" issues of the day because, Parrington wrote, he "came late to an interest in sociology, held back by the strong literary and aesthetic cast of his mind."[11]

Parrington today is read as a primary source and not for his critical analyses. Few critics share his unmodified enthusiasm for naturalism or his schematic division of literary history into two dialectical opposite camps contending through United States history. His stress on literature as documentary evidence to be judged against a discoverable historical record, however, is less a subject of debate among historians. It is this limitation in the conception of a literary text that a second method of linking history and literature has most recently addressed. Known as the New Historicism, this tendency has paid closer attention to the "literariness" of literary texts. Less willing to discard critical attention to narrative technique and the status of language, scholars in a wide variety of fields have adopted a closer reading of literary texts than did Parrington and those who followed in his wake. These techniques and interests are then marshaled toward a historical end—discovering how history forms and, in some cases, is formed in the literary text.

It would be a mistake to group all new approaches under a single rubric of interpretation. As Emory Elliott has demonstrated, what is being called the New Historicism has a number of important variants, many of which are ultimately not resolvable to a unified view.[12] One strain, which has parallel aims to those of intellectual historians, has been termed "ideological" criticism. Ideological critics, working on the assumption that history inheres in the literary text itself through the language deployed, identify the prevailing ideology of the text—what the text values and the ways in which it values. For such critics literature is in part a structured response to the historical situation amid which the author lives, regardless of whether that situation is spelled out in the text. The novel is a complex way of participating in the political and social conditions surrounding its making. Because the ideology of a text is rarely, if ever, directly given, the critic, alert to the contemporary uses of language and prevailing modes of ideology, must have recourse to a panoply of discourses in economics, law, and sociology, which have traditionally been the raw materials of intellectual history.[13]

Though historians can indeed profit from this second method, not all its implications are conducive to the interests of historians. Historians must be alert to assert their own uses of the past. First of all, there is often a tendency in the New Historicism to see parallel discourses as context, a kind of illuminating background that shows a correspondence with the literary text but has no causal relationship. In their dazzling—one might say promiscuous—use of companion discourses, some New Historicist critics obscure the linkage between history and the text. Since almost any discourse can be shown to be parallel to the text, the end is that none truly influence or affect it. Contextualization looks like it is addressing the problem, but lacking mechanisms of interplay and, to use a word out of fashion these days, causation, its final result is detachability—the divorce of the text from mechanisms that reproduce social life. Indeed, for some especially influenced by French theories of deconstruction, the very idea of causation is suspect, a throwback to the false positivism of nineteenth-century science. Some of these critics have taken note of the similarities in language and narrative between the novel and studies of the past and have concluded that historical accounts are just as metaphorical and indeterminate as fiction. Only historians, clinging to a view of language that holds that words unambiguously represent the objects and events that they purport to describe, either do not know these limitations or refuse to acknowledge them. Ironically one result of these new criticisms is to make history a monolithic whole that is virtually impervious to human aspiration and action. At the same time that their work denies a hierarchy of causes in favor of a multiplicity of them, some New Historicists also assert the impossibility of even partially escaping or transcending history. Walter Benn Michaels, for instance, contends that novelists cannot comment on or criticize their own times, for that implies being above or outside them. All an author can do is exemplify his or her historical moment. In effect history, rather than an author shaped by an interacting with history, writes the novel.[14]

Historians as well must bear in mind a difference in emphasis between themselves and literary critics. For literary critics the major focus is the text itself. New historical work in literary criticism has turned to historical information to formulate fresh and enlightening interpretations of texts. Though historians ignore such endeavors at their own peril, they primarily want to know what texts can tell us about the past. Intellectual historians in particular are interested in understanding how historical subjects understood their historical situation. This difference of analytical stance is subtle, for any writing of history that includes inadequate analysis is one that disqualifies itself from serious consideration, but drawing significant generalizations about the past is the work to which historians have committed themselves. Historically based literary criticism reverses the emphasis, asking What does this text mean? This disciplinary difference is not simply a matter of the literary critic's paying more attention to the text than the historian does. It is also that the fundamental question a historian poses is Why did x happen and not x' or y?

The emphasis that New Historicists have placed on interpreting texts has sometimes obscured another aspect of the impact of history on literature, the historically specific way in which the text was written. Whereas the text itself is seen as problematic, riven with contradictory discourses and silences on key terms and at crucial moments, the making—the actual process of writing— goes uninvestigated. Whatever the validity of excluding history from an interpretation of the text, people write fiction for people. Hence in the process of producing a text authors inevitably enter into relationships with their material, their audience, and the society as a whole. To cite a number of possibilities that is by no means exhaustive: writers may either create or report their material; they may preach to their audience, guide it, or engage in egalitarian discourse with it; and writers may see themselves as direct defenders of the existing order or in opposition to their society. We may refer to this complex of relationships, following Raymond Williams, as a "practice."[15] Whether or not the author explicitly conceives of writing as a practice, each novel poses an answer to the problems of the nature of the novel-writing process, the constitution of the intended audience and the methods of insuring comprehension, and the social purpose of literature. The way the narration is formed, the language deployed, the particular stance toward events—all these textual elements—are the result of the specific set of problems around writing a novel at a given time.

This is by no means to contend that only a single practice exists at a given time or that a practice dictates in some rigid fashion a genre. Otherwise only a single genre would prevail and all texts in a genre would closely resemble each other. Clearly realism was not the only genre of the late nineteenth century and, as we shall see, not all realist texts follow the same principles. It is to argue, however, that all variants of realism bear a familial relationship by virtue of similar choices made by their authors, and it is these choices that are influenced by the particular history in which they are made.

One advantage of this third mode to the study of history and fiction, which is the approach of the present study, is that it grounds literary production in historically determined structures. Not only the text, but also its making, is historical. Concentrating on literary practice allows us to discern both the purposes of a literary text at a given time and how those purposes were enacted within a history that both liberated and limited communication. This emphasis calls our attention to the ways in which novelists confronted their own history, by reminding us that the confrontation was conducted in specific historic circumstances. The issue under investigation is less what was produced than how was it produced. The answer to the latter question can then throw additional light on the former problem, for it gives us a clue to what kinds of expression were possible.

Using the concept of literary practice enables us to reopen the problem of genre. Traditionally explanations of genre have concentrated upon common philosophical tenets. Texts within a given genre share a common view of reality or history. H. Wayne Morgan gave a representative opinion in his *American Writers in Rebellion*: "Both Realism and Naturalism are attitudes of mind rather than techniques of writing."[16] Those who have tried to answer the question of why realism emerged in the late nineteenth century have often pointed to the prevailing cachet of science and its stress on observation and exactness. Realism borrowed from this ideology and sought to mimic the new technologies of reproduction that industrial advances made possible. But we can also see genre as a shared response to the historical problems of writing at a given period. From this perspective what made realism was that its practitioners formulated similar answers to a set of problems. These answers committed them to specific types of texts and not others.

Readers will note that I make little distinction between varieties of realism. Conventional critical theory demarcates a literature that is concerned with the average, common, and typical from one involved with brute force, animality, and the subhuman. The former literature is designated realism, the latter naturalism.[17] Yet realists and naturalists, for all their sizable differences in viewpoint, posed similar answers to the problem of novel writing. From different generations and facing different historical problems, they nonetheless had fairly similar ideas about the value of literature, the nature of the work process, the relationship of author and audience, and the social position of the author. That different types of texts could result from these realist techniques suggests that the process of writing left open a series of possibilities for the novel that were significantly broad.

My approach is not, strictly speaking, biographical. Individual differences are registered, but they are registered faintly. There are two reasons for this deliberate choice. First, we have an excellent set of biographies for the major American realists. Leon Edel's majestic five-volume biography of Henry James, Edwin Cady's two-volume study of William Dean Howells and Kenneth Lynn's one-volume work about the same author, Justin Kaplan's study of Mark Twain, and R. W. B. Lewis's work on Edith Wharton are definitive and handle the particular and individual pressures with aplomb. Only Frank Norris and Harold Frederic lack modern treatments, and the paucity of materials makes such a venture problematic. Second, and more importantly, my intention is to demonstrate that the structure of realist practice superseded individual differences. Individual predispositions gave final and differentiating qualities to the novels, but it is the contours of realism, not the individual texts, that lie at the heart of this book.

This concentration on the determinations of the broad boundaries of literary realism is why I have made little mention of the two pivotal factors of race and gender. These are not simply and solely biographical elements of authors that add distinguishing marks to their fiction. Race and gender can also be considered as structural influences of behavior and thought. No complete history of literary discourse in the United States can ignore these two dimensions of both authorship and readership.[18] Women and Afro-Americans belong in the roll of important contributors to literary realism. Edith Wharton and Charles Chesnutt were major practitioners of the genre; so too were Sarah Orne Jewett and Mary Wilkins Freeman, who have sometimes been derogatorily referred to as "local colorists," as if they were somehow unworthy of the more serious title of realist. I have instead concentrated on the primary structural relationships into which racial and gender factors ultimately entered. As I have indicated, this book does not aim to be the full story of literary realism. It deals less with the crucial themes of realism or the historical makeup of the United States in the years in which realism flourished than with the structural elements that shaped the problem of writing a novel in the late nineteenth century. I have tried to isolate the factors that all realists confronted regardless of their race and gender. Black and female authors still faced the problems of commodification of literature, the fragmentation of discourse, and the social purpose of literature. As realists, their responses tended to tally with other realists'.

I do, however, concentrate on three major and diverse authors: William Dean Howells, Henry James, and Frank Norris. Although Stephen Crane, Mark Twain, Harold Frederic, and Theodore Dreiser figure in the study, their careers and writings are less central. The selection may seem arbitrary, but the choice of Howells (1837–1920), James (1843–1916), and Norris (1870–1902) rested on their efforts to justify writing as a profession and a calling. Not only do the three represent different variants of realism, but they attempted to derive a systematic theory of realism and its practice. Despite their differences, Howells's *Criticism and Fiction* (1891) and *Literature and Life* (1902), James's "The Art of Fiction" (1886) and countless other essays, and Norris's *The Responsibilities of the Novelist* (1901) stand as the first postbellum American works in which major novelists sought to explain in precise terms the nature of their craft. Collectively they fashioned a theory of how to write a novel under the conditions imposed by the mass market in literature. Translating these strictures and attitudes into actual prose invariably led realists to employ many of the formal elements associated with the genre. In a real sense the tenets of realism owed much to novelists' writing through their problems in the course of production.

The chapters that follow detail the practice of realism—the techniques and relations that were unique to its time. Chapter 2 defines the genre and begins a brief history of previous literary practices in the United States. Chapter 3 describes the literature industry of the late nineteenth century and how it posed for writers the problem of defining literary value. Chapter 4 investigates the work process of realism and how the theory and practice conflicted. Chapter 5 explores the problems of audience fragmentation and the beginnings of authorial celebrity. Chapter 6 traces how ambiguous social position gave rise to "political" novels that sought psychological, rather than political, solutions. Chapter 7 places the sum of realist practice in historical context.

CHAPTER TWO

The "Simple, Natural, and Honest"

American Literary Realism in
the Late Nineteenth Century

*It remained for realism to assert that fidelity to experience and probability
of motive are essential conditions of a great imaginative literature.*
—William Dean Howells

N
o history of the late nineteenth century is complete without citation of
the impressive statistics on the growth of railroad mileage, steel tonnage, and
kilowatt hours or a listing of such remarkable new inventions as typewriters,
telephones, dynamos, linotypes, and blast furnaces. It is not simply the
changes in material life that have struck historians as significant about the era.
They have also noted the bewildering and sometimes sudden change in social
conditions and living patterns and have extensively chronicled the contours of
a new and puzzling urban life, the explosion of violent class conflict, and the
emergent features of a mass society.[1]

The understanding that an older way of American life was disintegrating and
a new one was being born is not just a retrospective view. Nineteenth-century
Americans also believed that their social world was in flux. This same turbu-
lence spawned a new set of discourses that aimed to explain more completely
the changes that industrialism had wrought. The history that featured monopolies, strikes, and mass consumption also brought to prominence new disciplines like sociology and updated established ones like history. Encompassing
such diverse explorations as the sociology of Lester Frank Ward and Charles
Horton Cooley, the history of Henry Adams and Charles Beard, the economics
of Richard Ely, the philosophy of John Dewey and Charles S. Peirce, and the

jurisprudence of Oliver Wendell Holmes and Louis Brandeis, the late nine-
teenth- and early twentieth-century intellectual ferment shared a new methodology and a new object of study. Believing that the older disciplines could
explain neither the new social relations nor the new sources of cohesion and
discord of industrial capitalism, American intellectuals set out to reformulate
both the concepts by which Americans understood their lives and the methods
necessary to live intelligently in a world that seemed at times beyond human
control.

Linking these varied investigations was an insistence that intellectual life
must rest on the compilation of facts about the external world from which
trained minds could formulate laws. Rejecting the older belief that the purpose
of intellectual discourse was to confirm preexisting standards of knowledge
and ratify eternal laws, the new disciplines stressed detailed and systematic
observation of an external world, the components of which constituted reality.
Only through conscientious adherence to a methodology patterned on that of
natural science could intellectuals understand how people actually behaved.[2]
In these new investigations facts themselves took on a new status. Information
was important for its functional value as well as its truth. The value of theory
was not its pristine worth as a completed system but its ability to help men
master their circumstances. If William James's notion of "the cash value" of an
idea often became in less open minds simply an apology for profit-seeking
behavior, its primary thrust was to stress that ideas first and foremost had uses.

These new intellectual discourses shared more than a common methodology; they also shared a vital new concept—society. The older disciplines had
failed fully to explain human conduct, not only because of their reliance on
ideal, rather than observed, categories but also because they were limited in
what they investigated. In "society," the new intellectuals of the late nineteenth
century hit upon a concept that described a space between the State as described in political theory and Man as understood in philosophy. The recognition of society as a rule-bound entity that was greater than the sum of its
individual parts enabled intellectuals to investigate both private and the public
spheres, as the latter was composed of the same elements as the former. This
discovery of community, which was the unity of self and others, as George
Mead noted in an appreciation in 1930, was the most important contribution of
the turn-of-the-century social scientist Charles Horton Cooley. "These ideas
[of self and others] differ from each other as they exist in the conscious
experience of different people, but they also have cores of identical content,
which in public consciousness act uniformly. . . . The 'other' lies in the same
field as that of the 'self.' It can be recognized as quite immediate as the self."[3]

Thus rooted, the concept of "society" allowed American thinkers to discover new and regular patterns of behavior and to explain how the pursuit of private ends did not result in anarchy or chaos.

Although literary realism did not fashion the claims to scientific precision that sociology did, it was an essential component of the intellectual movement of the late nineteenth century. Steeped in the intellectual environment of the period and drawing upon many of the same sources as the new or revitalized disciplines, realists brought to literature the same concern for the mapping of society and its behavioral rules and the same method of observing the concrete rather than replicating the abstract. Although realists often anticipated the new developments, they were equally eager to apply insights from other fields. In his capacity as editor of *Harper's*, William Dean Howells reviewed William James's *Principles of Psychology* (1890) and Thorstein Veblen's *Theory of the Leisure Class* (1898) and urged his fellow novelists to heed the analyses contained therein. The familial relationship between literary realism and the new sciences of society did much to bolster realists' claim that the genre was the literary form best suited to chronicle its own moment. Realism, Howells argued in *Criticism and Fiction* (1891), his explication of the genre, depicted "the simple, the natural, and the honest." It rejected the idealized portraits of a desiccated romanticism and took up the gauntlet of fidelity to experience and probability of motive. In the same way that romanticism had once broken with classicism to "widen the bounds of sympathy, level every barrier against aesthetic freedom, and escape from the paralysis of tradition," American literary realism presented itself as the modern form of literature.[4] Armed with new subject matter and representational techniques, American realists argued that the truthful treatment of material meant picturing men and women as they were, not as the writer wished they were. Where romantics had read Keats to indicate that Beauty was Truth, realists reversed the emphasis and contended that truth was beauty.[5]

As a discourse the realist novel had two distinct advantages over other disciplines. Unlike sociology, philosophy, or political science, the realist novel had no need to compartmentalize knowledge along disciplinary lines. As Howells argued in his lecture "Novel-Writing and Novel-Reading," novelists were to record all that they saw around them. Nothing was foreign to their experience and nothing could be automatically disregarded.[6] In addition, the novel was a popular form and not the province of specialists. Its practitioners were not striving to establish their scientific credentials or attach themselves to the academy, and its consumers did not require extraordinary or special train-ing. "Literature," Frank Norris exclaimed in a typically enthusiastic outburst,

"is of all the arts the most democratic; it is of, by and for the people in a fuller measure than even government itself."[7]

The realists drew concerted fire for their attack on prevailing literary conventions. Regarding realism as "common," "vulgar," and destructive of the highest ideals, men like Noah Porter, Hamilton Wright Mabie, and E. C. Stedman, who combined philosophical rigor, a pride in proper technique, and a belief that great art ennobled, saw in realism mere copying and a whiff of materialism.[8] Mabie discerned a defect of warmth and imagination in William Dean Howells's work. Howells and the realists, he felt, were too eager to let observation do the work of the insight. The realist novel consisted of surfaces but not essences and was consequently inferior work.[9] The popular press was even more critical. In *The Forum* William Roscoe Thayer labeled realism "obscene" and complained that it dehumanized life through its insistence on determinism. Maurice Thompson, who began his career as a disciple of Howells, turned on his sponsor in the 10 July 1886 issue of *The Critic*. In an article entitled "The Analysts Analyzed" he railed at the supposed stress of realism on "foibles and peccadilloes of character," its aversion to happy and pleasing endings, and its worship of the vulgar.[10]

Thompson's denunciation and those like it did not slow the advance of the new literature. The year before Thompson's attack, American literary realism had scored its greatest popular success. In 1885 *The Century*, arguably the most august general circulation monthly, had published serials of William Dean Howells's *Rise of Silas Lapham*, Mark Twain's *Adventures of Huckleberry Finn*, and Henry James's *Bostonians*. The triumph of the realist triumvirate (James's work was less an artistic and financial success at the time than the other two) was not a matter of overnight change in sympathies or a sudden jump in literary methods. It had been twenty years in the making. Drawing on the concern of American intellectuals that literature match the glories of American republican institutions, Rebecca Harding Davis, John DeForest, and Edward Eggleston moved tentatively to explore new materials and methods. Although DeForest's *Miss Ravenel's Conversion from Secession to Loyalty* (1867) and Eggleston's *Hoosier Schoolmaster* (1871) did not entirely forgo formulaic plots, stereotypic characterization, and authorial editorializing, their refusal to confine themselves to materials from the drawing room made their efforts protorealist novels. Protorealism soon became realism. Beginning in the mid-1870s with William Dean Howells's *Their Wedding Journey* (1872) and Henry James's *Roderick Hudson* (1876), American authors undertook a series of new fictions that declared a departure from a literature that they believed had become so rarefied and study-bound that it simply trotted out

archetypes and caricatures for inspection and acclaim. Honing its representational techniques and developing its theoretical justifications, realism matured during the 1880s. Although the simultaneous appearance of Howells, Twain, and James may be reckoned as the literary high point of classical American realism, the movement possessed both vitality and diversity.

All three continued writing until the second decade of the twentieth century and influenced such notable practitioners as Edith Wharton, Henry Blake Fuller, and Robert Herrick. But American realism mined veins other than the one that Howells, James, and Twain had opened. Impressed with the power of the impersonal forces of environment and heredity to determine the behavior of men and women, Stephen Crane, Harold Frederic, Frank Norris, and Theodore Dreiser produced a literature that stressed "scenes of coercion."[11] Naturalists, believing that chance was simply another name for our lack of knowledge of causes, in effect charged realists of the 1880s with not being realistic enough. By the 1920s the Howellsian current had run its course. Although writers as diverse as F. Scott Fitzgerald and Sinclair Lewis followed realists in their concern for social portraiture, few championed the originators' causes. In his Nobel acceptance speech in 1930 Lewis ridiculed Howells as "a pious little old maid whose greatest delight is to have tea at the vicarage."[12]

The history of literary realism in the United States has more than its share of ironies and contradictions. Proclaimed as a literary revolution of the first order, it suffered setbacks in the marketplace and in the academy with unfailing regularity. Although the genre appeared prominently in the nation's leading publications (*Century* in the 1880s, *Harper's* in the 1890s, and essays in the *North American Review* in the first decade of the twentieth century), which by and large regarded themselves as custodians of past intellectual achievements and therefore should have been hostile to the changes that realism proposed in literary life and conduct, it never attained unquestioned supremacy among writers, critics, or readers. Labeled crude and immoral, most realists led personal lives of late Victorian propriety and rectitude. Seen as the harbinger of radical change by both its opponents and proponents, realism was the epitome of middle-class observation and aspiration. Proclaiming itself as natural and lacking artifice, it nonetheless required great practice and work.

Despite the campaign on its behalf in the 1880s, realism barely qualified as a coherent literary movement. Realists did not uniformly rally around a single set of principles. Two of its leading lights, Mark Twain and Henry James, had little use for and appreciation of the work of the other. A younger generation that came to maturity in the mid-1890s found its elders decidedly timid and "unrealistic," despite the pioneering efforts of Howells and James. Even the very term "realism" introduces confusion. Late nineteenth-century authors

used it to indicate that their form of writing dealt with the "real," and hence was the "truth." Grounding the narrative in the concrete and the reproducible represented a significant step toward truthful art. Yet romantics, while denigrating a literature bound to description of the tangible, never thought of themselves as writing lies. In the romantic tradition, which extends as far back as Plato, what was "true" was the deeper, eternal truths, not the perceivable and measurable. Observed phenomena were merely the appearance that truth took.[13]

As a creed, "the simple, natural, and honest" provides as many perplexities as guidelines. Although seemingly straightforward, the classic terms of Howellsian realism are by no means self-explanatory. Howells's strictures tell us more of what he valued than what realism accomplished; how one arrived at such a literature and what a simple, natural, and honest novel would look like remained vague. Howells did not remark on the matter, but the three terms are by no means unproblematic when juxtaposed. A "simple" presentation may obfuscate or obliterate actuality and thereby undercut the goal of "honest." And one need not be well versed in philosophical debates to see the difficulties inherent in advocating a literature that celebrated the "natural." The concept is a human construction that depends upon its polar opposite, the "unnatural," and it bespeaks a human condition in which men and women feel separated from their surroundings. The "natural" therefore is neither obvious nor objective. Further complicating Howells's project of producing a natural literature to describe a natural world is the implication that the world is somehow basic and permanent, an assertion that made representing the "truth" of change problematic.

Although the realists were the first group of American authors to produce a full body of theory about the purpose, function, and quality of literature, they violated their theoretical premises as often as they observed them. Fidelity to everyday life and to probability of motive were easier to theorize about than to realize. The classic texts of American realism boast more than their share of intruding narrators, improbabilities and coincidences, and cataclysmic or heightened moments of life deployed as plot devices. In addition to these textual qualities often associated with romanticism, realism also pointed ahead to modernism with the use of subjective narration, a stress on the fragmented self, and forays into symbolism and impressionism, all of which contradicted the realist dictum of an anchored reality.

The inability to isolate a specimen of pure realism has led to problems in classification. Some critics have rigidly separated realism from its younger and cruder cousin, naturalism. For them the 1890s represent a watershed in American letters in which one side of the divide, tame and literary, looks back to the masterworks of early American literature and the other, more vivid and uncontrolled, anticipates twentieth-century developments. For Lee Mitchell, writing in the *Columbia Literary History*, for instance, a crucial difference can be seen in the different conceptions of the self contained within various texts. Mitchell, among others, contrasts the realist sense of "a more or less unified" self with the naturalist assertion that there is no disjunction between "outer events and inner disposition."[14] While Walter Benn Michaels aims to dismiss the "old debate" over genres, arguing that it plunges the critic into the trap of positing a space between culture and literature in which the latter has the ability to comment on the former, he does admit some important differentiations between the two. He sees, for instance, in naturalism a concern over double identities that are necessary in order to have any identities at all. By this assertion he means that naturalism hints at the ways in which a category and its opposite are inextricably mixed. Starvation by death becomes the satiation of desire in Norris's *Octopus*; production and consumption become nearly identical in Gilman's "Yellow Wallpaper," and so on. He goes on further to note that whereas realism aims to "minimize excess," naturalism does not.[15]

Naturalists themselves were uncertain whether they merely extended the inheritance of the realists or stood for something new. On the one hand, Norris derided the tame and timid "tragedy of the broken teacup" of Howellsian realism in his famous "A Plea for Romantic Fiction," charging realism with a failure to acknowledge the deeper, elemental forces of life. On the other hand, he adopted the realist credo that the "function of the novelist of the present day is to comment upon life as he sees it."[16] In "An American School of Fiction?" he was full of praise for Howells, whose *Rise of Silas Lapham* and *A Modern Instance* had begun the task of constructing a legitimate American literature. Unfortunately, Norris noted, Howells had had no successors, and a false romanticism had arisen. Norris felt obligated to "protest against what I am sure every serious-minded reader must consider a lamentable discrowning."[17]

Some literary historians have explained the rise of realism as a product of material changes. As Eric Sundquist notes, realism was the literature of industrial development. "In the journey between the regions of rural and urban life, most of all in the tension that binds them together, lies the substance and spirit of American realism. Held in balance by the emerging techniques of industrial labor, by racial and class antagonisms, and by the twin energies of commerce and social progress, the period's fiction speaks eloquently of the moral complexity and paradoxical freedoms of modern American life."[18] Yet realist aesthetic principles, as the modern literary history of France indicates, need not be developed in an industrial society. Balzac hardly lived in industrial times. Unlike European realism, which emerged in the early portion of the

Dean Howells's Bartley Hubbard of *A Modern Instance*, and Dreiser's Carrie Meeber are typical without solidifying into rigid types. For all their representativeness, they are not reducible to the social class or group to which they belong. Paralleling developments in psychology, literary realism placed great stress on exploring the contours of the specificity of individual personality. Nor was realist characterization limited to a constrained social stratum. The goal of mapping society led realists to broaden the boundaries of characterization. Previous American literature had employed "low" characters, but had done so for comic relief or as a vehicle for class ridicule.[20] Breaking with the ruling principle that "low" characters stamped a novel as vulgar and cheap, realists gloried in the "common," equating the average with "the simple, the natural, and the honest." Howells's belief that like the scientist, the novelist could not ignore any fact or any existence and Norris's contention that the stuff of literature was present even in New York's Lower East Side were indicative of the justifications that gave rise to a rich roster of characters.[21] The nouveau riche mineral-paint king of William Dean Howells's *Rise of Silas Lapham*, the frightened private of Stephen Crane's *Red Badge of Courage*, the troubled, even pathetic Methodist minister whose plight provided the title for Harold Frederic's *Damnation of Theron Ware*, and the ragamuffin Huckleberry Finn were a few of the characters that previous American literature had deemed not to be of central interest. Finally, American realisms devalued the traditional notion of heroic character. By expanding the social basis of characterization and locating the narrative within specific social settings that inevitably exerted constraints on human action, realists eliminated the larger-than-life, elevated, central character. In his place stood the realist protagonist, who was more likely to embody his or her moment rather than stand above it and more likely to incorporate the forces that shaped daily life than to resist them. As Eric Sundquist has argued, even an exception like Frank Cowperwood, the central character of Dreiser's *Titan* and *Financier* who crushed everyone who opposed him, is not so much a hero as an embodiment of a historically specific will to power. His heroic status derives not from his difference from others but from his exaggeration of typical American traits.[22]

Because it emerged during the dynamic phase of capitalism, realism was vitally concerned about the relationship between humans and things. At the same time that men and women lived their lives in a human environment, they also were surrounded by things. Indeed many of the New Historicists argue that the confusion of the two categories is central to an understanding of American literature in the middle portion of the nineteenth century and to realism in particular.[23] Incorporating in their texts the explosion of artifacts, realists presented characters awash in objects. The elevated train of Howells's

Hazard of New Fortunes, the skyscrapers that tower over and enclose the action in Henry Blake Fuller's *Cliff Dwellers*, the sparkling and seductive furniture that comprises the central motivation of Henry James's *Spoils of Poynton*, and the appearance of the bicycle, the telephone, and electricity in *A Connecticut Yankee in King Arthur's Court* are not simply mentioned; they loom throughout the texts. As human beings struggle to connect themselves with these things, they find that these objects influence and slowly determine their lives. Realist texts soak their characters in this environment, which in turn exerts pressures on individuals. Though not the historical materialism of Marxism, which stresses history and not environment, American literary realism employs a determinism of environment that limits the possibilities of human action. The impress of the slums on Crane's Maggie, the determination of genetics on Norris's McTeague, and the results of Christopher Newman's nationality on his fate in Henry James's *American* all point to the way in which realism saw men made by their circumstances as well as making them. It was no coincidence that American realism, for all the influence it drew from local color and regional literatures, became predominantly an urban literature. Not only did the city allow realists to trace the new social relations, but it also opened the way for the depiction of the flood of artifacts and commodities that inundated men and women.

Howells's dictum that the novel should be "simple, natural, and honest" applied not just to its content but also to its form. In order to insure its understanding, the novel should in itself be a natural object and not be immediately identified as an artifice. In its use of language the realist novel aimed to eradicate signs that it occupied some special realm. Realists jettisoned rhetoric—a stylized language of elevated expression designed to demonstrate that the writer had mastered the tradition of polite letters—for everyday speech. Believing that rhetoric distorted the impact of literature by announcing that its material was lofty, distant, and privileged, they chose a linguistic style that more closely resembled "normal" or "average" usage. Attempting to approximate word and thing, they strove to convey to readers the existence of a reality "out there." In discarding the circumlocutions of earlier literature for a direct and simple presentation, they hoped to make the novel read as if it were an account of actual events. Aiming for a direct impression that corresponded to the way in which readers experienced their lives, realism in the United States generally avoided the temptation to invest things with contrived meaning. Using the most neutral language possible allowed things to speak, as it were, in their natural voice and with the meaning that human purpose actually assigned to them. To rely upon an artificial language and contrived construction to convey the natural struck realists as an obvious intellectual inconsistency.

This tendency toward mimesis extended the language of characters as well. In an effort to place character, realists employed dialect rendered as exactly as possible and liberal dosages of everyday speech. In *Huckleberry Finn*, for instance, Mark Twain explicitly acknowledged that he drew upon a number of distinct dialects.

> In this book a number of dialects are used, to wit: the Missouri negro dialect; the extremest form of the backwoods South-Western dialect; the ordinary "Pike County" dialect; and four modified varieties of this last. The shadings have not been done in a hap-hazard fashion, or by guess-work; but pains-takingly, and with the trustworthy guidance and support of personal familiarity with these several forms of speech. . . . I make this explanation for the reason that without it many readers would suppose that all these characters were trying to talk alike and not succeeding.[24]

Realist language was the most important tool in the effort of the genre to build a unique form of narration. Realist narration disdained the intervening narrator, who paused and commented upon the action. Such a device, realists generally thought, only called attention to the artificiality of the text and undermined its credibility as an authentic document. In its place they substituted a removed and unacknowledged intelligence that controlled the flow of events. Realist narrators were generally disembodied, coherent sources of the novel that traversed the entire range of activities they related. Occupying a privileged position by virtue of this omniscience, only some of which was revealed to the reader, the realist narrator was able to present the narrative as a fluid, proportioned whole. Descending into the consciousness of characters and withdrawing to a vantage point without, realist narration aspired to as much coverage as possible while preserving the fundamental goal of naturalness. In such a manner realists hoped to convey to readers the sense that the novel unfolded of its own accord. As with language and characterization, realist narration set as its goal the illusion of everyday experience.[25]

These characteristics of the genre were tendencies rather than ironclad principles. No single text displays all of them; many texts do not consistently follow them throughout the course of the entire narrative. As we shall see, the fundamental precepts of realism often pushed in contradictory directions with the result that realist novels are laced with tensions. The realist goal of unalloyed experience, for example, represents an unachievable end. Because a novel is, after all, a human production, it will always bear marks of its creation. Completely eradicating the narrative presence and reproducing pure experience would require eliminating all such phrases as "she said," as they mediate the experience. Given the possibilities inherent in the principles, disputes over whether a particular author should be classified as a realist are numerous. These disagreements cannot be resolved solely through a more rigorous definition of what constitutes a realist novel. Even if one could declare previously classified realist work as nonrealist on the basis of a different standard, one would still be left with the problem of trying to understand how it was that these standards evolved at a particular time. Only by placing realism within a broader history of writing as a special act of communication can we begin to understand why realism in the United States contained such tensions and counterforces. By locating the entire writing process in the history of the late nineteenth century, we can understand what problems realist theory was designed to resolve.

The central historical determinant of the realist writing process was the consolidation of the literary marketplace as the locus of literary production, exchange, and circulation. Realism came to prominence in an era in which the written word was also a commodity, bought and sold like other articles of commerce.[26] Such had not always been the case. Prior to the Civil War the literary marketplace had not been the sole medium in which American writers practiced their craft. In addition to the literary marketplace, which was employed for popular tales, sermons, political tracts, and slightly discredited genres like the novel, American writers had recourse to a second track in which texts circulated among coteries of peers. Based on such forms as diaries, letters, essays, and poems, this noncommercial literary system generated a highly elevated discourse known as belles-lettres, which stressed the proper use of rhetoric and language. Writers in the belles-lettres tradition considered the function of writing as the elevated expression of ideals and experience. One did not simply sit down to write but received training in the proper methods. For the men and women who schooled themselves in such English instruction manuals as *The Wit's Academy* (1667), *The Young Secretary's Guide* (1687), and Hugh Blair's *Lectures on Rhetoric and Belles Lettres* (first American printing, 1790) and who used Addison and Steele's *Spectator* as their model for the proper essay, writing was not an idle endeavor but an essential component of their social role. Writing to the *Pennsylvania Gazette* in 1733, Benjamin Franklin expressed the manner in which those trained in the noncommercial ideals regarded the social function of writing:

There are few men of Capacity for making any Considerable Figure in life who have no frequent Occasion to communicate their Thoughts to others in *Writing*; if not sometimes publickly as Authors, yet continually in the Management of their private Affairs, both of Business and Friendship: and since when ill-express'd, the most Proper Sentiments and Justest Reasoning lose much of their native Beauty and Force, it seems to me that there is scarce any Accomplishment more necessary to a Man of sense than that of Writing Well in his Mother Tongue.[27]

Writing for an audience trained in the rudiments of elegant prose, colonial and early republican writers exchanged their texts with men and women who were writers or potential writers themselves. Producers and consumers operated within a framework of shared assumptions about what constituted a valuable text and what a text was to accomplish. Honing their skills in literary clubs that consisted of the leading members of the professions, the writers of the early republic saw composition as a directly collaborative effort in which the interplay between author and audience was direct and immediate. They made no absolute distinction between public and private performances.[28] As a consequence their texts have a remarkable consistency. Thomas Jefferson's *Notes on the State of Virginia* reads remarkably like his private correspondence. Such was not the case with the realist novelist William Dean Howells, who felt uncomfortable with personal expression. Howells confessed to the illustrator Howard Pyle that "letters are not my natural expression, though literature is; I feel that I don't get myself out in them; my phrases hide me."[29]

Given the perceived necessity of writing and the stress on elevated expression, belles-lettres took on a political function. Hugh Blair saw in eloquent expression evidence of the dawning of a new era in human affairs. That men now settled disputes through the force of reasoning rather than the force of arms marked "the progress of society towards its most improved period." From this, Blair argued in a book that underwent thirty American printings in forty years, "it must follow, as a natural consequent, that they [educated men] will bestow more care upon the method of expressing their conceptions with propriety and eloquence."[30] Unstated in Blair, but made clear in later works, was the contention that eloquent expression was necessary to rule. Those who mastered the intricacies of rhetoric had a tool that was indispensable for government.

This melange of elements—restricted class participation, a direct author-audience relationship based on an agreed framework of assumptions, a stress on language as the bastion of social stability, and the resulting reliance upon rhetoric—made the writer who thought in terms of a coterie audience an articulator of social values. The identity that writers felt with their audiences, the naturalness of the task, and the requirement that writing give proof of polite learning and exquisite writing meant that the eighteenth-century writer eschewed conceptions of writing that stressed the need for personal expression. Romantic creation, which stressed the uniqueness of the composition and the composer, was foreign to literary clubs and correspondence networks. No white heat of writing guided the composition of the belletrists. Any urgency that existed stemmed from the pressing nature of the problem addressed, not from the writing process itself.

For much of the eighteenth century and the first two decades or so of the nineteenth, belles-lettres was the most prestigious and elite discourse in the United States. Rooted in European models and disdainful of popular expression, belletrists during their heyday took little notice of competing literary forms. Envisioning their task as bringing civilization to an unformed nation, they rested comfortably in the notion that they had avoided corruption of both their art and themselves. Belles-lettres and the conditions that sustained them were, however, not to withstand the growing importance of the literary marketplace in the nineteenth century.

CHAPTER THREE

Fifth Avenue Takes Command

Fiction as a Literary Commodity

The offer came unexpectedly about the beginning of this month, and in such form that I could not well refuse it, when I thought it over. It promised me freedom from the anxiety of placing my stories and chaffering about prices, and relief from the necessity of making quantity.
—William Dean Howells to C. E. Norton

Although the sale of belles-lettres in the United States dated from the installation of the first printing press in Cambridge in 1638, belletrists considered literature first and foremost a private exchange among educated peers. The conditions of authorship that were distinctive to that mode—a personal, though not emotional, relationship between author and audience, limited class participation, and the goal of elevated expression of social ideals—remained primary for its practitioners. Most of the accomplished stylists of the early republic availed themselves of the literary marketplace, but the requirements attendant upon a system of the sale of literary texts, though not ignored or shunned, held a diminished attraction for them. Supporting oneself through the sale of the written word struck many belletrists as either odd or vulgar. When they took to the literary market, they did so to reach a larger audience than was available in local private exchange. They did not, however, alter their conceptions of this larger audience. They wrote for men and women from the writer's class and with the writer's outlook and presumed those who were not trained in belles-lettres were readers eager for instruction from their betters.

Such a literary system was hardly conducive to the development and advance of the novel. The sermons, essays, and poems of American belles-lettres, like the European models upon which they were modeled, encoded within their formal structures these conditions of authorship. Speaking in a voice that drew its authority from tradition and entrenched power, early American writers wrote to display their knowledge and to ratify existing social values, not to indulge audience response. Writing for an audience that shared their level of education, republican writers relied heavily upon complicated and stylized conventions of expression that immediately identified the text as "literary." This restricted discourse was, as Cathy Davidson has recently pointed out, designed to implement the Scottish commonsense tradition, which feared that undisciplined imagination would undermine social order.[1] The emphasis of form over content was designed to keep the latter within acceptable bounds. Its elevated and special language, deployed because authors took for granted that readers knew the codes of expression, kept American belles-lettres circulating within a small circle and confined to socially approved subjects.

The novel in its formal elements stood in direct contrast to polite letters. Where coterie-based literature had been reserved, the novel was emotionally open and psychologically vivid. Although not all belles-lettres were exercises in logic chopping, even the great works circumvent warmth. Late eighteenth- and early nineteenth-century novels, on the other hand, are chatty and intimate. Readers are invited in and made to feel at home, a convention necessary because, unlike the readers of polite letters, novel readers were not naturally or automatically friends of the household. Where belles-lettres enforced its conventions through the use of rhetoric, novelists employed language that deliberately shunned elevation. Rather than heightened moments, the novel stressed material life, everyday occurrences, and the fate of an individual protagonist. Encoding in one shape or another the entertainment function of writing, the novel aimed for accessibility. Inclusive in its implied readership, rather than exclusive, the novel challenged the ruling assumptions of what constituted material for literature and what literature should do. Though it may be an exaggeration to contend, as Davidson does, that novels empowered those who lacked influence, the genre did cater to the emotional response of audiences.

Such a form could not easily coexist with a literary system that depended upon exclusivity and personal interchange among the educated elite. A new set of writers and readers, meeting each other through a series of new relationships, was necessary to usher in the new form.[2] The literary marketplace provided the impetus for literary change. Expanding the boundaries of literary consumption and emphasizing the literary needs of readers, the marketplace created a space in which the novel could develop. As more readers unfamiliar with or uninterested in belletrist conventions purchased or rented books, the strength of the coterie system declined. The distances in time and space that separated production and consumption upon which the novel depended became more generalized. By the end of the second decade of the nineteenth century the coterie system and the literature upon which it was based had lost much of its vitality. With the success of Washington Irving's *Sketch Book* (1819) and James Fenimore Cooper's *The Spy* (1821) the literary marketplace for indigenous work passed an important milestone. Financial success for individual authors was never assured in this period, but the continuation of the literary marketplace was. The bulk of the books purchased in the 1820s and 1830s was still belles-lettres, but many, although by no means all, belletrist conventions had lost their power to persuade or evoke approval.[3]

Most American belletrists regarded the new genre as a literary and social abomination. Although some exceptions were made for Fielding, Sterne, and Scott, the literary elite condemned the novel as a lie that gloried in its dishonesty and deception. Belletrist critics charged that the novel consciously admitted that the events it described had not happened but treated those events as if they were real and palpable. Condemning all novels when he primarily meant the domestic novels of female practitioners, Samuel Miller contended that the genre portrayed events as "wild imagination paints them."[4] In *The Progress of Dulness* (1772) John Trumbull satirized the fantasy life that novels induced in the unsuspecting:

Thus *Harriet* reads, and reading really
Believes herself a young *Pamela*,
The high-wrought whim, the tender strain
Elate her mind and turn her brain:
Before her glass, with smiling grace,
She views the wonders of her face;
There stands in admiration moveless,
And hopes a Grandison, or Lovelace.

Just as worrisome to belletrists were the social and political effects of the habit of novel reading. They baldly asserted that novels were subversive to individual morality and social cohesion. Thomas Jefferson claimed that the passion for novels resulted in a "bloated imagination, sickly judgment, and disgust towards all the real business of life."[5] With its emphasis on the primacy of emotion and on meeting the demands of the ego, the novel attacked the ideal of civic affiliation at the vitals. By ratifying the claims of the self against those of a repressive society, the novel undermined the republican concept of civic virtue, which held precisely the opposite. For this reason, the late eighteenth-century vogue of Goethe's *Sorrows of Young Werther*, whose protagonist was so lovesick that he committed suicide, prompted new heights of condemnation. Class and social considerations also entered into belletrist ire. The common tone and untrained audience of the novel rankled those who saw themselves defending a civilization that depended upon elevated expression. The salacious flirtation that went on between the lines, as it were, was simply unseemly pandering that gentlemen and women eschewed. Those accustomed to thinking of literature as a venture best pursued among the classically educated regarded the literary pretensions of those with one dollar and fifty cents who spent it on fiction as vulgar.[6]

Even native novelists endorsed or made concessions to the belief that the novel corrupted youthful morals and introduced foreign ideas. Many works were freighted with introductions that were designed to assure readers that, unlike other works of fiction, the present volume was a warning against seductions and lies. Relying on the most practiced clichés, novelists swore their allegiance to civic virtue and national glory. In the preface to *The Algerine Captive* Royall Tyler wrote that "novels, being the picture of their times, the New England reader is insensibly taught to admire the levity, and often the vices, of the parent country. While fancy is enhanced, and the heart corrupted. The farmer's daughter, while she pities the misfortune of some modern heroine, is exposed to attacks of vice, from which her ignorance would have formed the surest shield. If the English novel does not inculcate vice, it at least impresses on the young mind an erroneous idea of the world in which she is to live."[7]

It is instructive to note that both Trumbull and Tyler associated the habit of novel reading with gender. Not only was there a basis for such assumptions (young girls of the middle class do seem to have been the most avid novel readers, as the rise of the "Feminine Fifties" was to reveal), but one hears certain sexual anxieties in their complaints. Issues of gender relations became intertwined with those of intellectual comportment. Because the novel treaded upon ground that the male-oriented essay had previously occupied and because it stressed responses thought to be feminine, Trumbull and Tyler clearly regarded the rise of the novel as a gender-based attack on their authority and position.[8]

The belletrist condemnation was largely ineffectual in preventing the novel from becoming a popular literary form.[9] Despite the intellectual prominence of the genre's detractors, Americans took to the novel. Statistics tell part of the story. Between 1744 and 1789, 56 foreign novels were reprinted in the United States; the interval between 1789 and the end of the century saw 350 more. Indigenous production increased as well. Although no one has dated a North American venture before the Revolutionary War, the number of native written novels had reached double figures by 1792. By mid-nineteenth century,

Americans were writing novels at the rate of 150 a year.[10] Samuel Goodrich, with a touch of exaggeration, estimated the value of American fiction at $3.5 million by 1830.[11] To this number one must add the countless editions of foreign novels printed and reprinted in the United States.[12]

The full interplay between commercial exchange and the novel was not reached during the early republican period. A number of bottlenecks and contradictions existed. Not all citizens instantaneously became readers. Many of the most consistent buyers were belletrists, who nevertheless were not eager to further the cause of the novel. Dissemination was a local and regional affair; multiple and overlapping productions were common. One reason for the disorganization that haunted book production was the absence of a true publisher—a middleman who coordinated relations between printer, author, and bookseller. Jobbers, printers, booksellers, and authors often performed similar roles. The possession of the plates, the establishment of the discount (the difference between retail and wholesale price), and the setting of prices remained confused. What constituted literary property was seemingly negotiated anew with every manuscript. Because many authors had to finance the publication of their books themselves, publication effectively became the province of the well-to-do or the well-connected.[13]

If the confused organization of the book market retarded the growth of the American novel, so too did the absence of an international copyright agreement that would have allowed foreign authors or their agents to negotiate for the production and sale of novels. With no copyright law, multiple editions of British novels flooded the American market at cheap prices. American works, protected by a domestic copyright agreement passed in 1793 and amended in 1830, sold at significantly higher prices than British works. At one point in the 1840s Cooper's books cost five times as much as Dickens's.[14] Hence the antebellum market displayed the anomaly of underdevelopment: foreign luxury goods had domestic prices and domestic goods sold at luxury levels.

The maturation of the indigenous fiction market in the years following 1820 brought full-time publishers into the field. Although publishers, like Isaiah Thomas, who had plied their trade before that date often took a commission to circulate an author's book and allowed the writer to pay for its printing, those who flourished afterwards, such as Scribner and the Harpers, had accumulated sufficient capital to enable them to expand their purview and to take the entire risk of production. Distracted by the mundane and tedious details of business, authors were generally willing to cede financial responsibilities. Although true consolidation awaited the twentieth century, the antebellum experiments with discounts, methods of payment to authors, and distribution systems gradually forged the American book system. By eliminating redundancy in sales effort, antebellum publishers became the pivotal agents in the conversion of written work into commodities.[15]

In *The Wealth of Nations* Adam Smith had argued that "in opulent and commercial societies to think or to reason comes to be like every other employment, a business, which is carried on by people who furnish the public with all thought and reason possessed by the vast multitudes that labor."[16] American publishing, however, retained vestiges of its noncommercial heritage. Loath to view themselves as businessmen of words, publishers eagerly adopted the mantle of literary patrons and imagined that they were continuing older traditions. Gathering literary circles around their firms, early publishers melded business methods with gentlemanly patronage. Rather than stressing quick turnover, a disastrous strategy in such a fragile market, they relied on the backlist, classics whose active sales period was years rather than months. By striving for "symbolic capital," a term the French sociologist Pierre Bourdieu has coined to denote strategies of firms that seek to accrue prestige that could be translated into sales, antebellum publishers banked on the slow but steady sales of "valuable" books.[17] Eschewing higher financial outlays and immediate profitability for long-term returns and symbolic capital, New York, Boston, and Philadelphia publishers cultivated local opinion leaders, who were most interested in extending the belles-lettres tradition. Only when the success of novels demonstrated the existence of an audience for fiction did they abandon the symbolic-capital strategy for one that stressed quick turnover of topical commodities.

Patronage and symbolic-capital strategies were not the only ways in which antebellum publishing failed to develop full business relations. Publishing arrangements themselves deflected the imposition of a literary division of labor. Because many authors paid in part or in whole for the printing and bore the discount, not all antebellum writers regarded publishers as a separate and opposing class. Authors of wealth and position, who could risk selling the whole lot of their printed books rather than the copyright, had a direct say in discounts, rate of payment, and even typeface and margins.[18] Such financial involvement practically made authors publishers. Although G. P. Putnam's declaration that writers, publishers, and sellers shared mutual and identical interests was overstated, the "partnership" in an author's book made that claim credible.[19] Because authorship required capital or connections, the antebellum publishing environment drew cohesion from the similarity in class background between author and publisher. The intricate system of class-linked outlooks that evolved did much to dampen the differences.[20]

Equally important in forestalling a full free trade in antebellum manuscripts was the "courtesy" system. Devised in the 1840s to prevent the re-occurrence of cutthroat competition for American editions of foreign works, the courtesy system was a gentleman's agreement that the announcement of a foreign edition conferred upon the publisher who made the announcement the exclusive American rights. A source of pride among mainline publishers, who regarded it as proof of the moral rectitude of the profession, the courtesy system ostensibly applied only to foreign authors, who were unprotected by copyright. American publishers, however, enforced it with American authors as well. Authors dissatisfied with their current publisher were limited in their ability to find another, as publishers were bound not to "steal" another publisher's "author."[21] Although the manuscript was formally available to the highest bidder, in practice such was not the case. The courtesy system did increase author-publisher tensions and thereby undercut the forces that stressed a unity between the two functions, but it was above all a system that shielded an immature industry from the adverse effects of a free market.

These countertendencies did not reverse the general trend toward the conversion of literary products into commodities. Even the most literate and sympathetic publisher who catered to the most elevated audience was mindful that market signals could not be forever ignored. The firm of Carey and Lea had kept James Fenimore Cooper as a loss leader in the 1830s; the Harpers were less eager to do likewise with Melville in the 1850s. Existing demand had to be honored. Nathaniel Hawthorne noted in his entry for 16 March 1843 that he was under a good deal of pressure to produce certain types of works. "As for this Mr. ———, I wish he would not be so troublesome. His scheme is well enough, and might possibly become popular; but it has no peculiar advantages with reference to myself; nor do the objects of his proposed books particularly suit my fancy as themes to write upon."[22] Problems with publishers affected Hawthorne's fiction. William Charvat has argued that pressure from his publisher Fields to write the better-selling longer fiction exacerbated one of Hawthorne's literary problems—his inability to sustain the breadth of coverage required in a long work of fiction.[23]

The literary marketplace gave rise to a new type of writer: one attuned to the financial possibilities of writing. Alexis de Tocqueville recognized that the marketplace made the old literary ideals obsolete: "Democracy not only infused a taste for letters among the trading classes, but introduces a trading spirit into literature. . . . Democratic literature is always infested with a tribe of writers who look upon letters as a mere trade; and for some few great authors who adorn it, you may reckon thousands of idea-mongers."[24] No doubt echoing the complaints of his belletrist informants, Tocqueville saw as inevitable both the abandonment of the fastidious standards of aristocratic countries and the sale of books nobody much esteemed. Whereas in an aristocracy "style will be thought of almost as much importance as thought, and the form will be no less considered than the matter; the diction will be polished, measured, and uniform," democracies with their multiplicities of taste would favor novelty, and "style will frequently be fantastic, incorrect, overburdened, and loose, almost always vehement and bold." Authors "will aim at rapidity of execution more than at perfection of detail. . . . In democracies it is by no means the case that all who cultivate literature have a literary education and most of those who have some tinge of belles-lettres are engaged in either politics or a profession that only allows them to taste occasionally and by stealth the pleasures of the mind. These pleasures do not constitute, therefore, the principal charm of their lives, but they are considered as transient and necessary recreation amid the serious labors of life."[25]

American belletrists concurred with Tocqueville's critique of mass literature as insufficiently attuned to difficult beauties. W. O. Peabody, the minister of the Third Congregational (Unitarian) Church of Springfield, Massachusetts, noted in 1830 in the *North American Review* that unlike the ancient era, the brave new world of publishing encouraged the belief that no special powers were required for poetry. "The time which Johnson prophesied, in no good humor, is come in this country, if not in his own, 'when the cook warbles lyrics in the kitchen, and the thresher vociferates his dithyrambics in the barn.' " Americans believed that "well-meant exertion" deserved praise, with the consequence that vast quantities "of merchantable poetry . . . have been thrown into the market every year; or rather, we should say, have been produced." Peabody saw the dawning of a period in which everyone fancied himself or herself a poet: "We are evidently approaching a state of independence, even beyond that contemplated by the American system; when not only our nation shall cease to be indebted to others, but every individual shall furnish his own supply." The problem, he explained, was that producers no longer required themselves to work at their craft. "Those, who believe that no industry is required," he complained, "fall into direct and servile imitation, and that not of the best models." Men avoided Milton; "as such works are not so popular as those which are less admired, the judicious race of imitators choose a nearer way to applause, and copy the marvels of the hour."[26]

For their part, authors had widely divergent reactions to the prominence of the new literary system. Some, like Nathaniel Parker Willis, eagerly exploited the opportunity to become a businessman of words. By his own admission, Willis was not interested in everlasting fame. He frankly said that he meant to please enough people to achieve wealth and prestige. He was good at the game and parlayed his main chance into a career well-paying enough to afford a country estate from the proceeds of his writing.[27] The young Nathaniel Hawthorne originally rejected authorship as a career on the classical grounds that writing for money led to personal and artistic degradation. By 1841, however, he gave serious consideration to professionalism because it provided the possibility for better returns than the alternatives of clergy, law, or government service. "Whatever may be my gifts, I have not hitherto shown a single one that avails to gather gold. . . . Other persons have bought large estates and built splendid mansions with such little books as I mean to write; so that it is not perhaps unreasonable to hope that mine may enable me to build a little cottage, or, at least, to buy or hire one."[28]

Other major authors found the literary marketplace an encouraging sign. Because he felt that artificial standards of literary value could no longer be maintained, Orestes Brownson saw in the triumph of the literary marketplace the blessed end of the viselike grip of the elite, who fawned over English style. The choices that the marketplace in literature made available opened possibilities for a truly American literature. Although Brownson believed that great literature would arise from the social fermentation of the full-blown struggle of the men of wealth and the simple laborer who actually produced it, he regarded the demise of the coterie elite as a first and significant step toward a unique American literature.[29]

The classic antebellum authors found that the literary marketplace did not always reward their efforts. Melville, for instance, was presented with a bill for $143.83 against his advance on *Moby Dick*. Even Washington Irving averaged only $4,000 a year from his writings, prompting the poet Bayard Taylor to sputter in disgust that this salary was unworthy of a chief clerk.[30] The ease with which the race for recognition could be lost to inferior work chastened many. Hawthorne expressed his sense of marginality in *The Scarlet Letter*: "It is a good lesson—though it may often be a hard one—for a man who has dreamed of literary fame, and of making himself a rank among the world's dignitaries by such means, to step aside out of the narrow circle in which his claims are recognized, and to find how utterly devoid of significance, beyond that circle, is all he achieves, and all he aims at."[31]

Poor returns were not the only complaint that antebellum authors leveled against the new literary environment. For a number of classic authors the very process of turning words into commodities damaged literary communication. The commodification of literature, they charged, drained the human element from writing, dictated that consumption of the text be made smooth and easy, and reduced all truth to a bland sameness. Emerson, Thoreau, Hawthorne, and Melville all at one time or another penned sentiments that rejected the effects of the literary marketplace.[32] This dissatisfaction can be directly observed in the texts of American Romanticism. In *Pierre* Melville lampooned "Young

America in Literature" as degrading and oppressive. Drawing upon older traditions of propriety, he charged that the new literary system attempted to put a price on the pricelessness of art and valued only the voracious and unreliable appetites of consumers. Inundated with pleas from literary hucksters upon his arrival in New York, Pierre "could not but feel the sincerest sympathy for those unfortunate fellows, who, not only naturally averse to any sort of publicity, but progressively ashamed of their own successive production—written chiefly for the merest cash—were yet cruelly coerced into sounding title-pages by sundry baker's bills."[33]

Faced with a fate of marginality, a number of writers fashioned a compensational faith in authorial "genius." The idea had originated with English romantic poets like Shelley, Blake, and Wordsworth, who had envisioned the writer as endowed with metaphysical gifts. For American belletrists writing was part and parcel of the everyday activity of a social elite; for romantics, it was a specially endowed activity that made its practitioners a class unto themselves. Larger than life, the romantic poet transcended the corrupting and mundane considerations of the market. His was the realm of spirituality and mystery, not that of capitalist rationality. "Imaginative creation" stood in contrast to the alienated labor of the market. Where the capitalist calculated, the writer intuited. "Genius" was therefore a political ideal that protested the apparent disregard for things of the mind.[34]

Although American writers did not hold the belief as stridently as English poets and French bohemians did, antebellum literati did make special use of the concept. As a guiding ideal, "genius" simultaneously acknowledged the writer's powerlessness in the material world and asserted his or her elevation. The "genius" operated in a separate sphere beyond the perception of ordinary beings but could not control the visible world. The purpose of the writer, proclaimed Edwin Whipple, whom Edgar Allan Poe once called the greatest American critic of the day, was "to operate on unseen substances, working silent and mysterious changes in the inward man without altering his external aspect."[35] Emerson asserted in his "American Scholar Address" (1837) that the "office of the scholar is to cheer, to raise, and to guide men by showing them facts amidst appearances. . . . He is the world's eye." If this duty meant "poverty and solitude" and would require the author to live in a state of "virtual hostility" to society, Emerson accepted this result as inevitable.[36]

Hawthorne's insistence that he wrote romances, not novels, paralleled Whipple's and Emerson's concern with genius. Associating the novel with a concern with "very minute fidelity, not merely the possible," Hawthorne aimed for a literature that was not bound to portray a petty, earthbound world. For this task the romance was perfect. A romance, which "must rigidly subject itself to laws . . . sins unpardonably, so far as it may swerve aside from the truth of the human heart—[and which thus] has fairly a right to present that truth under circumstances, to a great extent of the writer's own choosing or creation," gave the author a position of creativity outside the shackles of the marketplace. In line with the belief that the true artist should "mingle the Marvellous," Hawthorne saw the writing process itself as a triumph of the primacy of the nonvisible world over the visible one. In the Hawthornian and romantic vision, this inner faculty transcended its social determinants and established itself as an innate gift. In the preface to *The Scarlet Letter* Hawthorne explored the nature of the faculty of inspiration in a discussion of what the twentieth century prosaically terms a writer's block. For Hawthorne, his dry period was a matter of nature: "Nature, —except it were human nature, — the nature that is developed in earth and sky, was, in one sense, hidden from me; and all the imaginative delight, wherewith it had been spiritualized, passed away out of my mind." His "gift was suspended and inanimate" within him.[37] In his insistence that writing overcame the drabness of the visible, Hawthorne fashioned his fiction as a form of protest against the material forces that restricted his craft.

The Realist Literary System

In fashioning the concept of "genius" as a counterweight to the rational calculation of commercial exchange, antebellum authors had an ideology that corresponded to their actual situation. Powerless in the market, they were at the same time partially outside it. Unlike their successors, the major antebellum writers were not essential players in the market. Despite its growing strength, the literary marketplace had not swept all writers into its orbit. The antebellum book market was a small one, and only the most popular writers lived solely from their sales. Hawthorne and Melville drew only a portion of their sustenance from their writings. If such an existence was often precarious and rarely luxurious, it did shield the American romantics from the full brunt of commercial imperatives. As long as they could use family connections, government sinecures, and publishers' largesse to remain beyond the sometimes harsh operation of commercial exchange, romantics could draw upon the guiding principles of their noncommercial heritage, even in attenuated form. On the fringe, staring toward the expanding center of market relations, American romantics achieved their artistry by combining a distaste for popularity-seeking writing with a keen and sometimes bitter awareness of its attractions and potential. The unique juxtaposition of the material and the metaphysical that marked Romanticism owed much to the ambiguous status of romantic novelists.

As commercial exchange came to dominate all of literary work, the material basis for nonmarket literatures atrophied.[38] Though realists were not the best paid of the late nineteenth-century writers, they could not escape the new relations, even had they wanted to do so. By the turn of the century, the most prominent features of the literature industry had appeared. As markets became more organized and distribution systems tightened, noncommercial literature became a faint memory, and its ideals relics. Any writer who chose to ignore the literary marketplace chose for himself a future without readers, influence, or fame. The consolidation of the industry in New York among Fifth Avenue firms, a set of stable net prices, the elimination of cheap foreign competition, and the perpetuation of a publishing bureaucracy meant that Howells, James, and Norris could not toil with the apparent nonchalance of their predecessors. With the solidification of a system of royalties, editorial command, and advances, writing more closely resembled Adam Smith's vision of a capitalist knowledge business than it had previously. Despite the homage paid to past literary ideals, publishing, rather than coterie, relations ruled Gilded Age literary work.

The triumph of business relations in the creation of literature drew upon a number of underlying transformations in technology and society. Together they made possible a more potent marketplace for literary commodities. The invention of linotype in 1885 and monotype seven years later, the perfection of photoengraving, the decline in paper and ink prices, and new methods of rounding, backing, and binding made books easier to produce and more attractive to own. The large-scale expansion of railroads and telegraphs knitted together diverse local markets into a single national one. Increases in urban populations, leisure time, grammar school education, and real income enlarged the reading public, made bookstore owners and traveling dealers more accessible, and dictated a change in the material required to satisfy consumers. These developments were not the only ones that fueled the book market. Literacy and availability by themselves do not guarantee readership.[39] Just as important in propelling large-scale reading and book buying were the new needs in a mobile society. Although historians continually debate exactly when and if the United States became an impersonal, industrial society and the degree to which old communities broke down, it is undoubtedly true that post–Civil War America showed signs of significant transformation in social life. Reading was an essential component of this conversion, providing values and information to a society in which those needs were not fully met by relatives and friends. Reading in the late nineteenth century, however, was itself a changed practice. Gone for the most part was the direct reader-writer exchange and the "contemplative" intensive reading over and over of a small number of texts. In its place was a more diffuse, impersonal extensive reading. The former mode tended toward communal understanding, the latter toward individual appreciation. This was especially true with the novel, in which readers were educated to read not as if the account were literally true or an allegory dependent upon a master plot, but for typicality.[40] It was this set of conditions that the marketplace in literature exploited and extended.

With these new conditions came new practices for writers and publishers. In part these mores resulted from the new power of the publisher, who functioned to turn a literary manuscript into a marketable commodity. By fitting business practices to new business conditions, publishers developed a new environment in which the author dwelled. Gone was the confusing system of distribution in which as many as five different parties handled the book between its origin as a manuscript and its consumption by the reader. Publishers assumed new dominance in the distribution process, consolidating book channels, clearing the way for maximum exposure of their imprint, and turning to booksellers as the primary way in which an increasingly urban nation received its hardcover reading material. With the rewards potentially greater and the importance of the personal influence of the local literary tastemakers diminished or fragmented, publishers moved slowly toward a system in which they engineered, but did not dictate, the circulation of books.[41]

Foremost among their innovations was a new conception of the book-buying public. Unlike their antebellum counterparts, post–Civil War publishers operated with the understanding that belles-lettres had limited sales potential in these new conditions of publishing. They believed that rather than serving a united public confirmed in its literary tastes and preferences, they confronted a fractured and shifting readership. Not only were readers uncertain of what they wanted—estimates of those who entered a bookstore with no set notion of what to purchase ranged from two-thirds to fourteen-fifteenths—but each book had its own distinct public. The publisher Robert Sterling Yard claimed that there were hundreds of publics, each with its own standards.[42] By 1872 the stated purpose of the trade journal *Publishers Weekly* implicitly recognized the existence of a shifting and segmented audience. The journal existed to enable booksellers to "order knowingly and confidently books likely to sell well in their localities, and to obtain such information as to the character of new publications as will post them for calling the attention of *particular customers to books likely to suit their taste*."[43] Taste had become a matter of individual preference, rather than a community standard. Or so publishers reckoned.

Business methods and literary offerings changed accordingly. The transition was not smooth and conflict-free, but by the end of the nineteenth century the importance of the backlist had clearly declined. Postbellum publishers concentrated more of their offerings in fiction, which the new consumers preferred over all other types of literature. Given that until 1913, *Publishers Weekly* classified a book as new if it appeared in a new form, even if it had been previously published, statistics can only suggest the new emphasis on first-edition fiction. Nonetheless the trend is obvious. In 1880, for instance, 292 of the 2,076 new titles were fiction. The following year the figures jumped to 587 of 2,991. At the end of the decade nearly 30 percent of the new titles were fiction. With the passage of the International Copyright Act in 1891, foreign novels were no longer issued in duplicate or overlapping editions, and the percentage that fiction constituted of the total number of books published declined. Still, the raw number of fiction books increased. By 1907, 1,150 of 8,725 new titles were fiction; the following year 1,458 of 8,745. No other category challenged fiction for the top position. In second place, for example, theology and religion had only half as many new titles as fiction in both 1907 and 1908. Equally indicative of the importance of fiction was the proportion of publishers' advertising budgets devoted to novels. John Tebbel reports that between 1890 and World War I nearly 70 percent of book advertising went to fiction.[44]

Not surprisingly, fiction was responsible for the splashier commercial successes of the period. Seventy-four of the eighty-six best-sellers that Frank Luther Mott lists between 1870 and 1909 are novels or short stories.[45] Some did spectacular business. George DuMaurier's *Trilby* (1894) sold more than 1 million copies and created a national craze that made "Svengali" a part of the language. Elinor Glynn's *Three Weeks* sold 50,000 copies in three weeks.[46] Such traditional firms as Scribner's, Appleton, and Little, Brown suddenly devoted a large part of their production and sales efforts to fiction. Little, Brown, which had formerly concentrated on reputable nonfiction, scored a huge success with Henryk Sienkiewicz's *Quo Vadis* in 1896.[47] Even respectable and serious writers fared well. William Dean Howells's *Hazard of New Fortunes* sold 19,000 of its 23,000 first-run copies in six months.[48]

Indigenous fiction did not become an overnight success in the years following the Civil War. The failure of Congress to ratify the Bern Convention on protection of literary property in 1885 and the absence of an International Copyright Law until 1891 left the market open for the "pirates," publishers who flooded the American market with uncopyrighted editions of foreign novels. For all the moral indignation that Zola's work aroused, his novels went through at least twenty American editions. Disdaining the courtesy system, which they characterized as a device of monopoly, the pirates flooded the market with cheap paperbacks.[49] As Henry Holt noted to an English correspondent, the majors—the Fifth Avenue and Boston firms that held to the courtesy principle and had at least a 1 percent market share—had little faith that profitability could be restored to mid-level fiction.[50] Competing with cheap editions, American authors as a class found it difficult to sell without making major concessions on royalties.

Although the International Copyright Act removed some of the threat posed by uncontrolled foreign editions, the problem of overproduction did not vanish with the passage of the law. Despite the advanced marketing techniques and planned production that the act made feasible, American fiction still struggled.[51] Years after the passage, complaints in *Publishers Weekly* indicated that the glut, or more precisely the specter of the glut, still remained. This overproduction made a career as a novelist hazardous, even for the most respected. While the stars of literature prospered, the lesser lights had their difficulties. In 1901 *Publishers Weekly* estimated that only 6 percent of the fiction issued sold as many as 10,000 copies.[52] If Harper and Brothers' records are indicative of the trade as a whole, overproduction was continuous. Using a sale of 1,000 books as the break-even point, a study of the company's records indicates that nearly three-fourths of the novels published in that era failed to pay for themselves. No significant differences between the years immediately before and after the Copyright Act can be detected.[53]

It was not the pirates alone who escalated book production to an unprofitable level. Between 1860 and 1910, publishing firms increased fourfold. According to *Publishers Weekly* in 1901, more than one thousand firms published at least a single book in 1900. Major firms proliferated throughout the period. Because one best-seller was all that was required to maintain position, no one firm dominated the market. Harper and Brothers, the largest Gilded Age house, controlled only 2 percent of the market at the height of its success.[54] Although many firms agreed with the Doubleday and Page slogan "Fewer and Better Books," the exigencies of survival militated against a common strategy of limiting production. Attempting to steal a march on their competitors, publishers turned to constant production of fiction in hope of finding that elusive best-seller, with the result that few authors scored well in an overcrowded marketplace.[55]

Authors achieved some relief with the establishment of two forms of publishing that bypassed the congested channels of the book market. Ten-cent magazines and literary syndicates, which furnished fiction to newspaper Sunday supplements, became favored vehicles for many authors as they were uniquely suited to appeal to many reading publics and gave authors wider access to audiences that the book market did not reach. Adept at measuring audience preference quickly and fairly accurately, syndicates attracted a number of serious experiments in fiction. Stephen Crane's *Red Badge of Courage* made its initial appearance in the Bacheller syndicate, not in its Appleton edition. Syndicates also appealed to the writer's search for a better payday. Founded by entrepreneurs acquainted with modern managerial techniques, syndicates introduced new organizational principles into the staid world of publishing. Freed from responsibilities for the finances of their organizations by accounting staffs hired to oversee the balance sheet, the leading syndicators—Irving Bacheller (begun in 1885), Edward Bok (1886), and S. S. McClure (1886)—concentrated on corralling novelists and calling upon editors, who had the right to cancel a syndicate's service at any time it proved unpopular. Like the men who founded the ten-cent magazines in the 1890s, the syndicators, who themselves went on to careers in magazine publishing, saw not backlist but contacts as their business assets. Only by recruiting new authors through premium rates could these contacts be made.[56] As Rudyard Kipling, who received his introduction to American readers through syndication, noted of McClure, his business was "brains futures."[57]

Despite the opportunities for new talent and the better paydays that syndicates and magazines could offer, the book retained much higher prestige. Most authors regarded preservation between hard covers as the most appropriate course. Writers would first publish in magazine or syndicate and then conduct business with a publisher. The postbellum publisher, however, was not quite his antebellum predecessor. The greater output of books required the development of a staff of readers and editors, with the result that face-to-face contact with authors became less frequent. William W. Appleton, the head of the firm that bore his name, admitted that he read only a few of the books that he brought out each season and that his personal enthusiasm for his list was limited.[58] Such a confession belied publishers' claims in the late nineteenth century that they retained the personal relationships with authors that had characterized publishing earlier in the century. By the late nineteenth century quasi-patronage arrangements had given way to more formal and impersonal business dealings.

Personal friendships between author and publisher did not vanish in the postbellum literary environment, but they also did not cancel or modify considerations of profit. To an unprecedented extent the sales potential of the manuscript became the fundamental issue between the two parties. Publishers and editors (the latter group was a new development in the postbellum period) were less reticent to refer to themselves as procurers of a commodity. Roger Burlingame, for instance, defined the publisher's job as making "thoughts into print and paper, multiply[ing] them into thousands . . . and sell[ing] them for tangible dollars to creatures whose moody minds must translate the whole thing back into thought before they get their money's worth." A good editor would "see, as he looks at the untidiest manuscript, a printed, bound, advertised, and sold volume."[59] George Haven Putnam insisted that business considerations insured a fairness that personal relations did not: "It is certainly the case to-day that authors who can produce wares possessing commercial value find little difficulty in securing for them such value. Publishers are always on the lookout for real material, that is material possessing that indescribable quality which secures popular appreciation, and they can be trusted, on the ground of their competition with each other, if for no other reason, to pay for such material its market value."[60] What McClure thought most important about his syndicate was its ability to give the new writer the test of market value. The language of equitable financial exchange easily replaced that of art. McClure, with no trace of embarrassment, termed his wide acquaintance with writers and what they could produce as his "capital."[61]

Publishers' motives were no more pecuniary, and probably a good deal less, than those of their contemporaries who ran steel mills or rail lines. Having a genuine interest in books and literature, they were not a crass group. Given the relatively meager returns in publishing, a youngster with initiative and a mind set on acquisition would have made a significant miscalculation in entering the business. If publishers lived comfortably, they were hardly captains of industry. Their self-image as cultural patrons, however unrealized, is testimony to their uneasiness with openly business attitudes. No publisher wrote the equivalent of "The Gospel of Wealth" or uttered a sentiment on the order of "the public be damned." Despite their sense of themselves as partners in the high calling of literary enterprise, they found that the pressures of publishing for a mass market dictated their acceptance of the imperatives of commercial exchange.

Writers also considered their craft in commercial terms and began to define the basic building blocks of literature by their cash value. Because magazine contracts stipulated payment per word, writers began literally to worry about the value of their words. And because the work of different writers never became interchangeable, rates varied. The standard rate for quality magazines in 1890 was about ¾ cent per word, with unknown writers earning ½ cent. Howells earned about 10 cents per word for the 1890s; Crane earned about 3 cents.[62] By commercializing language, magazine publishers encouraged padding. As one writer admitted to McClure, he never used a long word when a number of short ones would do. Even respected authors who shrank from characterizing themselves as economic producers began to consider words as money-makers and word choice as instrumental in securing a large paycheck. Arguments over the correct word count were surprisingly frequent.[63]

The belief that the market validly determined the value of the product united publishers who disagreed on other matters. Although the "progressive" Walter Hines Page and the "conservative" Henry Holt clashed in the public press in 1905 over issues of professional propriety, neither man challenged the concept of literary property or the publisher's obligation to manage that property with an eye toward meeting demand. Despite their stated differences over what Holt termed "speculation"—the acceptance of books of dubious quality that were pushed with large publicity campaigns—the practice of the disputants was not that far apart. Page's seemingly aggressive pursuit of authors did not prevent him from spending much of his essay denouncing the literary drummers and consumer tastes that were forcing publishers to abandon their stately partnership with authors. Holt's practice did not always square with his enunciated standards. Although he lauded the publisher's role in creating good-natured fellowship with authors, he occasionally dropped a talented author whose previous work had not sold up to expectations, because, he admitted, the tastes of the prospective reader were the court of last judgment. By applying the yardstick of consumer sovereignty, Holt implicitly acknowledged that non-market-based standards were a private, not a professional, concern.[64]

Market strength, not instruction and elevation, became the criteria for acceptance decisions. Publishers, whose power rested in their ability to accept or reject manuscripts, favored emotional effect, which was crucial to a mass audience, over intellectual worth. McClure contended that he judged by his solar plexus, not his head. Personal preferences—and by all accounts publishers of the 1860s–1910s were joyously and unabashedly middlebrow—did not exercise undue interference. McClure's own taste ran to Robert Louis Stevenson, and he once said that the syndicate should be run as if it existed for the sole benefit of Stevenson. His need to meet the diverse demands of mass readership, however, dictated that his actual list be considerably more catholic. In 1889 he offered selections from both Henry James and Francis Marion Crawford.[65] His syndicate was a potpourri of styles, plying both realist and romantic texts.

The rule of the marketplace often caused personal dilemmas for those with belletrist backgrounds. George Ripley, a reader for Harper, recommended Lew Wallace's *Ben Hur*, even though he personally found it bombastic.[66] George Haven Putnam conceded that most publishers refrained from passing judgment on literary value and concentrated instead on determining whether a text balanced their lists, an admission that transformed the notion of patronage from sponsoring good literature to insuring commercial success.[67]

Many in the book world began to use "literary" as a derogatory adjective. Where eighteenth-century men of letters had associated the designation with their hopes for republican virtue, publishers and the new business men and women of the pen used the expression to signify threats to democratic equality. Reacting against signs of distinction and promoting a philosophy of the sovereignty of the consumer, a number of "progressive" publishers, the generation of publishers that came to maturity in the 1890s, used "literary" to connote an excessive concern with niceties of expression, pathetic insistence on outmoded formalities of composition, and dry, lifeless subject matter. "Literary" meant dull and boring at best and was often more sinisterly paired with "snob."[68] Page viewed literary men as hopelessly obsolete. Asserting that few publishers paid serious attention to the opinions of the self-anointed arbiters of literary value, Page taunted literati with their inability to affect sales and considered their love of Henry James as dramatic evidence of their self-imposed marginality.[69] McClure stated flatly that experience had taught him that the "only critic worth listening to is the publisher, the critic who backs his judgment with his money."[70]

By the 1890s literary reputation often proved a hindrance to acceptance. Putnam contended that personal recommendations from prominent men of letters did not alter acceptance decisions. Bok felt that literary men and women only tired the audience and that their stale pronouncements were a sure sign of stagnation: "A successful magazine is exactly like a new store, it must keep its wares constantly fresh and varied to attract the eye and hold the patronage of its customers." Even Holt, who prided himself on preserving literary tradition, felt that his most important contribution to American fiction was his discovery of new talent and his divesting his list of the same old literati.[71]

Novelty, which publishers called "timeliness," became the watchword in fiction. Repackaging and differentiating became cardinal virtues. An Appleton editor, Ripley Hitchcock, wrote to his English agent that Americans were in keen competition for new ideas.[72] "Progressive" publishers were especially restless with conventional offerings. It was the "idea"—the kernel at the heart of the fiction—that mattered to the new publishers. McClure's standards in fiction rested on "absorbing narrative" and "rapid movement," by which he meant minimal description of scene and little elaboration of character. The ten-cent magazine king, Frank Munsey, felt the same way. His advertisement for *Argosy*, his all-fiction magazine, requested stories, by which he meant "not dialect sketches, not washed out studies of effete human nature, not weak tales of sentimentality, not 'pretty' writing. . . ."[73]

Despite the abundance of manuscripts, editors and publishers found authors incapable of generating enough timely stories. Complaints about the triteness of submissions and the devotion to irrelevant details are prevalent in contemporary comments. Frank Norris, speaking from his experience as a reader for Doubleday and Page, noted that the majority of manuscripts were predictable, cloying, and without distinction. Even best-selling novelists were carefully scrutinized. Edward Payson Roe, who one survey indicated was a thousand times more popular than Henry James, often implored McClure to accept his work and ended his letters to the publisher with promises to be contemporary. Roe's novel-writing procedure, which can best be described as romantic empiricism, involved personal investigation of environments and characters but often generated topics that lacked McClurian "interest." His 1886 idea involved "the much-discussed fashion of women wearing birds, especially hummingbirds." Fortunately the manuscript is no longer extant.[74] Walter Hines Page became so discouraged that he proposed the establishment of postgraduate schools for writers.[75]

As the pitch of competition intensified, Page and the other "progressive" publishers and editors eschewed the gentlemanly or ladylike authorial submission for a more active intervention. Patiently waiting for the magic manuscript to materialize was a recipe for commercial doom. Too much was at stake to allow the untutored author a free hand. Consequently publishers and editors beseeched writers for any available manuscript or any work in progress, signed contracts on the basis of synopses, placed orders for specific treatments, and demanded significant and drastic revisions as a condition of publication. More thoroughly organizing the entire production process than had their predecessors, late nineteenth-century publishers encroached upon what had been the domain of the writer. Even the major realists found that the author alone no longer determined the subject of composition. Norris contended that the public was unaware of how much fiction was written to order: "The publisher again and again picks out the man . . . suggests the theme, and exercises, in a sense, all the functions of the instructor during the period of composition." Nor were publishers shy about requesting such changes. Norris suggested campaigns on the order of political canvasses. George Doran openly admitted that publishers initiated ideas and ordered specific treatments.[76] Writers could and did benefit from these changes. Howells, for instance, recognized the new importance of scenarios and attempted to secure contracts for promising young writers who had attractive ideas.[77] This benefit did not obscure the new power of publisher in manuscript production.

That power extended beyond suggesting topics and treatments. Publishers and editors exercised far greater power to revise than they had in earlier periods of publishing history. The function of editor had arisen to fill the void left by the decline of coterie-based groups. Supervising the final form of the manuscript, editors provided the consultation and instruction that coteries once had. To be sure, the goals of instruction were different. Coteries suggested changes that made the work conform to convention; editors were concerned with insuring audience reception. The role of the editor underwent a change in the postwar period. The classic antebellum-style editor, who survived into the twentieth century, worked with the author, suggesting and never ordering, as Scribner editor William Brownell told Roger Burlingame. Brownell, who was a noted critic in addition to being an editor, allowed his authors to work out for themselves any problems with their writing, on the theory that the editor and writer were partners.[78] The "progressive" publishers and editors, on the other hand, assumed a dominance in the process. Their suggestions, although not quite commands, carried more weight as their power to reject increased. Nearly all aspects of composition fell under their purview. Endings, style, and especially structure became subject to editorial approval.[79] Antebellum authors had had their share of quarrels with proofreaders and copy editors, but postbellum authors faced more radical surgery. Postbellum editors especially devoted themselves to the elimination of wordiness. Bok's credo was that there was no manuscript that could not profitably be reduced.[80]

Willingness to be edited became the standard of authorial professionalism. McClure held that in his experience "only writers of meager talent and meager equipment" objected. "To a man of large creative powers, the idea is the thing; the decoration is a very secondary matter." When McClure cut the first five chapters of Stevenson's *Black Arrow*, the editor praised the author's concurrence: "Like all writers of the first rank, he was perfectly amiable about changes and condensation, and was not handicapped by the superstition that his copy was divine revelation and that his words were sacrosanct. I never knew a really great writer who cherished his phrases or was afraid of losing a few of them. First-rate men always have plenty more."[81] Although many realists balked at such editing, there were times when they accepted the blue pencil. Howells, an editor himself, urged young contributors to accept the editing that he himself did not always find agreeable. Twain's proof sheets, Howells once observed bittersweetly, were a veritable mush of concession.[82]

Editors and publishers were not above wrenching an ending for their own purposes. Holt, for instance, once wrote Anthony Hope, the author of the phenomenally successful *Prisoner of Zenda*, that *Rupert of Hentzau* could stand a complete change. "Be patient with a suggestion that may strike you as inartistic. I have an idea that *Rupert* would probably sell two or three times as many, if somehow they lived happily ever after or that it would sell between its present chances and those brilliant ones if 'in death they were not parted.' You can keep the monument and all that, if you let it cover both of them. You might let up on the agony at the last, enough to spare that poor woman's widowhood!"[83] The American penchant for editorial intervention led Joseph Conrad to complain that "As to faking 'sunny' endings to my story, I would see all the

American magazines and all the American editors damned in heaps before lifting my pen for that task. I have never been particularly anxious to rub shoulders with the piffle they print with touching consistency from year to year."[84]

By virtue of their control of literary property, publishers commanded a coordinated package. Writers were an important, but by no means sole, cog in the machine. Howells remarked that with the improvement of the picture process in magazines, many authors were assigned to write stories that matched engravings rather than having the engravings match the story.[85] Contending that their primary qualification was their understanding of the book business, publishers justified their new prominence by their ability to keep "their ears to the ground." The mutual prosperity would thus be insured. Although writers who disagreed could sell their manuscripts elsewhere, this option proved more viable in theory than in fact, as publishers as a class had the right to refuse publication if editorial prerogatives were not extended or conceded. Indicative of the publisher's unquestioned control of literary property was the absence of tradewide policies on speed of decisions. Authors complained bitterly that publishers held on to manuscripts that they had no intention of publishing, often for an extraordinarily long time. Their cavalier attitude suggested their unacknowledged assumption that the manuscript was theirs to dispose of as they wished. When Colonel George Harvey took over Harper and Brothers at the insistence of J. P. Morgan, who bailed out the firm when it failed in 1899, he misplaced James's synopsis of *The Ambassadors* for nearly two years before he acted on it. That inattention ended James's business relationship with the house.[86]

Publishers came to regard their calling as career management, the proper packaging and marketing of text and author. Two favorite refrains among the publishers—that authors keep their books with one house and that authors reject agents—had their basis in the publishers' desire to have sole control of literary management. House jumping and agent intervention had the effect of undermining publishers' dominance and complicated the status of literary property. Career management, as opposed to the literary patronage of the antebellum period, resulted in varying personal relations. Publishers claimed that they were forced to walk a fine line between paternalism and objectivity in dealing with authors. Flattery in large doses could saddle a publisher with worthless commodities if the author proved incapable of producing another text that sold as well as the first. On the other hand, objectivity could dampen or crush a sensitive producer whose potential for an important book had yet to be realized.[87]

As Christopher Wilson and W. A. Swanberg have authoritatively demonstrated, one of the celebrated scandals in the annals of American author-publisher relations—the trouble of Theodore Dreiser with Doubleday and Page over *Sister Carrie*—was not the result of prudery and suppression, as Dreiser claimed, but a failed attempt at literary management. After initially accepting the work at the behest of Frank Norris, Page had second thoughts. He wrote to Dreiser that *Sister Carrie* was "not the best kind of book for a young author to make his first book" and offered encouragement and assistance.[88] Although Page proved to be an inadequate and unresponsive career manager, he did, contrary to Dreiser's contention, make at least a minimal effort to sell the books. The experience did not, however, convince Dreiser to abandon career management. In 1904, three years after the nervous breakdown that he claimed the failure of *Sister Carrie* had caused, he wrote to Appleton editor Ripley Hitchcock to inquire if Hitchcock and Appleton could take charge of his career: "What publishing campaign is it with which you are about to ally yourself? I wish I might in some way come under your friendly guidance for I have felt all along as if I might some day deal with you to advantage," he wrote. "All people have invitations of this sort. I do not know just how it is to be done, however, but I trust we may meet and talk it over."[89]

Hitchcock, in fact, was one of the most successful literary managers of the turn of the century. Not only did Dreiser seek his services, but so too did Stephen Crane. Hitchcock edited *The Red Badge of Courage* and attempted to win for the book and its author prizes, awards, and recognition. He requested that Howells nominate Crane for Authors Club membership and say a few words for the writer in *Harper's*, a request that was entirely unnecessary given Howells's unstinted admiration. Howells replied in the affirmative, telling Hitchcock that he was not afraid of Crane's becoming spoilt, but added in a postscript that he realized that Crane's career was not necessarily in his own hands.[90]

Vital to career management was the long-term contract. Publishers, eager to secure the exclusive services of well-known authors, committed themselves to contracts that often extended for five to ten years. William Dean Howells's contract with Harper in effect made his name a trademark of the firm. His 1885 contract gave the company exclusive rights to his productions. He was "not to write for any other person or firm, and not to act on or allow his name to be used in any editorial relation by any other person or firm during the agreement." In addition the contract specified the genre (novel and farce), the length ("not less than 300 pages of the size page of his novel *The Undiscovered Country*") and the rights concerning the plates and copies.[91] Publishers and editors had other uses for long-term contracts. Much like the re-negotiated contract in contemporary sports, the nineteenth-century long-term contract had the value of keeping an author from moving to a competitor.

Despite the guarantee of payment, authors found these agreements restrictive. Howells spent much of the 1890s attempting to persuade the Harper management to waive the terms of his contract. His correspondence with them constantly tested the limits of his right to place his material elsewhere. He wrote Ripley Hitchcock that his agreement with Harper precluded his writing an introduction to a collection of Daudet, a task that he most certainly would have enjoyed.[92] Stephen Crane felt ensnared and hired a literary agent to extricate him from a viselike grip:

> Now, one of the reasons for this is to get me out of the ardent grasp of the S. S. McClure Co. I owe them about $500, I think, and they seem to calculate on controlling my entire output. They have in their possession "The Monster" (21,000 words) and "The Bride Comes to Yellow Sky" (4500), both for the American rights alone. The American rights alone of "The Monster" ought to pay them easily, minus your commission. No, perhaps it wouldn't pay them fully, but it would pay a decent amount of it. Then the American rights of "The Bride" I judge to be worth $75. As for my existing contracts there are only two: I) to write an article on an engine ride from London to Glasgow for the McClures. II) to give them my next book.[93]

The career management under which Crane rebelled and Howells grew restless proved lucrative for those whom the public favored. As Norris noted, publishing had increased the forms of literary property. He listed eight different ways that literary pieces could be sold—serialization in the Sunday press, book form, Canadian edition, cheap cloth, paper edition, English edition, colonial edition, and Tauchnitz edition—and rejoiced, "eight separate times the same commodity has been sold, no one of the sales militating against the success of the other seven, the author getting his fair slice every time."[94] In royalties alone, George DuMaurier earned $52,000 in six months for *Trilby*. Lew Wallace took in over $100,000 in the first year after the publication of *Ben Hur*.[95] As early as 1872, in a suit against the publisher of a collection for the railroad reader who had used his name and stories without permission, Mark Twain claimed that his annual income was $25,000.[96]

These figures were unusual. Noting that a lawyer or doctor just beginning his career earned as much on the average as the literary practitioner of fifteen years, William Dean Howells concluded that the low regard that Americans held for men of letters had its origin in the poor returns they accrued from the sale of their work.[97] For every Lew Wallace, there were countless writers like Henry Blake Fuller, whose *Cliff Dwellers* earned him $409.35 in its first year. For every DuMaurier, there were many more like his friend Henry James, whose average Harper royalty was a little above $200 a year in the 1890s. While Richard Harding Davis could count on at least $2,000 a year from the sale of his books, not to mention more from the sale of his stories and articles to magazines, Ellen Glasgow could only manage $554.25 in royalties during her best year with Harper and Brothers.[98]

The postwar emergence of the royalty as the preferred method of author payment is evidence of the new strength of Fifth Avenue publishers. Royalties, which granted the author a fixed percentage of the retail price on each copy sold, signified that the publisher had bought the property rights to the manuscript, which allowed him to supervise the production of the commodity (the book) and control the flow of the money. By accepting royalties, authors also accepted the publisher's management prerogatives. The usual contract called for 10 percent on a $1.50 novel, or 15 cents per copy. For the years 1882–95, that came to an average of $43 per book for Harper novelists.[99] The fiction craze and the feverish search for best-sellers pushed royalty rates even higher during the last years of the nineteenth century and the first of the twentieth— known in the trade as the "Crazy Period"—when they reached as high as 20 percent. Donald Sheehan has noted that whereas only 5 percent of Harper's books were given royalty rates of 15 percent between 1870 and 1890, that proportion of the list grew to 22 percent in 1890. If sliding-scale agreements are included in the reckoning (these increased the royalty rate as sales surpassed given plateaus), the proportion was 28 percent for 1890–1900 and 29 percent for 1901–1914. Even more remarkable was the 14 percent of books published in the first fourteen years of the twentieth century that had royalty rates of 20 percent. Given that royalties were calculated on retail prices whereas publishers received only the wholesale price (retail minus the customary 40 percent discount), the author's share of net publishing income was 17 percent in the case of a 10 percent royalty, and 25 percent for a 15 percent royalty. Although these figures suggest authorial wealth, it should be remembered that sliding scales, additional costs, and high rates of failure limited the actual payoff. Sheehan points out that Harper and Brothers had an uncanny knack for setting the escalator on sliding scales just above the actual copies sold and therefore avoiding payment at the higher rate.[100]

Payment became a major source of contention between authors and publishers. Dissatisfied with their lot, authors pointed out that publishers grew rich from authors' work. William Dean Howells spent much of "The Man of Letters as a Man of Business" excoriating the "speculators" in literature who grew wealthy on the unearned increment. Harold Frederic constantly deplored the low rates he received from *Scribner's* for his stories. Rejecting a McClure inquiry about a work assignment, he wrote, "I am kept in a perpetual worry and annoyance by the slipshod money-methods of two-thirds of the American publishers I have relations with—and I am resolute about not widening the area of this unhappiness."[101] Norris complained about the very term: "Royalties! Why in the name of heaven were they called that, those microscopic sums that too, too often are less royal than beggarly? It has a fine sound—royalty. It fills the mouth. It can be said with an air—royalty. But there are plenty of these same royalties that will not pay the typewriter's bill."[102]

Despite the movement for uniform contracts, the continuous struggle between authors and publishers militated against homogeneity in such documents. Some contracts called for royalties after the first thousand copies had been sold; others began royalty payments immediately. Time of payment varied between six months and a year. In periodical publishing, the situation was even more uneven, with some authors paid on receipt of manuscript and others upon publication. When George Lorimer introduced the policy of paying on completion at the *Saturday Evening Post*, he earned the gratitude of writers and the enmity of his competitors.[103]

Royalties were not the only source of economic contention between the two parties. An interesting item in the standard Harper contract, which was as often deleted as imposed, was the additional costs that the publisher tried to make the author bear. Correction of galleys, indemnification against libel, and various other editing expenses were often charged against authors' accounts.[104] The size of the allowance for corrections became a negotiating item. These charges remained irksome to novelists and were one of the rallying cries in emergent efforts to organize writers in both the United Kingdom and the United States.[105]

Although publishers held important advantages in the relationship, authors benefited from the ease of entrance to publishing and the resultant intense competition among publishers. Publishers may have protested that despite authorial unfaithfulness and house jumping the courtesy system still stood, but the fact of the matter was that the courtesy system suffered an irrevocable decline in the years between the Civil War and 1914. Courtesy had fulfilled a business requirement, protecting an immature industry from engaging in competition for authors at the same time that it cemented author-publisher relations. Writers and publishers, aware that they were bound together, had personal and sometimes very cordial relations. With the end of cheap editions of foreign novels at the turn of the century, domestic courtesy served little functional purpose, for domestic property was now secure. As authors for the first time "shopped around" for better terms, publishers seemed ready to oblige them. When Walter Hines Page set up his own firm, he sought out Ellen Glasgow and Mary Johnston from the ailing Harpers and Joel Chandler Harris from the similarly afflicted Appletons.[106] Even Henry Holt, the most vociferous defender of the courtesy system, wrote his English agent that an author dissatisfied with another firm should be brought into the fold. George Doran reported that Alfred Harcourt, Holt's assistant, tried to pry away Arnold Bennett's *Old Wife's Tale* on the ground that it was more suitable for Holt's list.[107]

Although publishers blamed the greed of authors for the decline and professed to distrust house jumpers, they promoted the end of the system themselves as a way to bring in profitable writers and to jettison unprofitable old-line authors. Walter Hines Page's own prescriptions undermined his pleas to his fellow publishers to regard authors as clients and thus save the profession from becoming purely a business. By arguing that what the publisher owed the author was the guarantee of financial stability above all else, Page indicated that the financial protection of the house was paramount. For all that Page wanted to soften the harshness of the laws of supply and demand, he yielded to them in the end. To deride literary men for their lack of business sense and then to claim that antebellum hospitality should guide social relations was not hypocritical, but it was inconsistent. Noncommercial relations could hardly last the advent of national publishing. Publishers, understanding all too well the logic of literary property, had little use for the restrictions of courtesy.[108]

Authors with reputations, skill in negotiating, and perseverance were able to manipulate the literary marketplace to their advantage. Although the prospects for resistance had significantly declined, they could still use the system to gain space for their work. Publishers' mandates on royalties and editorial intervention had to be heeded, but these pronouncements did not always become the final arrangement. William Dean Howells, for instance, had the advantage of his respected name and his ownership of his plates. Both factors led to higher royalties, as publishers did not have to bear the cost of plates. Mark Twain, who sold more books than Howells did, even reversed normal procedure with James Osgood, the successor to the Boston firm of Ticknor and Fields, for *The Prince and the Pauper* (1882). Twain paid for the manufacture of the book and granted Osgood a 7.5 percent royalty for selling the book.[109]

The cases of Howells and Twain belie claims of the meaninglessness of literary reputation. Prestige still carried clout on Lower Fifth Avenue. Most authors, however, lacked the financial resources and the connections that enabled Twain and Howells to rise above standard royalty arrangements. What authors did have was their potential. As George Lorimer of the *Saturday Evening Post* realized, publishing was investment in future performances. The promising novice was at the mercy of the experienced publisher. Stephen Crane was blunt about this aspect of publishing. "Without vanity, I may say that I don't care a snap for money until I put my hand in my pocket and I find none there. If I make ill terms now there may come a period of reflection and so I expect you to deal with me precisely, as if I was going to write a GREAT BOOK ten years from now and might wreak a terrible vengeance upon you by giving it to that other fellow and so we understand each other."[110]

The speculative urge and the need to protect the future led publishing houses to grant advances. Nearly one-fifth of Harper authors between 1870 and 1910 received advances.[111] Although publishers like G. H. Putnam and Walter Hines Page condemned advances on the grounds that socially wasted labor should be borne by the man who expended it, none could afford to forgo advances that secured services before production. Putnam may have chided the British author Walter Besant for asserting that there was little risk in publishing and may have contended that there was a clear danger in the author's "securing for some first piece of labor more than it has actually earned," but he was fighting a losing battle.[112] Even the failures that publishers had with advances (Sheehan reports losses of $17,000 on thirty-six books in 1900, including volumes by H. G. Wells, Henry James, and Stephen Crane) and the looming possibility that no work would be done after payment did not stem the growth of advances.[113]

Authors not surprisingly viewed advances more favorably. Because payment was based on work actually done rather than on the basis of public reception, writers treated advances as a form of investment credit. Because advances spread the risk, authors also thought them more equitable. Their existence permitted stabler financial planning and a writing career. As a result, authors used advances to pace themselves at a more leisurely rate and to devote themselves exclusively to writing. With the generalization of advances, the number of writers who turned to other pursuits was demonstrably fewer. Norris confidently asserted that the advance was the facet on which postbellum authorship depended.[114]

Authors had other tools at their disposal to neutralize the publishers' inherent advantage of control of literary property. The emergence of literary agents, who performed functions for the author that mirrored those performed by publishers, enabled novelists fully to exercise their market position. American literary agents, who originated as contacts for British publishers after the passage of the International Copyright Act, used the advantage of their collective clientele to exploit the competition among publishers and secure the best possible terms for their authors. Like publishers, agents conformed to the logic of the literary marketplace and made their own literary tastes a private concern and not the basis of their profession. Paul Revere Reynolds, the first United States literary agent, maintained that the only legitimate function that an agent could perform was realizing his client's wishes. This action, argued the defenders of agents, would relieve the writer from the pressing demands of production and clear the way for a better literature.[115]

Reynolds virtually stumbled into a career of literary agency. After his graduation from Harvard he did editorial work for *The Youth's Companion* and reviewed books for *The Episcopal Churchman*. Upon the passage of the International Copyright Act he began work as a business agent for the English firm of Casell, establishing markets for the house's books and advising it on which American products were suitable for its list. Realizing that his contacts with American publishers and editors would be advantageous in placing American work in American magazines and taking a cue from A. P. Watt and J. B. Pinker, the first major English agents, he began charging a commission of 10 percent to sell American work at the best available price. The domestic side of his business grew slowly but steadily. As late as 1904, twelve years after he had begun, the bulk of his business still came from his English arrangements.[116] In the years that followed, an increasing number of American authors turned to agents to help them with complex transactions. In 1905 his 10 percent commission brought Reynolds $10,806.63. Four years later he transferred $16,029.31 to profit in his ledger.[117] Among his clients were Hamlin Garland, Booth Tarkington, Richard Harding Davis, Willa Cather, James Branch Cabell, Stephen Crane, Theodore Dreiser during the writing of *Jennie Gerhardt*, and, during the writing of *The Octopus*, Frank Norris.[118]

Reynolds owed his prominence to the significant results he achieved for his clients. Of 367 novels that he handled between 1910 and 1920, 213 (57 percent) received advances. At a time when 10 percent was the standard royalty, only 30 percent of Reynolds's clients wrote for that low a rate, and many of these were authors of first novels, which had untested appeal.[119] In individual cases Reynolds achieved some spectacular successes. After soliciting Richard Harding Davis's business with a claim that he would help make Davis the best-paid magazine writer in the country, Reynolds pushed Davis into the upper echelon, making him the first to earn $3,000 per story for the Sunday supplements.[120]

Authors were divided in their opinion of the new institution. Many felt that agents were extraneous and accomplished little that an author could not do for himself. Perhaps the most vehement was Hamlin Garland, who regarded Reynolds as another species of middleman. "Your system has always repelled me. You are no more value to me than a mailing agent unless you can find my highest market value and sell my goods at that price. Moreover, I can get prompter consideration of my Mss. . . . If I thought it would pay me to put it into your hands I would do so. But if I get a price say at $3000 and you sent it at that price, you are doing no more than I can do sitting here. And I'd be out $300. There is nothing in it for me unless you can get $350 more than I could possibly do so." Reynolds may have soothed Garland's feelings on the matter, for the correspondence continued for another three years, although Garland's complaining continued throughout.[121]

Theodore Dreiser felt differently. In the years following his disastrous experience with *Sister Carrie* he was unable to dispose of his stories by himself in what he took to be a glutted market and turned to Reynolds to get them read and placed. Agents, noted Dreiser, who understood the mechanics of publishing quite well and had no compunction about using all aids available to him in his quest for literary success, earned their commissions by developing a reputation for matching editors' needs with authors' products. Reynolds's stature, he believed, was precisely the ticket he needed to gain careful consideration.[122] Once Reynolds had made him known to editors, Reynolds could "browbeat" them for even better rates.[123]

Agents performed other services. Although Lorimer had introduced the policy of payment on delivery, Reynolds was credited with insisting that payment precede the delivery of the manuscript, thereby eliminating the complaint that authors worked without payment.[124] Some agents even advanced money to favorite novelists. The English agent J. B. Pinker lent Stephen Crane more than £2,000 in the course of their business association.[125] Perhaps most important was the general effect that agents had on the literary marketplace. By fostering competitive bidding, they aided even those who did not avail themselves of agents' services. Legitimizing the principle of sale to the highest bidder, they secured the right and the ability of the author to seek out the best terms. William Dean Howells used this ploy expertly in the 1890s, playing Harper and Brothers and Edward Bok against each other.[126]

Literary agents were the last in a series of late nineteenth-century institutions that consolidated writing as a form of commodity production. Not only did their extensive contacts abroad "internationalize" literary production, but agents put the final stamp on the principle that literary property was a fact of literary work and deserved the best possible return.[127] Whether an author believed in pandering to an audience or in conforming to predetermined elevated principles, he or she was an independent producer, inevitably integrated into a system that was ultimately concerned with financial returns. Given the ubiquity of commodity exchange, the only objective standard that could be applied to literary work was its status as literary property. The strength of the market in literature was such that its rule challenged previously held definitions of "literature." Noncommercial standards could not be sustained in an environment in which the market embodied personal, subjective choice in the written word. The search for profits did not, of course, mean that publishing concerns jettisoned "serious" authors, but it did mean that the firms were run under new principles. "Literary" writers received no direct subsidy. Like the other new business men and women of words, they had to test the marketplace and negotiate with an increasingly dominant publishing institution that in the final analysis judged their work by its popularity. While realists, on the whole, fared well, they voiced many complaints and found few alternatives. Romantic resistance meant a return to the shriveled realm of private circulation and a guarantee of irrelevance. George Haven Putnam's remark that authors required the "lash of low funds to produce quality work" may have struck some writers as vulgar and insulting, but it revealed a kernel of truth about the nature of compulsion in the postbellum literary environment.[128]

Not all major novelists chafed under editorial intervention or resisted the new system of literary commodities. Some saw it as a distinct improvement over the old, coterie-influenced publishing world. Harold Frederic appreciated the solicitations and suggestions that he received from Page, claiming that earlier editors had not responded at all to his submissions because he was not a member of the inner circle.[129] Others, however, worried that the new freedom that the novelist gained with the predominance of the literary marketplace carried with it new problems for the practice of art. Able to survive in the marketplace, they were concerned less about their own futures (although men like Howells and James never ceased to worry about their royalties) than about the future of the novel.

Literary Value and the Postbellum Market

As had Orestes Brownson in the antebellum period, the realists recognized the potential for a democratic and socially meaningful art in a time when the cultural elite could no longer dictate mass values. A literature that told of ordinary people's lives and reflected their interests had, the realists believed, the capability of liberating human awareness. To the degree to which the literary marketplace increased and encouraged new participation, realists gave it credit and honor. The problem, they came to realize, was that this institution did not act unambiguously. With its new freedom also came new costs. Much to their chagrin, realists found that marketing had also introduced manipulation and pandering. Invariably the novels that flooded the market were standardized, deficient in craftsmanship, and lacking in serious purpose. As realists surveyed the results of the literary marketplace, they saw an incessant demand for instant gratification rather than enlightenment, and a fiction that justified itself as a relief from boredom. Realists were therefore faced with the problem of preventing the exchange value of fiction from swamping its use value. Put another way, one object of realist writing on the problem of literary value was discovering how to rescue literature from the whims of the marketplace.

The elevation of popularity to an absolute value threatened the validation of realists' own work and the future of their form. They frequently bemoaned the present state of literary affairs and doubted a glorious future. James, for instance, envisioned a Gresham's law of art in which the bad drowned the good: "There are people who have loved the novel, but who actually find themselves drowned in its verbiage, and for whom, even in some of its approved manifestations, it has become a terror they exert every ingenuity, every hypocrisy, to evade."[130] After noting how the "horrid tumult of the swashbuckler" had silenced good work, Howells argued in 1900 that the "delicate something which we call tone, whether intellectual or ethical, must suffer from an orgy of [that] kind as it would suffer from an excess in opium or absinthe."[131] This concern led realists to derive a philosophical conception of art that would separate what they did in fiction from what the mere commodity producers sent out into the market. Anticipating in some respects the mass-culture critics of the 1940s and 1950s, realists aimed to confer upon art a status of special communication that transcended its position as merchandise.[132]

This struggle to designate some novels as more important than others is apparent in the changing language itself. From the mid-nineteenth century on, words designating the uniqueness of artistic endeavor appeared in the language. The use of "culture" to designate the works and practices of intellectuals, the rise of "aesthetic" to signify a realm beyond social use and social valuation, and the evolution of "art" to distinguish the activity of writers, painters, and the like from that of craftsmen are all indicative of the search for a secure meaning for art.[133]

Not all writers were disturbed with the status of the book as a literary commodity. Some, following in the antebellum tradition of Nathaniel Parker Willis, enthusiastically embraced the marketplace as the ultimate arbiter of literary as well as economic value. Francis Marion Crawford, a popular romanticist, defined a novel as a "marketable commodity of the class termed luxuries, not contributing directly to the support of life of maintenance of health," whose first object was to "amuse and interest." Although Crawford admitted that the novel had the power to educate and cultivate, he emphasized that it was "excellent to the degree in which it produces the illusion of a good play." The novelist's premier task, he contended, was to "sell the illusion."[134] In holding that the novel that best amused fulfilled its mission to the highest degree, he accepted the consumer-sovereignty logic of the market. Not only did he equate amusement with gratification rather than with truth, he assumed that the measure of amusement was the sum of individual choices that were best registered in the market. For men like Howells and Norris, who argued that the novel had assumed an importance approaching necessity, Crawford's position only relegated the novel to inferior status.

Crawford's view resembled the so-called marketing revolution of American business that originated during the turn of the century and grew into a school in the 1950s and 1960s. Marketing theorists contrast marketing with selling. Marketers give the public what it wants; sellers attempt to get the public to buy what they have. The former, the more "modern," approach shifts emphasis from producer to consumer values and wants, and defends that strategy with a pseudo-populist rhetoric.[135] What both Crawford's definition of the novel and the marketing philosophy share are an insistence that gratification is obtainable only as a commodity, the belief that pleasure is solely short-term gratification, and the contention that meeting all demands is a virtue. Crawford's reliance on consumer sovereignty is a far cry from antebellum aesthetics that emphasized standards to which both the reader and writer should conform.[136] Like the editors of *Publishers Weekly*, Crawford saw taste as individual and independent preference, not prevailing belief.

As Crawford was a working novelist who benefited from the national literary market, his views are not surprising. The most prominent literary critics and theorists were less enthusiastic. Believing that business contaminated art, a view that originated with aristocratic disdain for the rising middle classes, and subscribing to an aesthetic ideology that was distinctly idealist, literary intellectuals like Woodrow Wilson, Bliss Perry, and Daniel Thompson postulated an eternal or extrahistorical value for art. Arguing that the value of literature lay in its ability to reveal everlasting truths in imaginative and vibrant form, these theorists attempted to extricate literature from the vagaries of the marketplace by denying the import of commerce altogether. Seeking in art a way around the crudities of monopolies, industrial strife, and the ethic of material acquisition, they settled on elevated formulations: great art "feels the pulsation of the Infinite Heart" (Perry), or communicates "external harmonies" by exercising the "faculties of ideals, values and convictions" (Wilson), or is a "subtle, penetrative, and universal agent for the transmission of thought from poet to the people" (George Parsons Lathrop), or manifests in its forms "certain truths of human life," truths that are manifestations of general laws (Hamilton).[137] For all the differences between these conceptions, all share the belief and desire that true art is timeless and impervious to the imperfections of the moment. These idealist critics tried by fiat to make the use value of literature permanent and to quarantine literary value from the encroachments of exchange value.

Realists found neither the literary entrepreneurs' capitulation to the marketplace nor the literary idealists' arbitrary denial of its impact satisfactory. Although these two groups held diametrically opposite views of the purpose and means of art, both, realists believed, had failed to secure a significant basis for important art. Crawford's surrender to the changing fashions of literary consumers virtually reduced the value of literature to its exchange value; the idealists' fantasy of a permanent, ethereal realm made the value of fiction so evanescent as to render it irrelevant to those who read it. The history of the advance of the literary marketplace had firmly demonstrated the childish wish at the heart of the old contention that literary standards were impervious to the ways people actually behaved. A theory of literary value that took no notice of how fiction was actually valued had, the realists believed, little chance of making a contribution to the quest to establish a meaningful art. Denying the effect of the market by fiat and arbitrarily asserting the existence of universal standards was elitist and would result in an art that cowed its readers, rather than one that sprang from human needs and desires.

For Howells, James, and Norris, both the idealist justification for art and its pronouncements on the proper subject matter were outdated. The realists saw in the belief of an eternal sphere of artistic value the cloistered and dead feel of the study. Not unlike "progressive" publishers, Norris reviled the very word "literary" and associated it with the production of obsolete texts. Idealists, he said, would "make the art of the novelist an aristocracy, a thing exclusive, to be guarded from contact with the vulgar, humdrum, bread-and-butter business of life, to be kept unspotted from the world, considering it the result of inspirations, of exaltations, of subtleties, and—above all things—of refinement, a sort of velvet jacket affair, a studio hocus-pocus, a thing loved of women and of aesthetes."[138] Howells provocatively contended that the classical literary canon was as dead as its authors: "A superstitious piety preserves it, and pretends that it has aesthetic qualities which can delight or edify; but nobody really enjoys it, except as a reflection of the past moods and humors of the race, or a revelation of the author's character; otherwise it is trash, and often very filthy trash, which the present trash generally is not."[139]

Crawford's view, on the other hand, granted too much to the marketplace for their tastes. Although Norris and Howells were at one time or another employees of publishing firms, neither was willing to see art as a simple entertainment to be judged on its popularity or the author as a simple supplier of preexisting demand. To make of the author simply a reader of the reception of his novel and who mapped out future production accordingly was to make art a mechanical response. Striving after effects to achieve a predictable response from the audience made the author—as Howells put it, "merely a trained bear."[140] Though realists did not shun popularity and indeed thought that any great art needed to win the applause of the "common people," they argued that the literary marketplace could not demonstrate or register value. It measured preferences, which were not identical to value. "It makes one sick and sorry," Howells wrote, "often to see how cheaply the applause of the common people is won."[141] Taste—in the sense of personal preference—was a fragile reed upon which to support literary value, and Howells knew it: "Even the most refined, the most enlightened person has his moods, his moments of barbarism, in which the best or even the second best does not please him. At these times the lettered and unlettered are alike primitive and their gratifications are of the same simple sort; the highly cultivated person may then like melodrama, impossible fiction and the trapeze as sincerely and thoroughly as a boy of thirteen or a barbarian of any age."[142]

If the literary entrepreneur made literary value equivalent to popularity and romanticism found the source of literary value in universal truths, realists tried to mold a position in which art was simultaneously in the world but not of it. The valuable novel had to walk the line between rejecting outmoded conceptions and capitulating to the ways of the world, between hewing to outmoded conceptions and accepting the contaminations that the marketplace introduced. It had to establish itself as authentic and unmediated communication. "Fiction," Howells argued in his devastating review of the new historical romances of 1900, "is one of our most precious possessions, and if it is not good it is one of the worst things that can be. One cannot see it fall below the highest aim of the greatest novelists without a pang; and this highest aim of the greatest novelists has always been to move the reader by what he must feel to be the truth. For the civilized man no representation of events can give pleasure, or fail to give pain, if it is false to his knowledge of himself and others."[143] The assertion that the only justification for the novel was that it told the truth about life, the favorite refrain of Howells, James, and Norris, can now be seen as the realist effort to extricate the novel from the miasma in which its adherents found it in the age of the mass market.

According to realist theory, the realist novel escaped its commodity status by portraying the world of which it was a part so convincingly that it matched readers' experience of the world. "A novel," James contended, "is in its broadest definition, a personal, direct impression of life; that, to begin with, constitutes its value, which is greater or less according to the intensity of impression." Converting "the very pulses of air into revelations," the novelist would justify the work by its ability to "guess the unseen from the seen."[144]

The strength of the Jamesian novel was that, unlike a commodity, it was not reducible to a thing. Although the novel dealt with the visible, it succeeded when it saw beyond to that which was essentially unquantifiable.[145] Though the proliferation of literary commodities had had disastrous effects on the novel—"It has been vulgarized, like all other kinds of literature, like everything else today, and it has proved more than some kinds accessible to vulgarization"—the form itself, James insisted, "subsists and emits its light and stimulates our desire for perfection."[146]

For all their explicit hostility to marketplace valuation of literary work, realists found it difficult to segregate art from the intrusions of economic life. Being in the world but not of it made resistance to the world's ways difficult. Though they rejected explicit capitulation, the realists did have great difficulty in establishing an inherent quality of value in the novel that did not borrow from principles at the heart of the literary marketplace. Howells, James, and Norris all came to a position that the ultimate test of artistic value rested in the subjective measure of readers, who, like the participants in a market transaction, made free choices. Such a standard left open the possibility that art could lose its value altogether. Enshrining the sovereignty of the individual subject was the fundamental principle of the marketplace from which they had hoped to disengage literature. Their notion of literary value was, to be sure, not a surrender to the whims of the market, but it did rely upon the importance of subjective liking, which ultimately compromised their search for a permanently separate value.

In arguing that although approval is not an "infallible test of merit" any work that does not have the approval of the general populace is "not the greatest performance," Howells moved close to an unacknowledged acceptance, if not of the literary marketplace itself, then of its fundamental principle.[147] James came to a similar view. Literary value did not exist prior to the act of reading; it stemmed not from objective standards but from the responses of solitary individuals. "The sort of taste that used to be called 'good,'" he wrote, "has nothing to do with the matter: we are so demonstrably in the presence of millions for whom taste is but an obscure, confused, immediate instinct. In the flare of railway bookstalls, in the shop-fronts of most booksellers, especially the provincial, in the advertisements of the weekly newspapers, and in fifty places besides, this testimony to the general preference triumphs, yielding a good-natured corner at most to a bunch of treatises on athletics or sport, or a patch of theology old and new."[148] Arguing against Zola, whom he understood to believe that there were things that people ought to like and could be made to like, James countered that no reader could be compelled to like something. "Selection will be sure to take care of itself, for it has a constant motive behind it. That motive is simple experience. As people feel life, so they will feel the art that is most closely related to it."[149]

Howells, who made the most concerted effort of the three to derive a comprehensive and unified theory of the social position of fiction, hoped to establish an objective standard. He began his attempt to prove the everlasting value of literature with the assertion that art should be a privilege performed by those "who have a proven fitness to exercise it," with its "results free to all." The writer lived in shame, knowing that "emotions pay for the provision bill." For Howells the very act of selling cheapened the production, regardless of how necessary for the author's livelihood it was and irrespective of the motivations that prompted the writing. That literature was sold like soap and shoes robbed it of some of its transcendent value. "It is perfectly true that the poem was not written for these dollars," he wrote of Emerson and Longfellow, "but it is perfectly true that it was sold for them."[150]

Given this original fall, literature had a hard time maintaining value at all. Literature, Howells noted, was a peculiar commodity. Unlike the basics of life, it had no objective value, only a subjective one. The basics were necessities— objects men could not live without. Literature was not of this class. Both the evaluation of a given novel and the demand for the genre as a whole were variable. What was gold to one reader was dross to others. The desire for a novel depended upon mood. This uncertainty raised for Howells a difficult problem. How could such an article become a commodity? How was it to be priced and fairly marketed? "The only thing that gives positive value . . . is acceptance with the readers," he asserted. He also conceded, however, that "acceptance is from month to month wholly uncertain."[151] The status of the printed word vacillated between dependence upon the market to establish its value and the understanding that the market undermined any chance for value in transcendent terms. The conclusion, which Howells resisted, was that literature as a commodity was at times worthless, not wanted by consumers.

Salvaging literature required Howells to shift his emphasis to its making, not its selling. As a made thing, the novel had a dignity that literary hucksters could not confer. Artists, he wrote, were "paid for the labor they have put into the thing done or the thing made." Literary labor, then, gave the novel value, and the vagaries of the marketplace could not undo that condition. Taking recourse in the populist distinction between those who made and those who sold and lived off the direct producers, Howells sought to reinvigorate literary value by making it rest on the privileged condition of its producer. This move, however, could not fully overcome his earlier assertion that the "only positive value" in the novel was its "acceptance." He was trying to identify the author as a worker distinct from the vendor, but he could not envision a natural economy where value existed independent of the market. He inevitably returned to the marketplace for demonstration. "If he is sick or sad . . . the author earns nothing," he argued, going on to say that "the wage he commands depends on skill and diligence." For Howells wages were market determinations, and he found himself in the position of rejecting and accepting the market as the final determinant of value. He could only conclude that "the author will never be at home in the world."[152] So ingrained was his acceptance of some sort of market framework that he counseled the young writer that though the novice might feel uncomfortable about it, brute liking was the final test, and the artist needed to study the springs of feeling in others.[153] Whereas the coterie elite and the romantics had postulated that literary value extended beyond individual tastes, Howells eventually asserted that it was the sum of those individual tastes that mattered.

In effect, Howells's literary theory applied populist thought to literature. The familiar rhetoric of the virtue of the true producer and the simultaneous identification of the market with manipulation and freedom marks both mature populist thought and Howellsian theory. Stymied by the impersonal and unpredictable nature of the rewards bestowed by commerce, the populist explanation for the failure of true value to receive just returns was fraud and unfair advantage. On the one hand, Howells worried that marketing art resulted in the corruption of the artifact and the exploitation of the true producer. On the other, he defended the market and the formal equality of exchange as democratic. The commodity form itself escaped analysis. The tensions inherent in this position led him simultaneously to attack and protect the market. Fourteen years after he pointed out the shame of commercialism and the literary system that made it possible, he argued that only the novelist could drain art of its true value by commercializing what he or she did.[154]

What constituted art in an age when the novel was clearly a commodity proved a central problem for realists. Loath to compare important work with slapdash, run-of-the-mill production for entertainment only, they hoped to establish a firm basis for art in an era of mass-market best-sellers, sliding royalties, and large advances. As writing novels came to be like every other business in its complexity and goals, Howells, James, and Norris aspired to free serious writing from the danger of irrelevance in the market. The possibility that good literature would only be this year's fashion filled them with dread. Struggling to differentiate what they did from what the business men and women of words did, realists turned to their aesthetic theory. How to write a novel to satisfy that theory posed yet more complex problems.

CHAPTER FOUR

The Novelist at the Desk

Realism and the Problem of Craft

No one is expected to strike off the whole novel in one continued fine frenzy of inspiration. As well expect the stone-mason to plant his wall in a single day. Nor is it possible to lay down any rule of thumb, any hard-and-fast schedule in the matter of novel-writing. But no work is so ephemeral, so delicate, so—in a word—artistic that it can not be improved by systematizing.
—Frank Norris

Writing in the April 1888 *Forum* on the topic of "The Element in Life in Fiction," the best-selling novelist Edward Payson Roe advanced a common sentiment of the late nineteenth century. Writing, he contended, was rarely, if ever, a matter of genius: "It is a very obvious fact, that if genius alone should produce our books, publishers would be few and printers would starve." Nor did he believe that writing entailed only the inventive powers of the novelist. "The power of invention, like that of imagination, is a natural gift, and in a greater or less degree essential to the novelist; but it is a power that can be increased by acquaintance with what people are doing, and how they do it." This increase suggested to Roe that writing is something that the novice could train to do, if one applied oneself diligently and systematically to the task.[1]

Roe's prosaic approach was a typical example of the late nineteenth-century conception of the writing process. Jettisoning the metaphysical approach of earlier times, theorists of writing preferred to stress that writing was an activity comparable to many other skilled endeavors. The concept was applied to anyone who wrote for a living, regardless of the quality or genre of the production. Both the writer who churned out newspaper paragraphs and the most rarefied poet relied upon some form of literary labor. Implied by the formulation was the suggestion that journalists, novelists, essayists, and poets shared a common socioeconomic position that seemed to unite them far more than the genres in which they worked seemed to divide them.

Some writers, including William Dean Howells, went so far as to make of authors another species of worker. Yet such a usage was not analytically precise. Unlike the emerging industrial proletariat, writers did not suffer erosion of work skills, sell their labor, punch a time clock, or toil under direct supervision. For all the editorial intervention of the Gilded Age, they kept control of their work process and retained the ability to initiate production. Even the most harried paragrapher did not turn out a standardized product in the way that a machine toolmaker did. The notion that the writer was a laborer did, however, have an ideological function. Unlike antebellum writers, who had no use for anything so common as work, postbellum writers delighted in the implication that they, like farmers or craftsmen, were an integral part of American life. In claiming that their value was in their productivity, they ceased to be "aristocratic" dabblers and became useful citizens instead.

For realists, the concept of literary labor had special significance. Using "labor" as most accurate description of the writing process allowed realists to focus attention on the way in which the valuable text was produced and to differentiate realist work from that of their predecessors. Romantics had explained their creation through the concept of "inspiration" or "revelation"— the merging of the writer with a higher force. For them, writing was a matter of drawing upon predetermined gifts as the moment warranted. Realists countered this mystical notion with one firmly rooted in everyday human activity: "work." For them, writing as it was actually conducted involved diligence, dedication, and exertion.[2] Actual writing was honest toil that required careful attention to detail and meticulous planning. Writing had a regular, rather than fitful, pace. The realist object in so designating the writing process was to match the work of writing with the effect produced by the novel. Both the method of production and the text that emerged from it were to approximate everyday experience. A natural process, realists seemed to contend, would produce a natural novel.

Realists did not hold that work itself was sufficient to create valuable texts. The "writing as work" ideology was not exclusively a realist one. Nearly every variety of late nineteenth-century novelist claimed affinity to this new ideal. As a result, realists were forced to assert that the "work" of writing had to be of a special kind. Although their critics charged that realists lacked a sense of craft, most who wrote in the genre held to some notion of literary skill, which they saw as essential to their self-definition as artists. It was, however, a skill that rested less on beautifying words and clever turns of phrases than on keen observation and the ability to realize the possibilities inherent in the material. In their reworking of the concept of craft, realists attempted to imbue the value of work with distinction and in the process separate themselves from those that they regarded as solely commodity producers.

Observation and the realization of the possibilities inherent in the material created for realists a bind that set the limits on realist narration. On the one hand, they contended that the author was a simple servant to the material, for the material dictated the story. The author simply let it unfold. The realist goal of natural stories led, like the commodity production that it was, to the effacement of human intervention and the removal of touches of human creation. On the other hand, skill in observation, according to realist theory, was essential, and it was nearly always individual.

Put another way, the realist theory of the work of writing was divided between an industrial and a preindustrial conception. The industrial conception took as natural the existence of a commodity divorced from the world of human action and subjective intervention. The preindustrial or artisanal mode stressed the individual and human touches necessary to demonstrating that work had gone on. The realist text therefore simultaneously had a life outside the author's hand and yet required the author's touch. The stress on work thrust the writer into the novel at the same time it recalled the author from it. The result of this double bind was that realist novels had a formal irony. Two discourses—one in which the objective narrator provided the natural material, and the other, more covert, in which the writer fashioned the material— operated simultaneously. In the end, life, which seemed so self-evident that realists did not bother to define it, became a problematic entity.

The Diligent Writer: The Work Process and the Eclipse of Inspiration

The emphasis that realists placed on the human and natural origins of writing was a far remove from antebellum conceptions. Though not denying that writing consisted of effort and fully aware of the necessities of responding to the existence of the marketplace in literary commodities, Emerson, Whitman, Melville, and Hawthorne all counted at some point on a quasi-divine spark, an inspiration that enabled the specially endowed writer to pierce the world of phenomena and penetrate to the noumena, the true essence. For Emerson, reclamation of the human project could come about only through intuition. As Michael Gilmore has pointed out, the attempts of the American Romantics to escape the pressures imposed by the marketplace in literature often borrowed from the very principles that they hoped to overcome.[3] Nonetheless, few antebellum authors consciously and deliberately admitted that writing was a common activity. The dictates of the market may have forced the writer to disguise the nature of authorial work, making it more palatable, but for the Romantics, writing a valuable text required skills that were different both in kind and in degree from simple prose composition or popular novels.[4]

The sense that for the Romantics writing had a timelessness can be discerned in Emerson's view of the poet's task as recapturing the time before human activity occurred:

> Criticism is infested with a cant of materialism, which assumes that manual skill and activity is the first merit of all men, and disparages such as say and do not, overlooking the fact, that some men, namely, poets, are natural sayers. . . . For poetry was all written before time was, and whenever we are so finely organized that we can penetrate into that region where the air is music, we hear those primal warblings and attempt to write them down, but we lose ever and anon a word, or a verse, and substitute something of our own, and thus miswrite the poem. . . . The sign and credentials of the poet are that he announces that which no man foretold. He is the true and only doctor; he knows and tells; he is the only teller of news for he was present and privy to the appearance which he describes.[5]

Whitman's "Song of Myself" contains a related view of the poet as the inspired articulator who drew his images from his ability to merge with his surroundings. As he formulated the matter, the key to the artist's enterprise was more nearly repose than exertion.

> I sing of myself and what I assume you shall assume
> For any atom as good as belongs to you.
> I loafe and invite my soul;
> I lean and loafe at my ease,
> Observing a spear of summer grass.

Although the poet may have ranked highest in the antebellum intellectual hierarchy, many novelists shared the poet's belief in the writer's mystical gifts, in earthly repose, and in trust in interiority and spirituality. In practice antebellum novelists devoted nearly as much time to composition as did their successors. Hawthorne, for instance, wrote nearly nine hours a day during the creation of *The Scarlet Letter*.[6] The difference, however, was the formal weight that Romantics gave to labor itself. What counted was not the work of writing, but the special insight. Drawing upon the remnants of the British aristocratic tradition of amateurism and at times hesitant to see writing as human labor (to substitute something of the author was for Emerson to mis-write the poem), they presented the image of the nonchalant author who awaited the muse rather than forced a way through problems. As they wrote of their writing experiences, Romantics stressed that if inspiration was not forth-coming, then no amount of coaxing would deliver the story. Hawthorne's work ethic more closely resembled modern-day colonial workers' than that of Max Weber's bourgeoisie. "As to the daily course of our life," he wrote in his *American Notebooks*, "I have written with pretty commendable diligence, averaging from two to four hours a day. . . . I might have written more, but I was content to earn only so much as might suffice for our immediate wants."[7]

Edgar Allan Poe's sense of the dangers inherent in a work method controlled by the marketplace—a condition that paralleled his actual situation—is clear in his parody of contemporaries who lacked inspiration. The very title, "Thing-um Bob, Esq.," suggests that the danger that the literary marketplace held would turn men into things—draft horses of words—loomed large in the fears of men imbued with the spirit of elevated art.

> How I laboured—how I toiled—how I wrote! Ye gods, did I not write? I knew not the word "ease." By day I adhered to my desk, and at night, a pale student, I consumed the midnight oil. You should have seen me—you should. I leaned to the right, I leaned to the left. I sat forward. I sat back-ward . . . and, through all, I wrote. Through joy and through sorrow, I—wrote. Through hunger and through thirst, I—wrote. Through good report and through ill report, I—wrote. Through sunshine and through moon-shine, I—wrote.[8]

This antebellum nightmare approximated postbellum normalcy. By the time realists came to maturity, the irregular tempo of antebellum fiction writing and the reliance on the faculty of genius that flowed from it were pleasant, if unattainable, relics of a bygone era. Unlike their antebellum predecessors, late nineteenth-century writers had to be constantly attuned to the demands of increasingly demanding publishers and a novel-crazed public, and not a smaller group of like-minded readers, in order to maintain even a modest standard of living. Maintaining this standard required a continual pace. In responding to the demands of the market, realists insured the eclipse of inspiration, genius, and the uneven production rhythms of antebellum writing. As a consequence their theory of the writing process resembled their theory of literature. What mattered was the concrete, the nonmetaphysical materiality of the process.

Realists were insistent that writing was above all "work." In their writing about the process of composition, they stressed not sudden bursts of insight but the harder and more difficult task of fashioning and shaping. In his seminal essay "The Man of Letters as a Man of Business" Howells repeatedly and forcefully contended that the writing was a process of exertion and human creation. Like the mechanic and day laborer, the writer lived by the sweat of his brow. "It ought to be our [writers'] glory," he declared, "that we produce something that . . . was not there before, that at least we fashion something or shape something new."[9] Norris likewise emphasized the necessity of training and work in writing and derided the view of writing as mystical visitation. Training, he asserted in "Novelists to Order—While You Wait," not "genius," accounted for quality literary work. Although he believed that the gift of storytelling was inbred, he argued that it had been systematically rooted out of the young by the nature of the maturation process. Understanding the mechanics of fiction required an "acute sensitivity" that could be acquired. All it took was "great patience and a willingness to plod, for the time being."[10]

Dismissing inspiration also meant dismissing the concept of genius. Howells labeled the concept a superstition that had its roots in the aristocratic domination of the literary arts. Antidemocratic to the core, the concept of genius boosted a favored class of writers whose "innate" abilities allowed them to parade their gifts before an overawed and subservient readership. This concept, Howells contended, had the effect of making literature distant and mysterious rather than human and vital. For him the only intelligible meaning that could be given to the term was "the Mastery which comes to any man according to his powers and diligence in any direction." Norris argued that the frequency with which "genius" was used to explain the writing process only indicated its uselessness in analysis.[11]

Lauding exertion in theory, realists were diligent in practice. Both their career production and day-to-day output were prodigious. Where Romantics negotiated the market with trepidation, uncertain of how enthusiastically to commit themselves to production, realists tended to accept the regimen of constant work. Romantics tended to produce few works in the course of a career; realists many. Howells produced a book and a farce a year for the duration of his Harper contract, and he was equally productive before and after the ten-year agreement. Only in his seventies did he slow his pace. James averaged nearly a book a year during his highly productive 1880s and 1890s, in addition to a prodigious short-story output.[12] Malcolm Cowley identified one mark of naturalism as its "delirium of production, like factories trying to set new records."[13]

Constant production prompted grand visions. Though some may have chafed under the pressure of the seemingly ceaseless demands of the publishing system, realists and naturalists responded with a zest for writing. Spurred by the desire to do big subjects, they embarked on a large number of epics and trilogies. Norris's projected trilogy, *The Wheat*, which was halted by his death at the age of thirty-two, rivaled in ambition and scope any previously announced project in American fiction. He proposed to do three novels that traced the human and social relationships bounded up in the production, sale, and distribution of the staff of life and to follow the course of the wheat from its production in the West to its sale in Chicago and then to Europe after its milling into bread. In addition he planned a trilogy on the battle of Gettysburg as a follow-up. Though no doubt his second project stemmed from his latent competition with Crane, whose *Red Badge of Courage* was an acknowledged standard among his cohorts, Norris was incapable of thinking small. As he wrote to his Louisville confidante, Isaac Marcosson, he enjoyed letting his kite fly as high as it could go.[14]

Not only did realists rarely pause between books, they seemed hardly to cease work during the writing of each novel. Harold Frederic wrote as much as 4,000 words a day. David Graham Phillips, who published seventeen novels in ten years and left behind the manuscripts for six more upon his assassination in 1911, once accomplished the almost unheard-of rate of 18,000 words in a single day. Upton Sinclair, who once wrote formula stories for the mass-publishing firm of Street and Smith, applied the rapid-fire procedures he learned there to his personal production.[15] The inconsistencies and infelicities that crop up more than occasionally in realist works owe much to the breakneck haste with which they were written. Even those whose style is considerably more graceful and construction more unified than Sinclair's and Phillips's hardly dawdled. Despite some moments of indecision and doubt, Twain was capable of a prolific daily output. Writing to Howells with barely concealed delight, he noted his vigorous production during the writing of *Life on the Mississippi* and *Huckleberry Finn*. "Why, it's like old times, to step straight into the study, damp from the breakfast table and sail right in and sail right on, the whole day long, with no thought of running short of stuff or words. I wrote 4000 words to-day & I touch upon 3000 & upwards pretty often & don't fall below 2,600 on any working day. And when I get fagged out, I lie abed a couple of days & read & smoke, and then go at it again for 6 or 7 days."[16] Even Sundays were not sacrosanct. Some Sundays Twain would rise and breakfast at

5:15 and work for five hours or so. "Nothing," he wrote Howells, "is half so good as literature hooked Sunday on the sly."[17] Although Howells himself had a reputation for stodginess and careful work and kept to a modest, Hawthornian daily three hours in writing his novels, he was capable of writing at a brisk clip. Kenneth Lynn reports that during the writing of *A Modern Instance* Howells reached 3,000 words a day, twice his normal rate. Only the illness, which Lynn conjectures was a nervous breakdown brought on by the complications of the plot, slowed his rush.[18]

Speed in writing did not mean a heedless or unprepared effort. Producing a large number of novels in the course of a career and a large output every day was not the result of indifferent devotion or unpredictable inspiration. Unlike antebellum authors, realists could not afford to wait until inspiration favored them. Their occasional offhand comments aside—Twain once referred to the refilling of his writing tank—few realists depended upon a muse. Regular work habits replaced inspiration as a remedy for "writer's block." Although few went to the length of Jack London, who kept a daily schedule and wrote steadily on a six-day work week, or the Englishman Anthony Trollope, whose writing habits reveal a typical Victorian compulsiveness, realists did have writing itineraries.[19] Henry James's careful schedule was typical. Dictation—his preferred method in later times—was performed in the morning. Recuperative walks around Lamb House in Rye followed this task. After his assistant had typed the text, James reread and revised. When he finished his revisions, he prepared for the next morning's work. Later he planned new stories and wrote scenarios, which formed the blueprint for his writing. Even the evenings did not go to waste. Leon Edel reports that they were devoted to philosophical contemplation.[20] For a writer whom Harold Frederic scorned as a peripatetic houseguest to the English upper class, James did a great deal of work daily.

Realists not only planned their days, they planned their books. Given the vast amount of material, the society-wide scope of the text, and their rush to write, no other approach could have guaranteed a coherent product. Their daily notes are filled with remarks on the regularity and order that they aimed to give the writing process. Though driven to write, they were loath to allow a white heat to govern composition. Process did not give way to uncontrolled reverie. Nearly all have left outlines and prepublication notes from which they worked. Although the writing of each book had its own particular tempo, the general pattern of planning and thought remain constant. Howells, for instance, often anticipated, if not resolved, details and problems before he wrote the text. Although he was ill while writing the climactic scene in *A Modern Instance*, in which Bartley Hubbard abandons his wife Marcia, Howells had sketched the outline long before he put pen to paper to give his idea representation—whatever the psychological resistance he may have felt toward implementing it when the time came. Influenced by a production of *Medea*, Howells vowed to update the play, and his notes indicate that he was well aware of the requirements of such a plan.[21]

Realists' preparation for writing differed from that of their predecessors. Romantics, following the dictates of "genius," had regarded the story as coming to the author, penetrating to that region, where, in Emerson's terms, "the air is music"; realists reversed the process and scoured their society for proper materials. Earlier writers had, of course, engaged in observation and had kept notebooks. Few, however, regarded the compilation of observed phenomena as an essential component of the writing, or more than a subsidiary moment in the process. What was essential was the transformation that inspiration effected, a transformation that was accomplished more readily in a rural retreat where the muse was more likely to make herself felt. Late nineteenth-century writers viewed the study as confinement, and they specialized in empirical investigation. Howells attended an Indiana divorce trial to gather material for *A Modern Instance* and spent months in New England shoe towns and in textile factories doing research for *Annie Kilburn*. Crane explored the slums of New York for the material that found its way into *Maggie* and *George's Mother*, earning notoriety and trouble for his efforts. Norris, using advance money provided by McClure, devoted nearly a year to ferreting out the details of the Union Pacific operations in California for use in *The Octopus*. Harold Frederic spent a number of months inspecting his native Mohawk Valley for *Seth's Brother's Wife*. Although the image of an impeccably dressed Henry James prowling the East End of London strikes an incongruous note, his introduction to *The Princess Casamassima* and his notes on the speech of the people attest to his firsthand observation of the English working class.[22]

This dedication to observation and the implied distrust of inspiration provoked sharp criticism from contemporaries dedicated to preserving literary traditions. Bliss Perry, for instance, took exception to Henry James's injunction that the aspiring novelist take plenty of notes. Perry, a turn-of-the-century academic, complained that this procedure made a fetish of facts and promoted the illusion that art was simply a process of observation: "If human imagination cannot freely master its material and remould fact in accordance with the demands of the higher spiritual truth, then facts may prove worse than useless."[23]

The stress on observation and the emphasis on work rather than repose meant that the realist was never quite off duty. Every moment bore fruit to store away for use in later novels. Although James felt that the reporter in Balzac often overwhelmed the originator, he honored the French writer as producing "the most organized and administered, and thereby most exposed to systematic observation and portrayal" fiction yet produced. Balzac's strength, James concluded, was that he had "a passion for exactitude, . . . the appetite of an ogre, for *all* the kinds of facts." The point was seconded in an item that appeared in the *New Orleans Times-Democrat*, which opined that writers were incapable of relaxation because their brains could never be turned off. They were "forever pursued by ideas insistent yet elusive. In the most subconscious way, mental note-taking goes on, even in idle moments."[24]

Consonant with the rejection of genius was the realist insistence upon polishing and revision. In part this was an accommodation made to the demands of the literary market and the intervention of editors. It was also quite consistent with their view of what constituted writing. Because they regarded the writing of the novel as a human activity and not something that came to the author from on high, realists were less likely to believe that a first draft was a perfect one. The novel did not come to the writer fully formed, but was always in the process of being made. It is true that some, like the very popular Jack London, claimed that they sent a story off once finished, regardless of quality. Most realists, however, did not follow this tack. Norris held that the great author tested and retested his formulations.[25]

Technological developments contributed to the changes in the nature of the author's professional duties. One reason that the late nineteenth-century writer could always be on duty was the invention of the fountain pen in 1884. Carrying its own supply of ink, the instrument allowed realists to record their impressions at any time. No longer limited to the spatial and temporal limitation that the study and the inkwell imposed, realists could expand work time and increase recording abilities. The ease of transport and the permanency of ink made the new invention superior to the quill and the pencil.

And although realists still generally wrote by hand, as had their predecessors, machinery and paid labor made their way into the writing process. Perhaps the most important landmark in the transformation of the means of writing was the invention of the typewriter in 1868. The realists' mastery of, or more precisely, experimentation with, the machine in part made possible their prodigious output. Those who had artisan and machinist backgrounds were especially enthralled with the new writing technology. One leitmotif of the Twain–Howells correspondence was the zeal with which the two authors took up the typewriter—both had once worked as typesetters—and their resulting unhappiness with the actual operation. For both men, the promise of increased speed was not always met. In 1874, when Twain complained of inaccurate spelling and malfunction, Howells wrote that he would gladly take the infernal machine off Twain's hands. Twain himself regarded the typewriter with the same ambivalence that his fictional Connecticut Yankee displayed toward the industrial changes in King Arthur's court. Lured to the machine by his hope that technology could unlock the knotty problems of life, Twain soon discovered that it was not the panacea he had hoped it would be. Even when he had mastered its operation, he complained that it did not aid composition. Twenty years after he had purchased his first typewriter, Twain grumbled to Howells that the machine was an inanimate and unhelpful encumbrance: "You can't write literature with it, because it hasn't any ideas & it hasn't any gift for elaboration, or smartness of talk or vigor of action, or felicity of expression, but it is just matter-of-fact, compressive, unornamental & as grave & unsmiling as the devil."[26] Both Howells and Twain complained at times that they felt they were in fact controlled by the machine rather than controlling it, and both eventually returned to pen-and-paper composition.

Few realists actually sat in front of the typewriter. Instead they relied upon an assistant who operated the machine to aid composition, particularly in making rough drafts that were eventually corrected and revised. The invention of the Pitman and Eclectic systems of shorthand in the 1860s and 1870s, and the more popular Gregg in the 1880s, allowed writers to retain competent stenographers, who took down their dictated novels and later transcribed the work on the typewriter. The advance of writing technology and the immersion into the literary marketplace combined to render anachronistic the individual artist who toiled by dint of inspiration to create a manuscript in the isolation of the study. David Graham Phillips managed his 18,000 words per day only by imaginatively shuttling between three different stenographers working simultaneously. In his case the individual writer resembled more a master craftsman than a creator.[27] Upton Sinclair and Jack London actually served as chairmen of a literary production process. Both farmed out parts of their novels and then did the final work and applied their names to the final product. Sinclair Lewis began his literary career when he successfully sold story ideas to London.[28] Employing labor did not divorce realist novelists from the production process. The ideas and the composition were fundamentally theirs. Hired help simply speeded the process. James often dictated to a secretary, one of whom, Theodora Bosanquet, wrote a book on her experiences in which she compared her work to a pianist accompanying a singer.[29]

Dictation, typewriters, and fountain pens refashioned the way novels were written, but their effect on the finished product was harder to discern. For some, like Phillips, dictation led to a brisk, almost cursory, rush of words and broad coverage. For others, like James, the result was the opposite, a thicket of prose that increasingly circled its object. James's dictation in his so-called later period no doubt made his works more prolix and full of pauses and circumlocutions that parallel the flow of language during speech. Yet the charge often made, that the new methods increased James's verbosity, is harder to sustain. More likely, the use of dictation and typewriter aided him in finding a method that matched his theories of language. James himself took great pains to deny that his technique of writing determined his style. The machine allowed him to realize his belief that the flow of language corresponded to the flow of consciousness; the increased speed of the typewriter enhanced the artist's ability to capture that swiftly changing flux. The problem of James's language was finally the problem of finding a language that matched reality. As reality became increasingly more complicated, the language became increasingly dense.[30]

The realists' continual production did not lead them to complain that the work drove them. Although Howells's comment to Twain that James "makes it go, but if there could be anything worse for me than a typewriter, it would be a human typewriter" suggests the possibility, realists seem to have felt little of the alienation typical of industrialization.[31] Though many found publishers' demands exorbitant and intrusive, none truly imagined himself part of a mechanical process beyond personal control, as a manipulated cog. Few complained of the helpless feeling of meaninglessness. Norris went so far as to dispute the possibility of overwork. "Rapid work," he wrote, "may cause the deterioration of a commercial article, but it by no means follows that the authors who are called upon to produce a large number of books are forced into composition of unworthy literature. . . . The writer's material is life itself, inexhaustible and renewed from day to day, and his brain is only the instrument that adapts life to fiction."[32] Nor for that matter did many realists commit themselves to constant work from either dire necessity or external compulsion. Crane, Twain, and Frederic did have debts to pay, and Howells had the burden of family medical expenses, but none wrote solely to pay crushing bills. To be sure, the cost of high living in Crane's case, the support of two families in Frederic's, and poor speculation in Twain's prompted those realists to write, but a more important reason seems to be the internal need to compose.

Although the necessity of satisfying the need of the publishing system for novels set objective boundaries on realist writing, realist novelists transformed the objective social condition into a personal goal. Writing gave them a social position and allowed them a personal definition. Realists wrote to live and lived to write. For James, writing itself was "soothing . . . the sacred and salutary refuge from all these vulgarities and pains." Most reacted as Howells did when faced with a problem in the text of *The Landlord at Lion's Head*. Not content to await the muse, he resolved to "keep working; keep beating harder and harder at the wall which seemed to close me in, till at last I broke through into the daylight beyond." Even Twain, who had found himself in the ironic position of having to write to pay off debts incurred in speculations designed to free him from constant production, showed this internal drive. Writing to Howells on the completion of *A Connecticut Yankee in King Arthur's Court*, he remarked, "Well, my book is written—let it go. But if it were only to write over again there wouldn't be so many things left out. They burn in me; & they keep multiplying & multiplying; but now they can't ever be said. And besides, they would require a library-& a pen warmed up in hell."[33]

The Skillful Author: The Art of Artlessness

By rejecting both genius and inspiration and stressing the uncelestial aspects of writing, realists aimed at matching the process of production with the effect they hoped to achieve. For them a writing process steeped in material reality was designed to create texts equally anchored. In the process, they opened themselves up to the charge that they lacked craft. Opponents who accused realism of being artless and crude were not only criticizing the sometimes shocking subject matter, its reluctance to idealize, and its apparent lack of moralizing; they were also deriding its apparently simple presentation. Even at its best, critics maintained, realism was "mere" reproduction, the transfer of the photographic principle to fiction. Rendering as exact a portrait as possible, the announced goal of the realists, was simply substituting quantity of observation for quality of design. Description, a necessary support to art, was not for most established critics of the late nineteenth century the essence of art; imagination was. Such was the burden of Hamilton Wright Mabie's review of Howells's *Rise of Silas Lapham* for the *Andover Review*. Noting the author's attempt to learn secrets through observation, the method of science, and not though insight, Mabie went on to delineate the novel's failings: "The patience and work involved in the making of some novels constructed on this method are beyond praise; but they must not make us blind to the fact that no method can take the place of original power."[34]

Mabie's commentary was one of the more reasoned critiques of the lack of craft in realism. A more intemperate attack that captured the more popular reaction appeared in the December 1894 issue of *The Forum*. Celebrating what he considered to be the demise of the "Epidermis School," W. H. Thayer catalogued the genre's literary sins. Realism, he said, abandoned the artistic principles of the Greeks—symmetry, grace, and beauty—in a false and misguided attempt at scientific precision. Not only did this attempt dehumanize the author and make the author incapable of making human judgments, but it sought to accumulate so much detail to "produce as sure an effect of reality as genius produces by using a few essentials." Kipling could do in one paragraph, he contended, what took Howells and James ten pages. Whereas the Greeks had lived by the credo of "nothing superfluous," Tolstoy operated on the assumption that art put in everything, and added a little more. The result, Thayer claimed, was dullness pure and simple, for realists had no craft.[35]

This charge was in accordance with prevailing standards of literary craft. Literary tradition held that craft required elegance in writing, restricted selection, and, above all, grace. Realists themselves did much to advance the charges against them. Explicitly attacking "pretty" writing as false, they contributed to the belief that realism required little in the way of special verbal ingenuity. In calling upon literature to abandon its pretensions and display life as lived, realists often gave the impression that the end mattered more than the method of achieving it. Their insistence on "truth," "life," and "experience," and the companion stress on the "work" of writing was a direct counter to the belief that literature was above all graceful. In place of glorious and special language, realists aimed at matching as closely as possible word and object described.

Yet it was not quite true that they believed that any words would do. Norris, who gave the essence of realist craft in an essay entitled "Simplicity in Art," rejected "elaborate phrase, rhetoric, the intimacy of metaphor and allegory and simile" and pointed out that readers and critics are prone to believe "that the more intense the emotional quality of the scene described, the more 'vivid,' the more exalted, the more richly colored we suppose should be the language." In fact, he argued, the substantives should speak for themselves. If the writing is done correctly, comment is superfluous. "If [something is] beautiful, we do not want him [the author] to tell us so. We want him to make it beautiful and our own appreciation will supply the adjectives."[36] Craft, therefore, constituted the achievement of effect without calling the reader's attention to itself. The "simple, natural, honest" account was art that appeared artless. And though the realists believed that human endeavor gave fiction value, they recognized that not all "literary work" was of the same quality. What prompted their hostility to the business men and women of words, who envisioned the writing trade as simply meeting existing demand, was that their art was far from artless.

Spurred by the promise of riches and the absence of formal barriers of entrance into the field, men and women took to novel writing in unprecedented numbers in the years following the Civil War. Though a precise reckoning is probably impossible, the evidence from publishers suggests a remarkable increase. Publishers and editors revealed that unsolicited manuscripts were on the rise. Many came from unlikely sources. Walter Hines Page confided that three-fourths of the manuscripts submitted were "novels that have been written by lonely men or by men who have no successful occupation and most of these are conscious or unconscious imitations of recent popular novels." Even a firm that published few novels, such as Putnam's, received more than 150 submissions a year.[37] The deluge grew to such proportions that Frank Norris, who intimately experienced the mechanics of the book market during his stint as reader for Doubleday and Page, facetiously wrote, "At a conservative estimate there are 70 million people in the United States. At a liberal estimate 100,000 of these have lost use of both arms: remain then 69,900,000 who write novels. Indeed many are called, but few—oh what a scanty, skimped handful that few represent—are chosen."[38]

The unquestioned popularity of novels forced those who saw their role as the defense of the pristine qualities of literature to reevaluate the genre. This change of opinion most likely further accelerated the popularity of the novel by removing some of the barriers to its acceptance. Noah Porter, the president of Yale University, urged that the inevitable must be accepted. Unlike earlier literary custodians, he did not condemn all novels. An indiscriminate attack on the genre, he reasoned, left those interested in moral rectitude at a disadvantage, for the charge that all novels were harmful in and of themselves was so clearly false that it discredited the entire argument about morality. Although no true advocate of the novel, Porter claimed to see the possibility that novels enlarged the imagination and extended the sympathies, "purifying and ennobling" attentive and watchful readers. Unable to bring the force of elevated opinion against the proliferating novel, Porter instructed his readers that "to hold intercourse with such creations, if the scenes be innocent and the transcripts are made from no vicious and degrading realities, cannot be unfavorable to pure and elevated moral feeling, even if there be no moral to the tale or poem and no religious enforcements of its lessons."[39]

The growing intellectual acceptance and the proliferation of novels made the question of literary goals a salient issue. For realists the proposition was not merely an academic exercise. At stake was the direction that American literature would take in the years that followed. If realists could not find some way to differentiate the work that they did from other kinds of literary endeavor, the standard would fail to provide a reliable guide and would have to be jettisoned in favor of popularity. Differentiating "good" fiction from "bad" had caused less trouble for antebellum literary arbiters. "Serious" fiction had conformed to various rules of language, subject matter, and philosophy. Those who prided themselves on their literary tastes immediately recognized inferior novels, and though they may have read them for leisure or amusement they never confused them with important art. The realm of art, if not impregnable, at least had specific boundaries that trash did not destroy. Although Hawthorne had bewailed the predominance of the "damned female scribblers," his complaint was economic in nature. The presence of the scribblers in the marketplace meant less opportunity for his books to attract consumers. He did not believe that standards were in jeopardy or that the existence of inferior writers canceled out the intellectual worth of his contribution. Because the novel was still a slightly disreputable form, literary arbiters had little difficulty in designating unseemly and worthless works.[40]

The postwar acceptance of the novel as a valuable genre was a victory fraught with problems. The advance of fiction into more respectable venues only blurred the distinction between taste levels. The fiction that appeared in the high-toned monthlies—*Atlantic*, *Scribner's*, *Putnam's*, and *Harper's*— was decidedly sentimental and ill-executed. For every story like Rebecca Harding Davis's "Life in the Iron Mills" (*Atlantic*, 1861), there were countless drawing-room dramas.[41] As Henry James appreciated, the large numbers of novels and the lack of standards made possible a time when the good would be drowned in the mediocre.[42]

Criticism of the quality of United States fiction had long been a staple of European writing. European critics charged that one hundred years after the Declaration of Independence Americans could reckon only Hawthorne as an authentic contribution to world literature.[43] Because Melville was generally unknown and Poe's personal habits disqualified him from serious consideration in an age that treated the character of the author as a crucial criterion of literary worth (although some of the avant-garde, like Baudelaire, did honor Poe's contributions), Hawthorne was left to carry the banner of American literary accomplishment by himself. Although the United States had produced curiosity pieces like *Uncle Tom's Cabin*, the general European consensus was that the nation was not distinguished. This meager output called into question whether the United States was capable of producing important literary men and women. Many foreign commentators drew the conclusion that the United States was the preeminent commercial culture, one that had fulfilled Tocqueville's prediction that a democracy infuses a trading spirit into literature.

That trading spirit had given rise to a culture predicated on instant gratification, or so foreigners hypothesized. The mass culture that emerged in the late nineteenth century was still in its infancy, and many of its participants could easily be branded as marginal—women, immigrants, and the young.[44] Their tastes were either undisciplined or incapable of training, according to critical Europeans. Matthew Arnold, who visited the United States in 1884, complained that Americans shunned Dickens and Thackeray for a native writer named Roe. George Steevens, who revealed his opinion of the republic in the title of his book, *The Land of the Dollar*, contended that the enormous wealth of the United States corrupted literature. Lord Bryce could not find writers of even the second rank and blamed their absence on the constant activity of American life. Knut Hamsun, the Nobel Prize–winning Norwegian novelist, bitterly deplored the stultifying effect of the immense quantity of books without distinction: "Literature is not a force in America, not an educational medium, but only a more or less diverting amusement." His opinion of Ulysses S. Grant, whose memoirs received much praise, was that he "could not even write his own language correctly."[45]

Such critiques hit deep with American literati who were concerned about their nation's cultural accomplishments. Ever since the founding of the republic, questions of literary value and national destiny had been intertwined. For some revolutionaries like Thomas Jefferson one proof of the merit of independence was the quality of American literature. Writing in *Notes on the State of Virginia*, Jefferson reacted sharply to Abbé Raynal's gibe that America had yet to produce one good poet: "When we shall have existed as a people as long as the Greeks did before they produced a Homer, the Romans a Virgil, the French a Racine, the English a Shakespeare and Milton, should this reproach be still true, we will enquire from what unfriendly causes it has proceeded, that the other countries of Europe and quarters of the earth shall not have inscribed any name in the roll of poets."[46] Philip Freneau echoed this lament in his poem "Literary Importation":

It seems we had a spirit to humble a throne.
Have genius for science inferior to none,
But hardly encourage a plant of our own:
If a college be planned,
'Tis all at a stand
'Till in Europe we send at a shameful expense,
To send us a book-worm to teach us some sense.[47]

This issue of American literary contribution seemed especially compelling in the postwar nationalism that followed Reconstruction. What began as a new series of calls for an American literature that matched the greatness of the nation's institutions became part of the debate over realism. In 1868, John DeForest issued what was perhaps the first plea for the Great American Novel. Promulgating a variant of realism that insisted one had to write of what one knew, by which he meant writing about American life, DeForest saw as the root cause of the literary malaise of the nation an inattention to the facts of

American life. To insure work comparable to European classics, American writers needed to inject the indigenous landscape into their work. In De-Forest's view, American authors were so blinded by outdated models that they did not notice the inapplicability of those models. Consequently they bent their work to make it conform. "Is there . . . a single tale which paints American life so broadly, so truly, and sympathetically that every American of feeling and culture is forced to acknowledge the picture as a likeness of something which he knows? Throwing out 'Uncle Tom's Cabin,' we must answer, 'Not one!' "[48]

Four years later T. S. Perry concluded on the basis of DeForest's own *Miss Ravenel's Conversion from Secession to Loyalty* that mere accuracy to American types was not enough. The writer had to make his characters live. In Perry's view, American fiction suffered not from the absence of Americanism but from a lack of vitalism. Mechanical application of the rules guaranteed mediocrity. "It is the bane of realism, as of all isms, to forget that it represents only one important side of truth, and to content itself, as complacently as an advocate, with seeing its own rules obeyed, and, generally, with the narrowest construction of the law. By insisting above all things on the novel being American, we mistake the means for the end." Like many critics who aimed to reconcile realism with portrayal of the ideal, Perry saw the redemption of American literature in a creative blending. "The idealizing novelist will be the real novelist. All truth does not lie in facts."[49]

It was H. H. Boyesen, Hamsun's countryman, who linked American literary prospects to literary sociology. In a *Forum* article entitled "Why We Have No Great Novelists," Boyesen argued that the American novelist's hunger for popularity delivered the judgment of quality into the hands of an ill-educated readership that required constant excitement from the portrayal of the abnormal. Particularly to blame, Boyesen felt somewhat contradictorily, was the delicate taste of women, who formed the vast majority of the readership. Following the realist contention that writers were products of the environment and their work, not born as geniuses, he argued that American women made American writers in the most repressive fashion. In a bitter diatribe he complained of the inordinate power of young women: "To be a purveyor of amusement (especially if one suspects he has the stuff in him for something better) is not at all amusing. To be obliged to repress that which is best in him and offer that which is of no consequence is the plight to which many a novelist, in this paradise of women, is reduced." Public taste, Boyesen charged, was in its reality that of the young American girl: "She is the Iron Madonna who strangles in her fond embrace the American novelist; the Moloch upon whose altar he sacrifices, willingly or unwillingly, his chances of greatness."[50]

The Iron Madonna was not the only blockade that the postwar literary marketplace erected to the achievement of literary value. Equally disturbing to realists was the tendency of the marketing staff to place commodities in rigid niches. Booksellers, publishers, and readers seemed to see books as stocks to be speculated in. Colonial novels, Down East novels, *Prisoner of Zenda* novels, bohemian novels fashioned on *Trilby*, and historical romances of the *Alice of Old Vincennes* and *When Knighthood Was in Flower* stripe followed each other in rapid succession. "B'gosh" fiction, the portrayal of rural eccentrics begun by Edward Westcott's surprise best-seller *David Harum* (1898), reigned supreme until Irving Bacheller's *Eben Holden* (1900) exhausted the market.[51] Other dog-eared tastes were constant throughout the shifting popularity of fads. William Dean Howells reserved particular venom for the vapid Christmas stories that adorned the year-end issues of the major periodicals.[52] Writers soon earned classifications based on their particular specialties. Literary magazines, encouraged by publisher's categorizations, were rarely content to refer to novelists; one was a sentimental, or children's, or Western, or Eastern, or adventure, or mystery writer.[53]

Both the nature of the audience and the segmentation of the market challenged the rewards that men of letters had claimed as theirs during the antebellum period. The classic antebellum author had aspired to influence on the basis of a personal mastery of all of the liberal arts. Thoreau, for instance, saw in the pursuit of exchange value a retreat from the author's office as aesthetic legislator whose detachment allowed him special insights. Self-sufficiency, not accumulation, gave the artist the capability of writing a text that would have real impact.[54] As the proliferation of knowledge made it more difficult for one to know it all and the spread of literary commodification stepped up its pace, the antebellum concept of fame—the standard by which men of letters judged their accomplishments—seemed more impossible to attain and progressively more irrelevant.

Writing from "The Editor's Study," William Dean Howells acknowledged that although money was not a fit reward for literature, "in the economic chaos of competitive society, there is no other way for authors to live."[55] Living required a receptive and paying audience. This truth invariably shaped the "work" of writing. Entertainment, rather than insight, became the quality that writers consciously pursued and hoped to embed within their product. Edgar Saltus, a short-story writer with a reputation for bohemianism, internalized this logic when he told John Brisbane Walker, the publisher of *Cosmopolitan*, "personally I consider the duty of the writer to entertain or be silent . . . as in all things, command me."[56] Saltus understood entertainment to mean not merely the pleasure to be taken from literature but the delivery of instant gratification. Francis Marion Crawford felt similarly and explicitly proclaimed that novelists "are nothing more than public amusers. . . . Let us, then, accept our position cheerfully, and do the best we can to fulfill our mission, without attempting to dignify it with titles too imposing for it to bear."[57]

Not all writers so openly stressed instant gratification. The writing career of Edward Payson Roe, the native writer upon whom Matthew Arnold heaped such scorn, offers an instructive example of the changing career patterns of postwar novelists. A Congregational minister whose pulpit was located in Cornwall-on-Hudson, New York, Roe became the foremost sentimental novelist in the United States. At the height of his popularity a survey of Midwestern book-buying habits indicated that he was one thousand times more popular than Henry James. In an age in which $600 a year was a princely royalty for novelists, Roe earned $15,000 annually from his writing. He had simply "fallen into" novel writing and never thought of himself as a true professional. Unlike most of his contemporaries in the writing trade, Roe enjoyed a career trajectory of sudden success. Rather than apprenticing as a newspaper paragrapher and then as a reporter and then jumping from journalism to short-story writing for magazines, he entered the field in one gesture.[58] Convinced that God's work was being done in the cleanup of the great Chicago fire of 1872, Roe booked passage on a train to witness the miracle firsthand. From his observations emerged *Barriers Burned Away* (1872), which became a runaway best-seller. Fourteen other novels followed in quick succession, and Roe became a staple of the literary marketplace until his death in 1888.[59]

Despite his disavowal of explicit religious intentions, Roe mixed his observation of contemporary life with an overriding belief in the efficacy of abiding faith. Intent on proving the relevancy of Christian beliefs in an age of dampened religious feeling, he employed the novel as a more efficient sermon. Like most late nineteenth-century romantics he was interested in the metaphysical truth beyond the observed facts. Despite the vaguely realist title of his only theoretical pronouncement on fiction, "The Element of Life in Fiction," Roe did not understand or care very much about the thrust of the realist critique. He argued that he was ultimately concerned with the "pulsations of the heart rather than the conventionalities impressed by time and environment." Although this belief has Hawthornian overtones, Roe was not a true romantic. His "pulsations of the heart" proved to be commonplace sentiments. The heart "remain[ed] practically unchanged"; the author's job was to "penetrate conventionalities and discern inner life." That inner life turned out on inspection to be the innate ability of men and women to accept Christ. The true author merely provided the vehicle that convinced the readership of eternal truths.[60]

These concerns did not preclude a rigorous writing method. Like the realists, Roe stressed accurate observation. For his slum novel, *Without a Home*, he spent a month in New York's Hell's Kitchen; for his Southern novel, *Miss Lou*, he traveled to Charleston, South Carolina, where he interviewed not only the white ruling class but also black servants and craftsmen. As he told a Detroit interviewer, he lacked genius and needed to make up for his amateur standing through rigorous observation.[61] Nor did he find writing an easy chore. Unlike Harriet Beecher Stowe or Elizabeth Stuart Phelps, Roe made no claim that God wrote his novels.[62] Without divine intervention, Roe spent a great deal of time worrying about his characterization and his plots. As he told an admiring reader, he needed to adopt strict methods to insure publication. He devoted himself to a systematic transformation of writing into an endeavor of rigid observation, composition, and revision.[63] Unlike realists who gloried in work, Roe viewed writing as a task better completed than performed. He often confessed that writing was not an endeavor that gave him great joy.[64]

Part of this struggle stemmed from his need to be constantly topical. For all his theological concerns, Roe made his concessions to an audience that was both more important and more impatient than the antebellum readership. Always pegging his stories to a contemporary problem—the requirement that shop girls stand throughout the day, the problem of Reconstruction, the rebuilding of Chicago, the necessity for chaperones—Roe was always vigilant to keep readers entertained. Writing to *Youth's Companion*, he explained that each chapter contained a "striking incident and that from the nature of the times and the character of the region at that date."[65] If literary sweat and toil made novels valuable, then by all rights Roe produced novels as important as any in the nineteenth century.

Roe and Crawford represented two different aspects of the transformation of literary goals that the marketplace enforced. Consumer-centered, both judged literature by what it could do, rather than its style or its revelation of personally acquired truths. Whether the stress was on entertainment or religious edification, both were interested primarily in the reception of fiction and its ability to tap the existing needs of readers, and not the elegance or insightfulness of its use of language. Both were examples of writers who successfully adopted the new standard of reader satisfaction. Justifications and guides to writing came from other sources as well, most prominently the growing number of journals and guidebooks dedicated to steering the novice through the difficulties of publishing. By reducing the realists' concern for the creative human effort to such catchy epigrams as "What counts in writing is perspiration and not inspiration," the new advice manuals preached a market sensibility. Counseling the tyro to "read" the market, the journals viewed problems of literary discourse as problems of market adjustment.

The most prominent of these journals was *The Writer*, which was founded in

1887 for the express purpose of providing helpful and instructive advice to newcomers, noting improved methods and laborsaving devices for literary workers, and discussing writers' problems in a "practical and useful manner." Representing the "Great Unpublished," as Norris termed literary aspirants, the monthly stood full force against the domination of literary life by scholars and aesthetes. Stressing that its articles would be "composed of plain, common sense ideas about the most effective use of the English language," the magazine embodied the "hack" credo that writing was another occupation. To this end, it offered short features on such subjects as the proper literary "workshop," the proper mode of manuscript preparation, and the proper writing instruments. Titles like "How to Write Short-Stories" and "Method Needed in Literary Work" were designed to give a sense that composition had a formula.[66] Recoiling from the antebellum image of the eccentric creator, the contributors emphasized the need for discipline, regular work habits, and an understanding of the requirements of publication. Literary dreaming and dark garrets were outdated remnants of an ancient day. Modern writers, on the other hand, needed a professional attitude toward their work.

That professional attitude borrowed the language of the realist ideology of the writing process but transformed it. For all the professionals' proclaimed concern with "quality" production, *The Writer* was not a literary journal. The battle over realism, the development of naturalism, the shifts in poetic style passed without formal comment in its pages. Although the realists and the contributors to *The Writer* both valued "work," the meanings that they attached to the term were opposed. Where realists employed the term to differentiate themselves from those who saw writing as supernatural, the guidebook writers saw mechanical response. Where realists envisioned work as creative practice, the business men and women of words saw mere activity and a royal road to success. Where realists emphasized the necessity for regular writing, the scribblers developed routine. Where realists saw the development of an individual voice or style as the pathway to truthful expression, the authors of *The Writer* saw adaptation to the market. "The professional," wrote A. E. Winslip in a January 1888 *Writer* article entitled "The Literary Focus," "comes to write that he may command a more abundant and lucrative market through a larger and better fame. . . . The amateur should patiently seek to know where his writing will be in demand, what paper, magazine or publishing house has readers to appreciate promptly and enthusiastically what he has to say as he said it. If there be no place where his thought as expressed is sought, it is well to wait some new thought or cultivate some other style." To eschew the elitism of the old amateur and to remove the stigma of foreignness from writing, the new professional had to manage himself in the real world and comport himself as a virtuous laborer. "It is no longer necessary," wrote A. L. Hanscom, "for a literary man to wear long hair, roll open his shirt collar like Byron, or have the delirium tremens with undoubted regularity. . . . Writing is a business. . . . The writer alone is apt to hold himself absolved from any such law and has the audacity to squeeze twelve hours of labor into one."[67]

The strictures of *The Writer* and the system it supported did not go unchallenged. A number of exposés of "Grub Street" appeared during the late nineteenth century. J. L. Ford's *Literary Shop* and J. G. Speed's "Confessions of a Hack" were among the most prominent muckraking efforts. Speed, who worked every day for an average monthly return of $435, worried that the low return was turning him into a drudge and that the constant need to write left him no time to revise or to ruminate. Ford placed particular blame for poor literature on the control that conservative editors had over the entire production process. Their staid and dictatorial methods meant that writers had to chop ideas into smaller bits and censor their expression. "I doubt," he wrote in a well-known passage, "if any system, either literary, political, or social—unless it be Negro slavery—has ever had a fairer trial in this country than has that of pruning-hook editing . . . and that system may be responsible, in part, for the fact that three quarters of the fiction offered in book stores today is the work of foreign writers, most of whom have been reared in the comparatively free and independent literary atmosphere of Great Britain and have always addressed their books directly to the public instead of the magazine editor."[68]

Accomplished in dealing with the publishers of Lower Fifth Avenue, realists were in no need of instruction from journals like *The Writer*.[69] Nor did they have any quarrel with financial success. Indeed many realists were envious of the popular success of writers they thought inferior, and they kept close watch on the amount of money and recognition they received.[70] And though they insisted that monetary gain was not the ultimate goal of writing, they felt that authors had, as Howells put it, "a right to live comfortably by their art, just as a physician or minister. Mr. James writes a novel from love of letters and the hope of recognition and the need to live."[71] Howells was perfectly correct about James's economic motives. Leon Edel and Michael Anesko have demonstrated that James, who has often been treated as if he would not have sullied the purity of art by considering its economic value, was well aware of his rates. Although extremely attached to Howells during Howells's tenure at the *Atlantic*, James did not hesitate to send his material to *Scribner's* when the latter magazine bid $1,200 for an unseen serial. When Macmillan, his English publisher, advanced only £70 instead of the requested £250, James issued a formal letter of business divorce.[72] Howells likewise paid attention to his accounts. Although he championed the literary virtues of his friend Mark

Twain, he refused what he considered an inadequate offer to write an introduction to Twain's collected works.[73]

Nor did the realists worry that the occasional mass-market work that swept the populace would eliminate their audience or pollute the interests of their readership. In the 1880s Howells thought that recourse to such lighter fare was a normal, if not admirable, response of the so-called literary elite that had become "tired of thinking" and sought "to find relaxation in feeling—feeling crudely, grossly, merely."[74] James understood the appeal of "escape"—Francis Marion Crawford's notion that art could ease life's pressures and present us with perfect men and women in difficult situations: "They [novelists] offer us another world, another consciousness, an experience that as effective as the dentist's ether, muffles the ache of the actual and, by helping us to an interval, tides us over and makes us face, in the return to the inevitable, a combination that may at least have changed. What we get, of course, in proportion as the picture lives, is simply another actual."[75] Nor did Norris disagree. "For the Million, Life is a contracted affair, is bounded by the walls of the narrow channel of affairs in which their feet are set. . . . They look to-day as they never have looked before, as they never will look again, to the writer of fiction to give them an idea of life beyond their limits."[76]

These sentiments did not put the major realists in the camp of pure professionalization. What separated realists from the contributors to *The Writer* was the purpose of writing that informed their work. No realist saw the ultimate end of writing in terms of success in the literary marketplace. The "honest toil" of the realist conception of the writing process was designed to aid in overcoming the machinations of the marketplace, not to ease integration into it. This task required, wrote Howells, a "sort of scientific decorum." The author "can no longer expect to be received on the ground of entertainment only; he assumes a higher function, something like that of a physician or a priest." Readers trusted authors "not to betray them or abuse their confidence."[77] For Norris, the key to authorial success was the sincerity of not mechanically responding to the signals of the marketplace. "The eye," he instructed, "never once should wander to the gallery, but be always with single purpose turned inward upon the work, testing it and retesting it that it rings true." An author should be able to boast that he never "took off the hat to Fashion and never held it out for pennies." Reception could not alter truth, which is all the author could legitimately achieve.[78]

Like Howells and Norris, James rejected both entertainment and moralizing as proper ends for the novel. "I should say that the main object of the novel is to represent life. I cannot understand any other motive for interweaving imaginary incidents, and I do not perceive any other measure of the value of such combinations. The effect of a novel—the effect of any work of art—is to entertain; but that is a very different thing. The success of a work of art, to my mind, may be measured by the degree to which it produces a certain illusion; that illusion makes it appear to us for the time that we have lived another life—that we have had a miraculous enlargement of experience."[79] At the vanguard of a broad movement that saw morality not as a formulated ethical system but as a sensitive concern with the whole quality of human experience, James saw no need for a series of Sunday school lessons. Quality performance was inherently moral. Defending Flaubert's *Madame Bovary* in 1876 against charges of immorality, James asserted that every "out-and-out realist who provokes serious meditation may claim that he is a moralist. . . . Excellence in this matter consists in the tale and the moral hanging well together."[80] Eight years later, in "The Art of Fiction," he repeated his contention that art was not consciously moral. Challenging the English novelist Walter Besant (who had asserted a moral function for art) to define conscious moral purpose, James argued that a novel had to tell what its novelist knew, not what people agreed to admit that they know.[81]

These critiques were a form of American Ruskinism, which held that a degrading work process resulted in a dreary and decaying literature. Ruskin had argued that destruction of the intimate relationship between man and material inexorably led to a doleful art. When makers no longer felt at one with their material and saw it instead as a separate entity to be manipulated and processed, the spontaneity and joy of art vanished. Amidst the scurrying of pens and the clanging of printing presses, the instinct of workmanship and the sense of standards, which had long been the pride of the craftsman, were fast becoming obsolete.[82] In his favorable review of Ruskin and William Morris, Howells told his *Harper's Monthly* readers that the lesson that both men preached was that joy in work was necessary for great art. No cynically rendered book could succeed. "Art, indeed, is beginning to find out that if it does not make friends with Need it must perish. It perceives that to take itself from the many and leave them no joy in their work, and to give itself to the few whom it can bring no joy in their idleness, is an error that kills."[83] In another context Howells repeated the point: "We hear much of drudgery, but any sort of work that is slighted becomes drudgery; poetry, fiction, painting, sculpture, acting, architecture, if you do not do your best by them, turn to drudgery sore as digging ditches, hewing wood, or drawing water."[84]

The realists were not the first artists to insist that the key to the process was sincerity. Worries about the corrupting power that money exercised over art preceded theirs by nearly two hundred years. They were, however, the first to suggest that a sense of craft that depended upon fidelity to experience and probability of motive would provide protection against artistic degradation and establish uncommodified communication. Art was best protected not by a conception of fine writing but by the use of language to convey the keenness of observation of life as led. Howells's notion of the "truthful treatment of material," James's of the "actual," and Norris's of "the truthful novel," which gave the impression of life, all generate their value from the ability of the novel to convey the sense of probable experience. Realists were under no delusion that this was an easy task. "The usual imbecility of the novel," James wrote Howells, "is that the showing and giving doesn't really come off—the reader never touches the subject and the subject never touches the reader."[85]

It was to this end, of constructing in words an experience that corresponds with nonliterary ones, that realists proposed that the "work" of writing was directed. Proper writing of this kind could not be taught in packages or prescribed. Howells deprecated the guidebooks as false. "To aim at succinctness and brevity merely, as some teach, is to practice a kind of quackery almost as offensive as the charlatanry of rhetoric. In either case the life goes out of the subject. . . . There is nothing mystical in all this; it is a matter of plain, every-day experience, and I think nearly every artist will say the same thing about it, if he examines himself faithfully." The secret of keen observation, Howells believed, was feeling strongly about the material and knowing it well. Style would take care of itself, "for style is only a man's way of saying a thing."[86] This contention was not very different from James's that the intensity of impression, which constitutes the value of the novel, will be absent "unless there is freedom to feel and say. . . . The execution belongs to the author alone; it is what is most personal to him, and we measure him by that." For this reason James opposed Besant's assertion that the laws of fiction may be laid down and taught with as much precision and exactness as "the laws of harmony, perspective and proportion."[87]

Joy in writing for its own sake, concentration on the realist task, proper treatment of the materials, and forsaking models and guidelines may all have differentiated realist literary "work" from that of the pretenders, but the theory was more complicated in actual composition. In fact, the concept of skillful work contained a series of contradictions that threw the entire realist project into question.

The Contradictions of Craft: The Problem of Narration

For all their rejection of a self-conscious craft and their insistence upon infusing a text with "felt life," realists did derive a sense of what constituted "good writing." For them the freedom to "feel and say" must eventuate in a novel that, like the material it shaped, gave no indication of its artificiality. Realist craft was at its base the striving for pure, direct communication. Any textual element that gave to the reader a sense that it was not natural failed to meet this end. The skill that the realists honored was the skill to obscure the effort that went into the writing and to naturalize the novel.

This was Howells's point when he remarked that "the narrator dwells in a world of his own creating, where he is a universal intelligence, comprehending and interpreting everything not indirectly or with any artistic conditions, but frankly and straightforwardly without accounting in any way for his knowledge of the facts."[88] James was at his most realistic when he asserted that the novel must produce an authentic experience, one that approximated the experience of other activities. "In proportion as in what she [Fiction] offers us we see life without rearrangement do we feel that we are touching the truth; in proportion as we see it with rearrangement do we feel that we are being put off with a substitute, a compromise and convention."[89]

The crucial litmus test of craft that realists applied to fiction revolved around the narrative presence. In general, realists opposed any narrative practice that called attention to its presence. When the narrator became in effect an additional character in the drama, the illusion of naturalness was forever lost. Any utterance that distanced the reader from the text reminded him or her that the text was artificial and under the writer's control. Instead realists opted for a narrator that closed the distance between narrator and narratee. A narrator that made readers believe the possibility that the characters and events described existed, even when the most sophisticated among them knew that the novel was technically made up, was the narrator that earned realist plaudits. The skillful author created, therefore, a narrator and a text that concealed its actual origins and did not foreground its artificiality.[90]

The realist most associated with the dictum that the narrator should call as little attention as possible to the teller of the tale was Henry James. The essence of realist craft, he contended, was to separate as much as possible the author from the narrator. A narrator that called attention to the artificiality of the story through asides and references failed to render the lived experience accurately. As early as 1874 James praised Turgenev for his "uncommented" drama. The virtue of Turgenev was that in his work "the poet never plays chorus; situations speak for themselves." By contrast, Anthony Trollope's penchant for reminding the reader that the story was only make-believe was "suicidal"; James set out a catalogue of such sins and their remedy. "He [Trollope] habitually referred to the work in hand (in the course of that work) as a novel, and to himself as a novelist, and was fond of letting the reader know

that this novelist could direct the course of events according to his pleasure. . . . It is impossible to imagine what a novelist takes himself to be unless
he regards himself as an historian and his narrative as history. . . . As a
narrator of fictitious events he is nowhere; to insert into his attempt a backbone of logic, he must relate events that are assumed to be real."[91] Saying that
something was beautiful, when it could be demonstrated, robbed the reader of
the experience and dictated in a way that was not encountered in daily life.

If the author was to be "nowhere" in the text, then the novel must unfold
according to the internal consistency of the material. The narrator simply
supervised the process. Having made initial choices, the realist author yielded
to the logic of the observed. In line with his rejection of "inspiration," Howells
regarded the imagination as a limited faculty: "It is a well ascertained fact
concerning the imagination that it can work only the stuff of experience. It can
absolutely create nothing, it can only compose." Once the novel had taken
form, the material upon which the imagination worked was no longer completely "fluid, flexible, and ductile. . . . The mind fathers creatures which are
apparently as self-regulated as any other off-spring."[92] Howells's ability to
follow this rule evoked James's highest praise in 1886. Howells's strength was
that he "hates an artificial fable and a denouement that is pressed into service;
he likes things to occur as they occur in life, where the manner of a great many
of them is not to occur at all."[93]

If the artificial fable and contrived story were general violations of realist
craft, the use of synthetic, untypical, and theatrical forms was a specific one.
In railing against traditional molds, conventions, and substitutes for actual
experience, realists advanced the proposition that the writing that had the most
craft was that which presented experience directly. It followed that writing that
announced itself as literary—primarily most highblown poetic tropes and
allusions—disqualified itself as realist writing. The typical realist sentence
can be extracted from the novel of which it is a part without identifying itself
as a sentence in a novel (James, here, remains a significant exception). Realist
criteria for skillful writing had as its end the removal of the burden of the
"literary"—the use of language that announced itself as distancing and therefore unexperienced.

This aspect of realist craft quickly brought charges that realism was not art
but mere copying. To the charge of copying realists vehemently pled not
guilty. In their denials they indicated that the author was not simply a filter
through which the material found its literary shape, but an active participant in
the literary process. Howells, for instance, insisted that the realist could not
merely heap up facts, could not map life, but must picture it. "Every true
realist instinctively knows this, and it is perhaps the reason why he is careful of

every fact, and feels himself bound to express or to indicate its meaning at the risk of over-moralizing."[94] Norris dismissed accuracy as "the attainment of small minds . . . a mere machine-made thing that comes with niggardly research." What mattered to the artist was what the novel looked like to "an interesting impressionable man." If a majority agreed that the impression was lifelike, then the artist had been true.[95]

Picturing, rather than mapping, introduced a new factor into realist craft: the shaping function that the writer performed. Without explicitly stating the point, realist theory separated the narrative function from the authorial one. The narrator—the teller of the tale encountered in the text—abstained from overt announcement of his presence. The author—the intelligence behind the narrator—was charged with providing the frame into which the novel should appear to have unfolded of its own accord. Though the divorce of narrator and author insured a logical consistency in realist theory, the separation of function led to the inescapable conclusion that meaning originated not within the material itself, but with the author. In an interview with Stephen Crane, Howells claimed that the novel "in its real meaning" adjusted the proportions and preserved the balances. This was, he said, the true morality of the novel and the task of the novelist.[96] It was for this reason that he criticized Emile Zola's "polemical delusion" that fiction ought not to be selective. "The fact was that he was always choosing, and always limiting. . . . His hand was perpetually selecting his facts, and shaping them to one epical result." Zola, Howells thought (as many did not), had a moral sense that made his books come alive.[97]

For all his strictures against the narrator's intruding in the narrative, James was a forthright advocate of the importance of the author in shaping the materials of the text. Confessing that he believed it imperative for the future of the form, he was in the vanguard of those writers who admired the ability of the author to give the novel a particular point of view. "The novelist is a particular window—and of worth insofar as he is one," he told Howells on the occasion of the publication of *A Hazard of New Fortunes*. Twenty-two years later, in summing up his appreciation for Howells's talent, he wrote in a similar vein: "The writer must use his hands playfully, quaintly, incalculably, with an assurance of his fancy and his irony and yet with that fine taste for truth and the pity and the meaning of the matter which keeps the temper of observation both sharp and sweet." Arguing that the author made sense of chaos, James argued that "the business of the artist is always to make a sense and to make it most in proportion as the immediate aspects (of experience) are loose and confused."[98]

These justifications unintentionally cast doubt on how "natural" or "real" the substance of realist novels was. Realists did not deny that the author worked on material, but they were uncertain whether the material itself was "natural." At times they wrote as if their novels simply drew their material from the world in which they and their readers lived. The real grasshopper, not the "romantic cardboard grasshopper," was the currency in which the realist novel dealt, Howells asserted.[99] Elsewhere they emphasized not the correspondence between life and literature, but the ability of the author to give symmetry and beauty to inchoate material, an entirely different matter. In emphasizing that narration succeeded when the reader granted that the writer "knows all about things that no man can imaginably know all about," Howells placed the emphasis not on the reality of the material but the reality of the performance to convince. In the end, the material did not actually speak for itself; it only seemed to do so.[100] Realist material thus exhibited both a natural anarchy and a hidden order. At the same time that realists championed the organic form as something that existed prior to the artist's work, they also believed that such a form was something that the artist imposed and, in doing so, made art.

The realist novel was therefore an anomaly: a naturalized artifact that was both created and given. What it presented to the reader was the sense that it came from nowhere. Behind this facade lay, disfigured and disguised, the actual work of writing. This bilevel approach meant that the realist author was constantly involved in a balancing act. It was essential to shape while yet making sure that the touches were not evident. The Jamesian author must select but could not rearrange, as if selection was not a form of rearrangement. In a passage on Flaubert, James caught the ambiguity of the realist novelist— pushed by the sense that the text was both man-made and natural. According to James, Flaubert's strength was his adamant refusal to turn his private feeling to literary account. The Flaubertian author was impersonal and his work "should consist exclusively of his subject and his style, without an emotion, an idiosyncrasy that is not utterly transmuted." James approved of Flaubert's prescription that the " 'artist must be present in his work like God in Creation, invisible and almighty, everywhere felt but nowhere seen.' " Like Flaubert, the writer must regard "as indecent and dishonourable the production of any impression that was not intensely calculated. 'Feelings' were necessarily crude because they were inevitably unselected, and selection (for the picture's sake) was Flaubert's highest morality."[101]

In a sense apotheosis was the only solution to the realist dilemma. Transcendent and immanent at the same time, the realist narrator obeyed a contradictory set of principles. The text must be "real," and by realist terms this meant an absence of the artificiality associated with both intervention and the narrator who becomes a character in the novel. At the same time, the text was "real" in its status as a product shaped by a designing human intelligence, whose position as human must consequently be signified and validated. Realist narration thus had simultaneously to give evidence of the presence of the intelligence that fashioned a thing that had not existed before, and to efface its traces.

In this conundrum realist narrative theory replicated the logic of commodity production as it tried to combine an artisanal or preindustrial view of work as personal and direct with a set of principles that took for granted a commodity-dominated world. As analysts as diverse as Marx and Emerson have noted, commodities have in addition to their specific and individual material characteristics an impersonal quality that allows them to exchange in distinct ratios for each other. This exchangeability tends to dominate human perception of them, and they tend to lose the marks of their origin in human labor and come to take on a life of their own. Human products that take their significance from the expenditure of labor for human needs, commodities seem given and part of nature itself. This is precisely the strain within realist narrative theory. On the one hand, the material seems to have a life of its own and comes to the reader without signs of the history of its making; on the other, it comes from a designing intelligence that cannot be denied. In the first moment, the narrator is a passive contemplator of a world that does not reveal his presence, or at least obscures it. In the second, the realist narrator resembles the craftsman in his shop, directly cognizant, or more nearly so than the factory hand, of his role in initiating the process of production. In the first moment, the creation (narrative) seems beyond the control of human beings; in the second, it is totally under their dominion, making up in theory an active dimension lost from the reality it confronts.[102]

The characteristic narrator of realist fiction, the omniscient, nonintrusive narrator, was a compromise between these conflicting impulses. An unstable compound, the omniscient narrator was always in danger of gravitating to one pole or the other. In an impersonal, matter-of-fact tone, the realist narrator conveys the naturalness of the material. By restraining from intervention, omniscient narration aims to present a window on the world, a picture uncontaminated by subjectivity. Only through a rigorous neutrality, realist theory held, could the narrator be successful as a transmitter. This formal neutrality, however, coexists with the subtle and undeclared intervention of the realist author. At the same time that the narrator refrains from editorial comment on the action, the realist author, one step removed, frames readers' judgments by establishing the categories of evaluation that readers used in coming to those judgments. In revealing or hoarding information and in setting in motion a distinct set of values that animate the text, the realist author could attach a personal signature to the text, intervening between reader and material. Despite its declared disavowal of involvement, realist narration constantly hints at the uniqueness of its observation.

The combination of narrative modesty and authorial intervention gave an ironic tone to realist novels. Employing two parallel discourses, one that was stated and one that was implied, realist novels pressed upon the reader the existence of authors that the texts explicitly denied. Except for the few first-person attempts, the texts lack formal narrators, yet the prose calls attention to narrators whose privilege resides in their exclusive knowledge. Authors, ensconced offstage, direct the spotlight to their bows in the wings. Such is surely the case in *Huckleberry Finn*, in which Twain undertakes to comment upon himself in the guise of the fourteen-year-old narrator. With his introductory note about the verisimilitude of dialect ("I make this explanation for the reason that without it many readers would suppose that all these characters were trying to talk alike and not succeeding") and the opening lines in which Huck acknowledges his fictionality ("You don't know about me, without you have read a book by the name of 'The Adventures of Tom Sawyer,' but that ain't no matter. That book was made by Mr. Mark Twain, and he told the truth, mainly"), the reader is aware that what follows is attempting to be an actual report but is also a conscious fabrication.

Although Howells tried to "hide the joint," as he once put it, the narrator of *The Rise of Silas Lapham* also calls attention to his work. His description of the Corey house just before the nouveau riche mineral-paint king visits the established Coreys is far from straightforward:

> The Coreys were one of the few old families who lingered in Bellingham Place, the handsome, quiet old street which the sympathetic observer must grieve to see abandoned to boardinghouses. The dwellings are stately and tall, and the whole place wears an air of aristocratic seclusion, which Mrs. Corey's father might well have thought assured when he left her his house there at his death. It is one of the two evidently designed by the same architect who built some houses in a characteristic taste on Beacon Street opposite the Common. It has a wooden portico, with slender fluted columns, which have always been painted white, and which, with the delicate moldings of the cornice, form the sole and sufficient decoration of the street front; nothing could be simpler, and nothing could be better. Within, the architect has again indulged his preference for the classic; the roof of the vestibule, wide and low, rests on marble columns, slim and fluted like the wooden columns without, and an ample staircase climbs in a graceful curve from the tesselated pavement. Some carved Venetian *scrigni*

stretched along the wall; a rug lay at the foot of the stairs; but otherwise the simple adequacy of the architectural intention had been respected, and the place looked bare to the eyes of the Laphams when they entered.[103]

On the first reading, the passage may illustrate the objective, natural aspect of realist narration. One is presented with a particular Boston street and a particular Boston house. Its stateliness and aristocratic nature are not only asserted; they are demonstrated by specific details ("slender fluted columns, which have always been painted white," "delicate moldings of the cornice"). The added touches of history ("evidently designed by the same architect who built some houses in a characteristic taste on Beacon Street opposite the Common") attest to its authenticity. The language links up with the material in such a way as to reveal as much as possible about the street and the house. The reader is almost tempted to hurry past, anxious to find out how the Coreys and the Laphams mix.

Such a response would, however, miss the tension embedded deep within this seemingly innocent passage of scene setting. A closer reading suggests that it is also a historical interpretation in which the narrator is fully embroiled. The narrator's presence is felt in the partial revelation of information and the assertions of value, which contradict the initial impression of a seamless whole existing independently of the narrator's "work." First, one might notice the framing of the passage. Images of invasion and decay pervade the presentation. Not only has the presence of boardinghouses disturbed the quiet of the "handsome" street (the key word here is "abandoned," which suggests a defeat or disgrace), but so too has the aristocratic seclusion vanished. This reference includes not only the boardinghouses and their presumed but unmentioned working-class residents but the arrival of the nouveau riche Laphams as well. Though "the sympathetic observer," presumably the narrator, decries the change in the neighborhood and by extension the history that underlies it, one might have chosen to look upon that history in other lights and from other points of view. Although Howells and his readers may have thought so, it is by no means self-evident that the historical forces behind the change were cause for lamentation. Nor is the morality that the narrator imputes to the architecture ("nothing could be simpler, and nothing could be better") as obvious as the flat statement might at first make it appear.

The author's historical, rather than natural, position is as much in evidence by what is not indicated as by what is flatly asserted. How and why the boardinghouses, of which little is said but on which much depends, have subtly disturbed the neighborhood is never made clear. They destroy the organic unity, but that unity is not a natural but a historical one whose time has passed. Further, the narrator remarks that the same architect built some houses in "characteristic" taste. "Characteristic" for whom? Certainly not the Laphams, who misread the interior in interpreting classic restraint as bareness. Most likely this "characteristic" taste belongs to the narrator and his assumed readers, who understand the language of that architecture and the values it embodies. One might say that Howells's narrator imposes by fiat and assumption a viewpoint that eases a turbulent history.

These fissures are not so much minor retreats from neutral narration as they are an indication of the way in which form complements content. The passage begins with a declarative statement that is immediately qualified in a different register. The indicative gives way to the past perfect and the conditional. Objective narration—the tending narrator who speaks with the authority of the material—competes with subjective narration in which the material derives from a perceived presence. At the same time, the viewpoint moves from outside and above to one that is more closely aligned, although not identical, with that of the Laphams. Indeed, the tension between the narrator who naturalizes the action and the one who admits his presence makes it difficult to determine precisely the location of the narration. Although we see what the Laphams see when they see it and share in their discovery, we are in fact watching the Laphams watch the street and the house. The viewpoints presented could hardly be theirs. Their lack of sophistication and inability to possess knowledge of either Mrs. Corey's father's beliefs or Boston taste prohibits them from precise judgment, except for the belief, only attributed to them, that the place looks bare. These narrative shifts from past to present and from exterior to interior (mirrored in the movement of the passage from outside the house to inside it) coincide with two important structural elements of the novel. The former prominence and stateliness of the neighborhood and its present condition bespeaks the historical transfer of class power from mercantilist to capitalist. The decay of the public power of the Coreys is written in the history of the neighborhood. Yet the interior of the house and the Laphams' failure to comprehend it reveal the ability of the Coreys to retain private power and the inability of the Laphams to "get inside" that circle of social power. Not only has the narrator positioned the readers toward the material, he has also positioned himself in accordance with the dual imperative that required him out of and in the text.

Having decided that literary value depended upon the "truthful treatment of the material," realists asked themselves how might one go about writing such a novel. Their response was that authors could no longer rely upon metaphysical aids as their predecessors had done, but must base their work in an honest toil attuned to the elements of life. "Work" implied two conflicting injunctions. On the one hand, it meant that a writer must be faithful to the material at hand and let it flow from its own logic. Truthful treatment was impossible if the writer allowed handiwork to show. On the other hand, "work" involved human intention, and to efface its traces was to obliterate the "work" and allow formlessness in the text. If the test of the novel was the test of execution, as James maintained, then some judgment of the skill in picturing was necessary. Realist narration, then, vacillated between a belief in an objective world and one in which the author was subjectively present. Recent commentators on realism have made note of the ideological change, born of the proliferation of things in the late nineteenth century, in which subjectivity invariably reigned.[104] They have argued that this subjectivity, which became the narrative concept of point-of-view, resulted from the confrontation of the writer with a history in which people became gradually separated from their materials and themselves. It was through the realist emphasis on the "work" of writing that authors experienced most directly the difficulties in identifying the sources and status of the material. As they puzzled how to write a novel, they found that the text was at once their own creation and the result of objective laws.

Norris argued that the essence of "work" was to pay no attention to the gallery, but he (and other realists) nonetheless made the relation with the audience the prime test of work. Denying that life could be ever known fully and completely, Norris sought to produce a novel that "the majority of intelligent people" would agree gave the impression of being lifelike. For his part, Howells made narration conditional on the agreement of the audience to accept it. In doing so both men focused attention on the author-audience relation. Realizing that no objective standard of art could be maintained in an era in which the literary marketplace held sovereignty, realists admitted that the ability to convince the readership was crucial. In effect, realist doctrine made value recoverable only at the moment of consumption. When the author was understood, the "work" of writing had been realized. The writer-reader relationship, realists were to discover, was one that the history of the late nineteenth century had transformed significantly.

CHAPTER FIVE

The Passive Reader and the Celebrated Author

Literary Discourse in the Age of Realism

In every novel the work is divided between the writer and the reader; but the writer makes the reader very much as he makes his characters. . . . the reader would be doing but his share of the task; the grand point is to get him to make it.
—Henry James

In banishing the narrator whose explicit commentary on the text called attention to its artificiality, realists did more than advance their notions of a natural text. Their insistence upon a narrator who left no traces of his handiwork contributed to a new reading experience. For all its pomposity, the device of the intruding narrator did function to establish the novel as a direct and personal communication between narrator and individual reader. Even when the address was not made to actual readers but to implied ones, the narrator who functioned as a character served in the attempt to make the antebellum novel a sphere in which engagement on an emotional level was a paramount response of actual readers. Designed to be read in the privacy of the study, freighted with conventions of intimacy, the antebellum novel thrived upon the reader's impression that here were confidential and intimate revelations of feelings and actions that were rarely discussed in society. As historians and critics have noted, the antebellum novel created a special sphere into which readers felt welcome. "Companionate readership," which featured the contemplation of the text, and intensive rather than extensive reading were prime components of the antebellum reading experience.[1]

In contrast to the directly identifiable and solid narrators of previous fiction, the realist narrator was an amorphous and intangible presence who provided a window upon a fixed and immutable reality. In its matter-of-fact presentation of what happened or was happening, the realist novel deliberately cultivated an apparent distance and smoothness. Gone was the formal invitation to the "dear and gentle reader," the contemplative co-constructor of the text who had been a staple of fiction since Richardson and Fielding. Gone too were the asides and commentaries in which the author invited the reader to share a personal observation and reflect on a break in the action. In place of all these, realists substituted a discourse that was at once impersonal and objective. Unable to pinpoint precisely the source of the narrative, readers found their interpretive space constricted and their role at times akin to that of a dazed spectator.

This change in the dynamics of reading had a strong link to the reconstitution of the actual audience. Though some realists, particularly Norris, were contemptuous of the contemplative reader, the realist reshaping of the reader-writer interchange was as much a reaction to the changing social framework as it was authorially instigated. The size and growing complexity of the readership in the late nineteenth century rendered unworkable the intimate narrator, whose confidences had their social basis in the assurance that in interests and position the audience and narrator were much alike. What had been for the Romantics a troublesome problem, which they pondered at great length, had become an established and encrusted fact by the time the realists came of age. Both the potential and actual audiences for the realists were fragmented and impersonal, separated from themselves and the authors by diverse interests, desires, and abilities. Where earlier writers had counted upon a language of shared assumptions, realists could not.[2]

The fragmentation of the readership was not the only change that separated writer from reader in the late nineteenth century. The spread of publicity to new levels made authors increasingly distant from their audiences. As the sources of information about authors proliferated in the late nineteenth century, the ironic result was that the actual authors became progressively unknowable. Invested with an aura of glamour, authors found their efforts to construct a dialogue increasingly stymied as celebrity interfered with the primary task of opening a channel of communication.

This new social basis for reading and writing circumscribed realists' attempts at constructing a dialogue with those who read their novels. Realism was not only an attempt to remove the ambience of unnaturalness from fiction; it was also an option that realists hoped would reconnect author and audience. Many of the characteristic formal elements of the realist novel—the use of everyday language, the attempt to construct a universe that the reader could test by his and her own experience, the rejection of elevated moments—can be seen as attempts to construct what history had undone. By concentrating on what readers knew (or what realist authors believed readers knew), the realists hoped that it would be possible to restore a kind of equality of function between author and audience.

Realists soon discovered that a unified framework of author-audience interchange was more difficult to achieve than the cheerfully rousing statements of principle suggested. This was especially true when large segments of the readership found realist experiments unpalatable and unexciting. In the face of such failures, realist novels and theories began to exhibit a certain slippage from earlier positions. Many authors, including Howells, who more than any other realist had put his faith in the possibilities of a new democratic movement in literature, grew silent. Only James persevered, but his eventual destination in the first decade of the twentieth century could hardly be termed a realist position.

A Nation of Readers: The Reconstitution of the Audience

Ever since the inception of the republic, foreign observers had noted with admiration the high degree of reading among Americans of all classes. If the quality of American writing was open to question, the quantity of American readers was not. Americans, they observed, were more voracious readers than their European counterparts. For large numbers, reading was a part of daily routine, as Crèvecoeur's American Farmer informed his correspondent. This reading habit was one legacy of the Revolution. An informed citizenry, republican leaders believed, was essential for the survival of the republic. Touring the country in the 1830s, Michael Chevalier applauded the dispersion of literacy in remote rural settlements, a social fact that he contrasted with the vegetative stupor of the French peasantry. Some fifty years later Matthew Arnold, despite his barbed comments on the lack of civilization in the United States, did concede that Americans read a remarkable number of books and newspapers. By the turn of the century the British novelist Arnold Bennett openly proclaimed that Americans were the most well-read people in the world. "Americans read vastly more than Englishmen," he wrote in an essay published in the *North American Review* in 1912 but penned earlier. "None but a nation of convinced, inveterate, and incurable readers could support the sixty-four page Sunday editions of the daily papers; a less studious race would sink under that massive weight of letterpress, illustrations, and advertisements. . . . The population of the United States is less than double that of the

United Kingdom, yet the circulation of the most popular books in the United States is three, four, and five times that of the most popular books in Britain."[3]

These impressions of a nation of omnivorous readers whose numbers and quality marched forward must be treated cautiously. Accustomed to lower-class illiteracy, Europeans may well have treated any signs of petty-bourgeois interest in reading as truly remarkable. Yet statistics, scanty and unreliable as they are, coincide with the travelers' impressions. On the simple criterion of ability to recognize names, official figures on literacy showed a decline in illiteracy from 20 per 100 in 1870 to 13 per 100 in 1900.[4] Using a higher standard, Lee Soltow and Edward Stevens have traced three major reductions in illiteracy in the United States during the nineteenth century, the first "following a decade of intense social reform, including common school reform (1850–1859), the second (more modest) appearing in the decade following the Civil War, when a number of states enacted compulsory education laws (1870–1879), and the third appearing in the decade following the passage of compulsory school attendance laws in most states and their enforcement in some (1880–1889)." Working from army enlistment files, they found that 89 percent of northern artisans and 76 percent of northern farmers and laborers were literate in the period between 1830 and 1895.[5]

While literacy may not have effectively increased from the end of the Civil War to the turn of the century, the number of literary commodities did. Whether this meant more readers or increased consumption by those who did read is uncertain, but book industry sources estimated that three in ten Americans purchased a book in addition to the Bible in any given year during the 1890s. Though this figure may not have represented an increase in percentage over previous decades, the larger population of the country as a whole meant more book buyers. Newspaper circulation almost trebled during the period. The rise of mass circulation dailies and the prominence of tabloids testified to the felt need to read, if not to superior discrimination in reading tastes.[6] The growth in magazine circulation was in some ways even more telling. Newspapers have a functional aspect, informing readers about everyday affairs and acting as a guide to living. Magazines, on the other hand, are for the more contemplative and require a considerable budget of time. Though not all magazines are for the studious, the medium as a whole requires greater attention than the newspaper, which can be browsed. The 200 journals that circulated at the outbreak of the Civil War had grown to 1,800 by the beginning of the Spanish-American War. According to *Publishers Weekly*, the 428 literary periodicals of 1883 had become 1,051 ten years later.[7] As early as 1870 nearly 3.5 million Americans received at least one religious periodical.[8] The rise of "cheap" magazines, which sold for ten or fifteen cents as opposed to the twenty-five cents required to purchase the more established *Harper's* or *Century*, led the circulation push. Propelled by the energetic promotion of its creator and publisher, *McClure's* broke the half-million circulation mark in 1898.[9]

Complementing the new mass book and magazine market was the growth in public libraries. State support for free libraries increased dramatically. In 1850 only New Hampshire, Massachusetts, and Maine had free public libraries. By 1870, 2,000 libraries of at least one thousand volumes existed throughout the nation. By the end of the century 5,400 institutions boasted that number.[10] More importantly from the point of view of those interested in increasing the interest in fiction, libraries catered to popular tastes. Unlike the old-style Atheneums and literary club libraries, the new public libraries stocked much current fiction. According to one report, nearly two-thirds of the books borrowed from the Boston Public Library in 1883 were novels. So prevalent was the fiction habit that librarians' conventions nearly always addressed librarians' fears about unrestricted circulation of fiction.[11]

The sources of this apparently dramatic increase in the number of both casual and avid readers lay in a number of social transformations of the late nineteenth century. More children attended school during the years following the Civil War than in the years prior, which guaranteed a presumably more able reading constituency. In 1870, 6.9 million students, 57 percent of the eligible school-age population, attended school on a regular basis. Twenty years later 12.7 million, 68 percent of the eligible population, were enrolled. If grade school guaranteed minimum competency, higher education allowed more adventurous reading, although it did not insure it. In the forty years after the Civil War more Americans attended high school and held college degrees than ever before. By 1900 nearly 10 percent of the population had at least one college degree.[12]

If the expansion of education provided a larger pool of readers, other post–Civil War developments made more reading possible. Increased privacy, expanding leisure time, and rising disposable income accelerated the opportunities for reading. The rise of cities as trade centers in an increasingly industrial nation necessitated a boom in housing. As Sam Bass Warner has pointed out, the haphazard and unplanned growth featured privatized dwellings. Although ghetto tenements rarely provided the requisite amount of private space for quiet contemplation, the small flats and new bungalows of the growing middle classes often included designated reading rooms.[13] Howells, who was fascinated with domestic architecture and interior design, often described household settings in his novelistic treatments of the middle class. Part of the

Marches' difficulties in finding adequate housing in *A Hazard of New Fortunes*, for example, is the dearth of suitable rooms for Basil's study. Adding to the new ease of reading were improvements in interior lighting. New gas and electric lights allowed readers to expand their reading hours.

Nevertheless, the burgeoning Industrial Revolution yielded mixed results in the creation of new leisure time. For factory workers, the intensive regimen of the workplace made reading difficult. The ten- to twelve-hour work day limited reading possibilities, and the strenuous exertion required for most jobs left the majority of workers too tired for more than recreational and light reading. This state of affairs was not lost on labor leaders. Agitation for the eight-hour day, which reached its peak in the May Day marches of 1884, had as its rallying cry "eight hours for work, eight hours for sleep and eight hours for study."[14] For the middle classes, by contrast, the late nineteenth century afforded more opportunities to read. The new strata of clerical and bureaucratic jobs were neither as physically draining nor as lengthy as blue-collar work. Middle-class women, who were primarily homebound and, as all commentators noted, the backbone of the reading public, benefited from such labor-saving devices as new cleaners and powders and sewing machines for the home. In addition, the reduction in family size meant less time rearing children and more time available for reading.[15]

Yet another necessary condition for the increase in readership—disposable income—expanded during the age of realism. The creation of hitherto unrealized wealth and the growing emphasis on the consumption of goods resulted in a new level of disposable income and a new propensity to spend such money. While the achievement of a "consumer" society awaited the twentieth century, the late nineteenth century witnessed a number of pressures to spend rather than save.[16] Although statistics are fragmentary and incomplete and open to conflicting interpretations, most sets of data suggest a rise in real income. Between 1870 and 1890 money wages rose by more than 10 percent. More importantly, the long economic trough in the last third of the nineteenth century depressed price levels to such an extent that books and magazines were in the reach of considerably more readers than had been the case in the antebellum period. According to the one estimate, the price index (100 in 1860) fell from 141 in 1870 to 98 in 1890. In effect, real wages rose between 10 and 20 percent in the 1870s and at least 25 percent in the 1880s. Though such bonuses were not uniformly shared, the sense of new prosperity was not unfounded.[17]

By themselves, technological advances and increases in literacy did not guarantee that those who could be readers would in fact become readers. People will not read simply because they have the capacity to do so, because books and magazines are more readily available, or because the physical conditions in which they read are more conducive to the practice. What does spur an increase in reading is a social need to do so. Studies have indicated that people tend to use their reading abilities when it becomes important both vocationally and socially for them to do so.[18] The crucial factor is thus the changes in society that make reading a perceived necessity. It was not, as Michael Schudson reminds us, in the most literate areas of the United States that newspapers grew, but in the most volatile antebellum locations, the coastal cities.[19] It was not so much that vocational requirements mandated reading, although those did exist; the deepest root of the late nineteenth-century reading explosion was a transformation from community relations to ones in which strangers figured prominently. New information, new curiosities, and new needs to control all contributed their part.

The growth of American readership did not escape late nineteenth-century novelists. For them the implications extended beyond the likelihood of sustaining their careers as writers. The growth of reading signified a new era in the history of the nation and new possibilities for social and political discourse. Norris accepted the prevalent view that the task of nation building had stymied the full blossoming of American cultural activity, but he saw in the completion of that task the stimulation of both novel-reading and -writing. "As a matter of fact," he wrote, "the American people are the greatest readers in the world. That is to say, that, count for count, there are more books read in the United States than in any other country of the globe in the same space of time. Nowhere do the circulations attain such magnitude as they do with us. A little while ago—ten years ago—the charge that we did not read was probably true. But there must exist some mysterious fundamental connection between this recent sudden expansion of things American—geographic, commercial, and otherwise—and the demands for books. Imperialism, Trade Expansion, the New Prosperity and the Half-Million Circulation all came into existence about the same time."[20]

If Norris saw Manifest Destiny in the reading statistics, Howells saw evidence of growing democratization and social progress. Hoping that the increase in readership would lead to a time when those previously intimidated would exert "the standards of arts" in their power, Howells argued that in the meantime the novel was fast approaching a kind of spiritual necessity for an increasing number of readers. This growth opened new possibilities for the genre and placed new responsibilities on authors.[21]

Achieving these new possibilities was by no means without problems. A larger, more diverse readership undermined the assumptions of discourse that authors had accepted during the antebellum period and required a new basis for communication between authors and audience. Personal address to a mass audience was much more difficult than to an audience that could be presumed to be like oneself and one's intimates. An author could no longer be sure that readers held similar standards or read with care. Henry James, commenting on the multiplication of books, wrote that the "published statistics are extraordinary, and of a sort to engender many kinds of uneasiness. The sort of taste that used to be called 'good' has nothing to do with the matter: we are so demonstrably in the presence of millions for whom taste is but an obscure, confused, immediate instinct."[22] In his popular lecture "Novel-Writing and Novel-Reading," Howells recalled the time a cabinet member, mercifully unnamed, confused him for the author of *The Story of a Bad Boy* (Thomas Bailey Aldrich). Another Washington hostess thanked him for the pleasure she received from reading *The Bostonians*. Still others thought him a dead Englishman and were astonished to discover him alive and an Ohioan. "I fancy," Howells reluctantly concluded, "it would not be well to peer into the chasm which parts authors and readers."[23]

Though earlier generations of authors may have had difficulties in finding enough readers to make writing a paying concern, they assumed that the audience for which they did write shared with them certain interests and desires. Realists, on the other hand, faced a gap that had to be bridged, which made such confidence more problematic. Earlier writers had to find their audience; realists had to create it. Even those rare readers who were both careful and engaged existed at a remove. Writing to a T. D. Metcalf whose comments about his work Howells found insightful, the author indicated that separation was a permanent condition that was only occasionally overcome. "What you say of the Altrurian greatly interests me, and I wish I might talk with you about all these matters. But life is short, and if we never meet, still I hope you will always think of me as your friend, and not read me as a personal stranger."[24] The quasi–face-to-face relations of previous eras had vanished in the flood of production and the expansion of readership, and to confirm the results of his venture Howells had to depend upon the few readers who did write to him.

Equally as complicating for the reader-writer interchange was the transformation in the reading process. Coterie readings had been collective endeavors; like-minded readers shared their perceptions and refined their understandings in common. Late nineteenth-century reading, however, was generally a private affair in which individual tastes confronted an authoritative text. In this privacy the reader's expectations, which varied from entertainment or instruction to revelation, received full play. The solitary public purpose of reading and writing was replaced with a myriad of private ones.[25] Whereas Crèvecoeur's

American Farmer had read aloud by the fireside, late nineteenth-century urban middle-class readers consumed their literature in rooms set aside for the purpose of private reading. The rural Midwest still retained its communal and oral culture, its husking bees and fairs, and many skilled and semiskilled workers, like garment workers and cigar makers, hired men and women to read aloud to them during their working hours; but most urban readers, many of whom were beginning to complain about the impersonality of city life, engaged fully with the written word through sight, not sound. Although the reading club increased in popularity throughout the nation during the course of the century, its purpose was to discuss assigned books or stories, not to read them aloud in a group setting. The active coterie experience of the early republican literary clubs became an increasingly marginal phenomenon. Even though public readings were even more popular than in the early part of the century, their function was considerably different. Rather than a communal experience designed to elicit some action or some new feeling or belief, the public reading became a vehicle for the celebration of the writer. When Twain, Howells, or George Washington Cable took to the podium to read from their works, they deliberately selected portions that they knew the audience loved.[26] Writers now concentrated on the psychological response of the individual reader and not the social results of a shared practice. Participatory dialogue gave way to passive reception, and novels were increasingly written *to*, not *for*, readers.

Howells saw the difference in terms of production and consumption. Readers no longer had the "craft" knowledge of writing that they once had possessed. The division of function had created different criteria of evaluation. Readers sought entertainment and fulfillment; writers evidence of craft and execution. Hence the pleasure that even a novelist took from another's text was the pleasure of performance. "The painter, sculptor, architect, musician," explained Howells, "feels to his inmost soul the beauty . . . but he feels more thoroughly the skill which manifests that beauty." The concern of the novelist with how a thing was done made an author the best critic; others might enjoy, "but he alone who has wrought the same kind can feel and know concerning it from instinct and experience."[27] Writers were consequently constantly on the alert for authenticity in ways that even the most educated readers were not.

Realists' difficulties in establishing a rapport with readers were compounded by the fragmentation of their audience along racial, ethnic, gender, and class lines. These differences had long been a feature of American life, but prior to the generalization of literary commodities they had not had much impact on the communication between author and audience. As a more diverse population came to readership, the possibilities that readers would misunderstand what novelists intended grew larger. Readers' diverse experiences resulted in different standards of, and expectations for, readership. Janice Radway and Philip Fisher have argued, for instance, that sentimental novels are read differently from other types of fiction. They contend that a distinct sentimental reading mode exists, which relies upon a different understanding of who the characters are and what the action signifies. Michael Denning has persuasively argued that most working-class readers read allegorically regardless of the official intent of the author. By "allegorically" he means that "the fictional world is less a representation of the real world than a microcosm"—in contrast to the novelistic mode of middle-class reading, in which one understands that the story is not literally true but typical. Taken allegorically, individual characters "are less individuals than figures for social groups." Behind each allegory is a master plot that is shared by a culture.[28] Such diversity in readers' expectations presented authors with a more difficult task than writing for coterie reading circles, which were unified by a common framework of assumptions about the nature of literature.

The view that the late nineteenth-century reading public was actually many reading publics was, as we have seen, an acknowledged working assumption of literary entrepreneurs. Book publishers, especially the newer ones of the 1890s, treated the audience not as a stable entity simply enlarging itself but as a kaleidoscope of interests that could be known only after the fact of purchase. It was common among bookmen to say that each book had to create its own constituency. The success of a given book rested upon its ability to merge reading blocs.[29] Part of the reason that ten-cent magazines achieved such a sudden success was their editors' uncanny ability to tap the emergent "new middle class." Like their readers, the editors were newcomers, and the magazines that they edited according to their own tastes played on their own and their readers' sense of being outside of social and cultural power.[30] Small wonder then that realists felt that addresses to the "dear and gentle reader" were fruitless, for they had little assurance that actual readers were "gentle" and had internalized elite conventions of reading.

Some of those "dear and gentle readers" were immigrants from southern and eastern Europe with whom the realists had little in common. Even had the "new immigration" shared the same regard for the novel (as opposed to the romance or the allegory) that the realists did, neither their sense of the "real" nor their literary traditions were the same as those that the realists counted upon touching in their readers. At one time or another nearly all of the realists revealed second thoughts and concerns about the new immigration. Even older immigrants provoked questions about the unity of the nation and the reader-ship. Howells, for instance, made derogatory remarks about the Irish control of Boston and about the prevalence of Jews in European spas.[31]

Henry James swallowed hard at Ellis Island and at the Lower East Side and immediately pondered the future of literary discourse in which it was one's "American fate to share the sanctity of his American consciousness, the inti-macy of his American patriotism, with the inconceivable alien." One felt, James suggested, like someone who has seen a ghost "in his supposedly safe old house."[32] He had little faith that the new immigrants could be easily inculcated with American literary style. In an anguished passage on viewing the Yiddish theater, he recorded his own audible gasp, "For it was in the light of letters, that is in the light of our language as literature has hitherto known it, that one stared at this all-unconscious impudence of the agency of future ravage. The man of letters, in the United States, has his own difficulties to face and his own current to stem—for dealing with which his liveliest inspiration may be, I think, that they are still very much his own, even in an Americanized world, and that more than elsewhere they press him to intimate communion with his honour." As he viewed "the mob sifted and strained," James saw the germ of a public that stimulated his "lettered anguish" as he turned his eye "from face to face for some betrayal of a prehensile hook for the linguistic tradition as one had known it." The East Side cafés were "torture-rooms of the living idiom." While believing that a new synthesis might emerge, James thought that literary discourse had forever changed. Realists must find a new way to communicate, for the old way was in eternal disrepair. "The accent of the very ultimate future, in the States, may be destined to become the most beautiful on the globe and the very music of humanity (Here the 'ethnic' synthesis shrouds itself thicker than ever); but whatever we shall know it for, certainly, we shall not know it for English—in any sense for which there is an existing literary measure."[33]

If the divisions of ethnicity gave rise to the realists' most strident and vocal laments about the fragmented audience, divisions of gender prompted a more pressing set of concerns. Women were the heart of the readership, and throughout the nineteenth century the number of women in this active reader-ship grew steadily. Only the least observant could miss the female presence in bookstores, lecture halls, libraries, and schools. Not only did women take a forceful hand in organizing reading clubs, but they supervised children's reading. Carl Sandburg recalled how his mother patiently saved a dollar and a half to buy for him *A History of the World and Its Great Events* from a subscription agent, only to have his father rail bitterly against the waste of money.[34] Prevailing theory held that "culture" was that realm in which the most cherished values and standards of the nation were dramatized. Because it insured morality and progress and relied on nurturing, "culture" was firmly placed within the woman's sphere.[35]

Many realists agreed with H. H. Boyesen that the female audience was the bastion of sickly sentimentality, and their complaints about the use of ideal models and their strictures on typicality were directed against sentimental fiction. Howells, as was his nature, was more resigned to this condition. Asserting that women made literary careers, especially in what he called "light" literature, he attributed their prominence in the audience to their education and their cultivated tastes. "If they do not always know what is good, they do know what pleases them."[36] With this in mind and speaking from his own experience as an editor, Howells advised writers not to try to violate the boundaries of acceptable taste: "Between the editor of a reputable English or American magazine and the families which receive it there is a tacit agreement that he will print nothing which a father may not read to his daughter, or safely leave her to read herself. . . . The editor did not create the situation; but it exists, and he could not even attempt to change it without many sorts of disaster. . . . It does not avail to say that the daily papers teem with facts far fouler and deadlier than any which fiction could imagine. That is true, but it is true also that the sex which reads the most novels reads the fewest newspapers; and, besides the reporter does not command the novelist's skill to fix impressions in a young girl's mind or to suggest conjecture."[37] Female custodianship of "culture," both high and popular, was a prime feature of realist novels. Twain, for instance, satirically presented Aunt Polly as the restrictive, controlling arbiter of manners and morals in *Tom Sawyer*. James's fiction of New York (*Washington Square* and *Watch and Ward*) often turned on the difference between downtown (male and business-oriented) and uptown (female and culture-centered).

The actual composition of the readership, as realists had reason to know, was actually more diverse. The concentration on the impact of female readers obscured the significant presence of males among the reading public. Their numbers were by no means astronomical, but men did read more than the conventional wisdom indicated. Clergymen, doctors, and lawyers, the heart of the old writing coteries, had by and large accepted the novel in the 1830s and 1840s.[38] By the age of realism, other professions augmented their numbers. A surprising number of businessmen joined the ranks of novel readers. One sign of this new interest was the growth in train-station bookstalls. Many operators testified that a large percentage of their customers were men who bought novels to wile away the hours during train travel.[39] Though not conclusive evidence of increased male reading in the late nineteenth century, the growing equation of the novel with literature and the new respect for the form suggest an upsurge in male readership. Some have pointed to this phenomenon as the cause of the well-discussed predominance of male over female authors. It does not seem farfetched to suggest that a similar trend occurred among readers.[40]

Realists in fact possessed concrete evidence that the gender composition of their readership was mixed. Though they did not emphasize the fact, many realists knew from the correspondence that they received from their audience that a good portion of their loyal readers were men. Howells, whose reputation was and continues to be as a writer about and for women, received nearly a majority of his readers' letters from men. They queried him on his plots, his characterizations, and his use of language. And though these letters are by no means a reliable measure of the size of male readership, they do indicate an eager and interested, if not necessarily completely sophisticated, male audience. Twain too had a large male readership. Having bypassed the genteel magazines in his early career, he brought his male readers with him when he finally made his appearance in the *Atlantic* and *Century*. Even the popular domestic novelist Edward Payson Roe had a more varied readership than the content of his novels has implied to later analysts. Roe believed his audience was nearly evenly divided between the sexes.[41]

In campaigning for the portrayal of life, realists had twin motives. On the one hand, they hoped to expand the horizons of the domestic novel and to deflate the conventions under which it operated. By including in their novels descriptions of the more "masculine" enterprises—paint production, dentistry, publishing, and finance—they aimed at acquainting feminine readers with the world around them. "There are," Howells wrote, "civic and moral and religious problems, from which no life is exempt, though they may not spectacularly tear at the heart like wolves. . . . They beset ninety-nine hundredths of us, and the other hundredth may be safely left to his question of conduct in matters which fiction, our American fiction, our Anglo-Saxon fiction, staggers round and coughs at behind its hand. The books which deal with the problems noted and with kindred questions are as powerful and as important as any which treat the emotional, or hysterical, or even the equivocal questions."[42] Indeed Howells's somewhat timid advice to the young contributor to accept the judgment of the editor applied only to magazines; books were another matter.[43] Authors of books were free to explore all sorts of subjects, although Howells did lament some of the results.

To this end, realists rejected the "love" story, at least in its contemporary form. In its obstinate concentration on the passions of love to the exclusion of all else, this staple of nineteenth-century fiction offended realists in its equation of romance with life.[44] "If a novel flatters the passions, and exalts them above principles," wrote Howells, "it is poisonous; it may not kill, but it will certainly injure; and this test will alone exclude an entire class of fiction of which eminent examples will occur to all."[45] In place of the traditional love story realists wrote inverted or transformed romances. Perhaps mindful of the economic importance of the female readership, they almost always included love stories in their novels, but they portrayed the romance in such a way as to debunk the accepted conventions and prevent the lovers from living happily ever after. The realist love story was an instruction in the actualities of courtship and the frailties of human relations. In *A Hazard of New Fortunes* Howells has his protagonist, Basil March, speculate on writing a different kind of love story, one that expanded the horizons of feminine readership. Basil asks his wife, Isabel,

Why shouldn't we rejoice as much at a nonmarriage as a marriage? When we consider the enormous risks people take in linking their lives together after not half so much thought as goes to an ordinary horse trade, I think we ought to be glad whenever they don't do it. *I believe that this popular demand for the matrimony of others comes from our novel-reading.* We get to thinking that there is no other happiness or good fortune in life except marriage, and it's offered in fiction as the highest premium for virtue, courage, beauty, learning, and saving human life. We all know it isn't. We know that in reality, marriage is dog-cheap, and anybody can have it for the asking—if he keeps asking enough people. By and by some fellow will wake up and see that a first-class story can be written from the anti-marriage point of view; and he'll begin with the engaged couple and devote his novel to *dis*engaging them separately happy ever after in the denouement. It will make his everlasting fortune.[46]

The other goal that realists had in mind in their attack upon domesticity was to extend full readership to men. Men may have formed a significant readership, but they did so on the sly or as less than honored participants. If realism presented itself as a guide to life in the late nineteenth century, it did so with the understanding that it would be a guide to lives of men as well as women. In his lecture on novel reading Howells made a case for the necessity of male readers. With their concerns taken from the daily paper, they added a new aspect to the dialogue between author and audience.[47] Though not always stated in terms of gender, the call for a literature that dealt fully with life was an assault on the "feminine" literature that did not. Norris, who was more militant on the subject than Howells or James, claimed that fiction "was not an affair of women, and of aesthetes." It was in fact "virile." Fiction led away from "the studies and the aesthetes, the velvet jackets and the uncut hair, far from the sexless creatures who cultivate their little art of writing as the fancier cultivates his orchid" to "a World of Working Men, crude of speech, swift of action, strong of passion." This "heart of a new life" was the stuff from which "must come the American fiction of the future."[48]

The realist call for a new readership oriented toward "male" as well as "female" interest began in the 1880s. Over the next decade the latent male readership of the 1880s became a visible force. For the first five years of the 1890s "masculine" novels were the literary rage. The appearance on the best-seller list of *The Red Badge of Courage* by Stephen Crane and *The Damnation of Theron Ware* by Harold Frederic in 1896 would have been inconceivable had "female" interests of hearth and home held unquestioned sway. Though women could and did enjoy these works, the novels were explicitly addressed to readers who had "male" interests.[49] The younger generation of naturalists—Crane, Frederic, Norris, and Dreiser—was most openly scornful of the "genteel and dainty" female reader and called for a masculine literature that was in touch with the vibrancies of modern masculine life. Without a male audience eager for a new kind of fiction and the decline of sentimentalism of the "Feminine Fifties," the posturing of London, Norris, and David Graham Phillips would scarcely have been possible.[50]

Class differences constituted the third division among the readership that the existence of the mass market introduced. Although the working class did not constitute a majority of the readership for realist novels, preferring instead story papers and "cheap" stories, realists did feel its presence in subtle ways. Hoping to include workers among their readers, they were faced with the need to open a dialogue with readers whose experiences, education, and reading assumptions were quite different from their own. The dialogue inherent in reading rests on an unstated but understood compact between author and audience in which both parties agree upon the meaning of certain conventions. Without such concurrence, the author's task of signifying intricacies of thought, time, and relationships becomes immensely complicated. Take, for instance, the opening courtship scene in Howells's *A Modern Instance*: "He made no reply, but she admired the ease with which he now turned from her, and took one book after another from the table at his elbow, saying some words of ridicule about each. It gave her a still deeper sense of his intellectual command when he finally discriminated, and began to read out a poem with studied elocutionary effects." Understanding these two seemingly straightforward sentences requires a number of unconscious but necessary inferences about the relationship of poetry and courtship, intellectual pride, and performance. For experienced, generally middle-class, readers the inferences are made without much effort or notice. For those less familiar with the techniques of realist narration, the communication is less assured.

Peter Rabinowitz has made a set of fascinating distinctions about implied audiences. He argues that rather than implying a single audience, texts imply several, and he especially distinguishes between the authorial audience (which shares a specific knowledge about the nonfictional world) and the narrative audience (which accepts without question the conventions of form about the novel). In most cases these two separate implied audiences bear a close resemblance to the kinds of readers who actually pick up the book. For the realists the problem in approaching the working class was that many workers were not part of either the authorial audience (they lacked the same knowledge that the author had, which was quite a bit different from lacking knowledge altogether) or the narrative audience (they did not read novelistically).[51]

These differences in class modes of reading provoked hostility from those who disparaged the working class. As early as 1868 *The Nation*, perhaps the most class-conscious American periodical of its day, informed its elite readership that the public could be classified into two classes: one that wished to give direction to the better sort of writer, and another, inferior class, which looked merely for amusement. In the editors' opinion, the thinking class was falling away from fiction. Once that genre had engaged in discussion of "vast numbers of difficult questions, questions which, for a generation or two, while yet they were new and in the merely picturesque state, made the subject matter of the novel and also were the cause why the novel supported itself so long in the position where the great founder of its dominion [Sir Walter Scott] was able to place it." With the advance of social science, "we are all sociologists, and sociology now leaves the novel where it used to amuse us, and which it used to make so interesting and important, and becomes the staple of the more serious, earnest, regularly appointed 'organ of opinion.' "[52] Such was not quite the view of realists, but Howells and James, both of whom contributed in their early years to *The Nation*, were to some extent influenced by its ideology. The precepts of realism were an attempt to regain for the form of the novel the seriousness that *The Nation* had bequeathed to sociology. Rejecting working-class modes of reading, realism depended upon typicality and on readers' educated sense of the nonfictional world.

The reading divisions between classes were not impermeable. In his youth Henry James had read Jacob Abbott's "Rollo" tales; late in life Thomas Wentworth Higginson praised the novels of E. P. Roe. More significant was the emergence of Mark Twain in respected Eastern journals. Much has been made of the restrictions that Richard Watson Gilder, the editor of *The Century*, placed on Twain. The relationship, however, may be seen in another light. For

all the attempts at domesticating Twain, Gilder and his readership were nevertheless unwilling automatically to bar a Western humorist and to cast him into
the ranks of the literary unwashed.[53] And if the "high" read the "low," so did
the "low" read or mimic the "high." Bowdlerized versions of Zola, Scott, and
Dickens circulated in cheap paperback editions. Lawrence W. Levine has
documented the ways in which Shakespeare was considered the playwright of
the general public of the nineteenth century.[54] Common reading material did
not, of course, guarantee similar understandings or uses of that material. For
realists, the problem of estrangement remained.

Realists were not the first American authors to write for an audience from
whom they were separated. Hawthorne and Melville had had their difficulties
with the expanding audience of the 1840s and 1850s. Unable to secure more
than a small band of loyal readers, both pondered the future of dialogue in a
writing process dominated by commodity exchange. Larzer Ziff and Michael
Gilmore have each argued that Melville's attempt to reinvigorate his relationship with an audience that either rejected his stories or regarded them simply as
bracing sea tales is central to understanding his work. In Ziff's conception,
Melville wrote not for an audience that actually existed but for one that his
writings would call into being. Not the popular audience, but an imagined
democratic one, was his target. "As a result," Ziff contends, "*Moby-Dick* could
not be a popular work, but it would be addressed to an assumed audience of
democratic readers, and with that assumption, shape an ideal audience even as
the ideal of that audience shaped it."[55] Melville's efforts yielded little immediate success and he withdrew from writing to the silence of the customs house
of the Tweed ring.

Coincidentally, the customs house provided Hawthorne with the site for his
literary reconciliation with the market audience. In the "Customs House"
introduction to *The Scarlet Letter* he outlined the elements of compromise that
enabled him to continue discourse with an unknown audience. When the
author "casts his leaves forth upon the wind," Hawthorne wrote, he addresses
"not the many who will fling aside his volume or never take it up, but the few
who will understand him, better than most of his schoolmates or lifemates."
Lurking behind this procedure was an inherent danger of narcissistic exhibition. Hawthorne admitted that some authors went so far as to indulge in "such
confidential depths of revelation as could fittingly be addressed, only and
exclusively, to the one heart and mind of perfect sympathy; as if the printed
book thrown at large on the wide world, were certain to find out the divided
segment of the writer's own nature, and complete his circle of existence by
bringing him into communion with it." Such self-revelation was scarcely
"decorous" and placed the whole project of communication in jeopardy. To

avoid benumbing utterance and freezing thought, Hawthorne himself had attempted to achieve a "true" relation with his audience by imagining that a friend, "a kind and apprehensive, though not the closest friend" was listening to the talk. This imaginary relation thawed the native reserve and allowed "prating" about circumstances around the author and even about himself, although the "Inmost Me" was kept behind that most Hawthornian of symbols, the veil. In such a way, neither the author's rights nor those of the reader were violated.[56] By conducting in the text an exchange between the imagined reader and a created author, Hawthorne sought to rescue literary discourse from the impersonal nature of commodity exchange.

As reading assumed its late nineteenth-century contours, the Hawthornian compromise lost some of its viability. Realists could no longer trust that their books or serials would find "kind and apprehensive friends." The sense that the author was part of the audience for which he or she wrote, so marked in belletrist prose and "The Customs House," began to fade. Though authors may still have shared much with their readers, their guesses about how much was shared were less confident than in previous generations. At times realists regarded their audience almost as a foreign entity, an undifferentiated conglomerate. Norris talked of writing for the "Million," which he saw as unenlightened and undiscriminating.[57] At other times they saw their audience as "types," rigidly separated by occupation. Howells could only imagine his readers in sociological categories: lawyers, housewives, doctors. Believing urban life was too chaotic, he envisioned his ideal readers as those in the "outposts" who had time for reflection and dialogue.[58] Howells's supposition about his audience was probably not far wrong. What is of interest is that realists came to an understanding of their audience only after the fact of consumption and had to make the effort to imagine them. Unlike the noncommercial writers, who either personally knew their readers or who wrote with the confidence that the audience shared an understanding of literature's qualities and charms, realists negotiated their way through a mass of readers. True communication would require a reeducation of the audience through lessons only a few would heed.

For all the breaks in the unified discourse of their predecessors, realists did not confront a totally baffling situation. A large number of readers did share with them many characteristic assumptions about writing. The likes of T. D. Metcalf (the reader to whom Howells responded so warmly) were not so rare as to be near extinction. Realists could personalize them as the reader for whom the text was meant. Many could be found among subscribers to literary magazines. Howells asserted that "most of the best literature now first sees the light in the magazines, and most of the second-best appears first in book form. . . . At present the magazines . . . form the most direct approach to that part of our reading public which likes the highest things in literary art. Their readers, if we may judge from the quality of the literature they get, are more refined than the book readers in our community; and their taste has no doubt been cultivated by that of the disciplined and experienced editors."[59] What is striking about this comment is that it discloses Howells's ultimate uncertainty about his audience. His division of the reading population into a cultured, magazine-reading community and an unruly, book-reading one reveals his anxiety about discourse. That the readership needs training, as he implies, betrays a latent assumption that the unity that had formerly existed between author and audience had now been broken. The missing term in the argument—the effects of the literary marketplace—raised doubts about the future of dialogue. Searching for a replacement for the discourse that the literary marketplace had sundered became a central concern for the realists. Gauging audience expectations was not just a market problem; it had become a literary one as well.

The Distant Author: The Writer as Celebrity

Though the antebellum writers had witnessed in a diluted form the growth of a diverse readership, they seldom experienced the kinds of publicity that came into prominence in the years 1880–1910. Publicity prior to the Civil War had primarily revealed the author's public self and presented those activities that pertained to the author's literary accomplishments. Even if known or talked about, as in the cases of Edgar Allan Poe and Lord Byron, authors' private lives generally received little public attention, especially when no norms of behavior were violated. The vast majority of reviews and literary profiles of that era concentrated on the author's ideas and career. Publicity in the second half of the nineteenth century, however, changed the focus of interest. Not only had the quantity of publicity grown and the venues by which it reached the public multiplied, but its aim was now to reveal the personal and private qualities of the author to an eagerly interested public. Book advertising, literary gossip columns, publicity tours, and interviews all pointed toward the creation of a glamorous person, a person whose life had aspects that were admirable or capable of being envied. Despite some initial reticence, authors themselves became active participants in the creation of their own images. For many, a literary personality, like the book itself, was constructed and public.[60] In striving to impress upon readers the glamour of the author, publicity ran counter to the realist goal of direct and equal communication. If the author was truly larger than life, then authorial activities were not work but something grander.

The promotion of celebrity in literature originated in the confusion of market relations. In a constantly overcrowded field the struggle for sales was also a struggle for recognition that no publisher could ignore. Gilded Age publishers were at first reluctant to engage in advertising because of its negative associations with patent medicines and undignified hoopla. Early book advertising had consisted of simple announcements of the title, the author, and the price. Publishers had relied on local booksellers to circulate the novel through their contacts with local opinion leaders, who would then create interest in a book. The few national sales efforts that did exist concentrated not on the readers, but on book wholesalers and jobbers. National fads and phenomena, such as Tom Paine's *Common Sense* (1776) and Harriet Beecher Stowe's *Uncle Tom's Cabin* (1852), had seized more upon word of mouth and political relevance than upon paid advertising. More than uneasiness over the dignity of advertising prevented publishers from employing it; practical obstacles stood in the way as well. The tenuous nature of national lines of communication and the comparatively small reading audience made national advertising counterproductive. The trade in pirated editions made any full-scale venture into advertising unthinkable. Because "pirates" could undersell established firms, any advertising of books by foreign authors amounted to advertising for a competitor as well. With the passage of the International Copyright Act in 1891, national advertising became a fixture of literary life. By 1900 firms commonly had annual advertising budgets of $75,000.[61]

Had backlists continued to play a prominent role in the economics of book publishing, advertising might not have reached such heights. The growing importance of the best-seller, however, made advertising a more feasible way to call attention to stock. As the old standards of literary value ceased to motivate readers and the institutions that determined taste ceased to hold sway, advertising presented a tool by which potential readers could be cultivated. Late nineteenth-century book advertising jettisoned the simple announcement of author and title and began to stress the excitement of reading a particular book. Advertisements became involved dramas in their own right. Instead of simple printed announcements, book advertisers now favored artwork depicting the most engaging moment of the work and copy claiming the extraordinary experiences to be gained from reading it. By varying art, type fonts, and decorative borders, book advertising could present each book as glamorous and special and thus sell not simply the book, but an aura that accompanied the book. Blaring headlines, vivid pictures, and heartfelt testimonials became regular features of book advertising in the last two decades of the nineteenth century. Although book advertising was circumspect compared with that for other commodities and restrained its exaggeration, Walter Lippmann's comment that advertising intensified feeling and degraded significance was as valid for advertisements for novels as for advertisements for soap.[62]

The new environment did not lack for critics. Old-line publishers and conservative litterateurs bewailed the turn of events. Two issues dominated the publishers' trade press for the last thirty years of the century. The first, which seems innocuous in retrospect, concerned the use of white space in announcements. As new advertisers began to increase the amount of "breathing space" for copy, some opponents saw in this development a waste of space and an indulgence in conspicuous display unbecoming to an exalted and lofty profession. The flashy presentation, they contended, ran counter to the dignity of the article advertised. Such proponents as Edward Bok demurred, pointing to the attractiveness of the new layouts. Bok, who prided himself on his ability to watch more carefully over the advertising content and the form of presentation than over any other aspect of his magazine, *The Ladies' Home Journal*, argued that the use of white space highlighted the information contained in the advertising and made the advertisement a special pronouncement that raised it above mere commerce. Heeding the fears and critiques of his opponents, Bok managed to deny that his innovations were a significant departure from tradition.[63]

The skirmish over the use of white space and ornamental borders in the late 1870s and early 1880s prefigured the heavy fighting that accompanied the promotional gimmicks and hyperbolic claims of the 1890s. The editors of *Publishers Weekly* fired the first shot. Claiming that the "booming of books" had demeaned the industry, the journal declared that "while this spirit of unsatisfied ambition has brought compensation and developed an activity not to be ignored, it has nevertheless been at the expense of certain elements of character which should not be abused or uncultivated. Dignity is very often forgotten." Retaining the view that literature should transcend mere trade, the editors posited that if "literature and art are to be treated as common merchandise . . . it will make commonplace the manners of our people and their intelligence will be restricted to the countingroom." What particularly irked them was the use of books as a premium for the purchase of soap in department stores, a strategy that signified that the novel was just another commodity and not a special artifact.[64]

To the new men who assumed leadership of the "progressive" firms, such an attitude was hopelessly stodgy. Though they issued caveats that the advertiser must first and foremost believe in a book, they nevertheless emphasized their ability to promote and to speak the language of commerce. Irving Bacheller, a sentimental novelist and literary entrepreneur, argued that "in the plain talk of commerce, he [the publisher] must find a chance to display and advertise the goods he has acquired and sell them to other people. I began to see advertising was part of the big plan of life."[65]

By the middle of the decade the debate had effectively been settled in favor of splashier advertising. The campaign conducted for Charles Major's *When Knighthood Was in Flower* (1898) was particularly spectacular. One advertisement showed an ancient castle with every stone printed over with a month and the amount of books sold that month. Another was a series of portrait layouts of writers with whom the publisher hoped Major would be compared: Shakespeare, Pepys, Scott, Dumas, and Anthony Hope. Still another displayed a medallion formed from old prints of the historical characters in the book. Even bookstores got into the act. The books were piled together in a shape of a castle on the floor of the store.[66] Unlike such earlier publicized works as Edward Bellamy's *Looking Backward* and George DuMaurier's *Trilby*, which earned their popularity among readers before the reams of publicity, the *Knighthood* publicity preceded the public interest.

The *Knighthood* campaign was one of the first to conflate popularity and quality. So too did one of the standard features of modern literary commerce, the best-seller list. Making its initial appearance in 1895 in *The Bookman*, a chatty journal about the literary industry and its authors published by the firm of Dodd and Mead, the list was the result of an improved communication and distribution system that had made more precise accounting of sales possible. Not long after the list made its appearance, book advertising began to announce that the advertised book had secured a place on the list. This innovation drew upon a curiosity made even more acute by the impersonal nature of urban life. Although best-seller lists (the *New York Times Literary Supplement* followed the lead of *The Bookman* a few years later) did appeal to the understandable desire to belong, it also testified to the ways in which selling books depended upon factors other than those that were, strictly speaking, literary ones. If publishers needed to know which books were doing the best business, readers had no intrinsic need for such information. By advertising the amount of sales, a campaign hoped to convince readers that they were missing out by not purchasing the book. Best-seller lists represented the culmination of the effort to make the sales campaign and the actual writing of the novel more unified. As "timeliness" and vitality came to be the guiding values in both the production and sales effort, the differences between the two activities became less pronounced. To the degree that authors incorporated these values into their novels, the literary marketplace exercised a stronger hold on writing than it had at any previous time.[67]

The *Knighthood* campaign consisted of more than advertising; it was a coordinated effort that included retailers, reporters, and publishers. The effect proved contagious. On the heels of *Knighthood*, books like *David Harum*, *Eben Holden*, and *Alice of Old Vincennes* demonstrated that "down home" material could be fodder for spectacle as easily as could historical subject matter. Even more literary-minded authors indulged in publicity schemes. Mark Twain, whose efforts at self-promotion were considered unsurpassed by his peers, released a complimentary copy of Pudd'nhead Wilson's calendar to coincide with publication of the novel.[68]

The "booming" escalated to such levels that publishers began to have second thoughts about the usefulness of advertising. When combined with the astronomical royalty rates of the "new prosperity," the large promotional expenses inaugurated what Robert Sterling Yard called a "crazy period" in publishing. The $75,000 advertising budget for Harold Bell Wright's *The Winning of Barbara Worth* (1911), and the $2,500 spent in one week on Frank Norris's *The Pit* (1903) convinced thoughtful businessmen that a fever in need of purging had infected the industry. Cautionary warnings that advertising was not a panacea became commonplace. The growing number of failed campaigns persuaded publishers that no amount of "booming" could convince the public to buy what it did not want. "If a work has any claim upon the interest of the public, continued descriptive advertising can nearly always be depended upon to produce an increase in sales," wrote George Palmer Putnam, "but it is often enough the case that such an increase is not sufficient to repay the cost of advertising."[69] Alfred Harcourt, recalling his early days with Henry Holt, remembered that many publishers saw advertising as a necessary evil "to impress and satisfy authors."[70]

These condemnations have the ring of the habitual drinker swearing off alcohol after a rough night: such afterthoughts are heartfelt and insightful, but they rarely translate into future behavior. Faced with the need to convince recalcitrant buyers to purchase, publishers had little choice but to continue advertising campaigns. As Christopher Wilson has noted, the attacks on advertising coincided with the broader movement to control costs through efficient advertising expenditures. The uncertain payoff had made publishers wary of overcommitment, and their attempts at reform meant a more thoughtful advertisement investment. At the heart of their complaint was the central uncertainty of the book business. No single publisher could use advertising to associate books with his firm the way Kodak meant "camera" and Band-aid meant "adhesive bandage." As William Ellsworth observed in *The Golden Age of Authors*, no customer would approach a book counter with the demand to

"Give me Scribner's and no other."[71] Because each book had to be promoted for its own unique attributes, the escalation in advertising was not reversed.

Critics who doubted the efficacy of advertising campaigns may well have been correct in their assessments. The complaints of publishers like Doran, Yard, and Putnam cannot be simply dismissed as diversions or falsehoods. Although the evidence is sketchy, most current studies suggest that advertising does little to persuade buyers to purchase new products. Advertising did establish categories of consumption and therefore educated readers in the prevailing genres. By presenting various types of books to readers, advertising encouraged them to think about books in terms of preexistent categories and indicated the kinds of experience available from each genre. Advertising led, and reviews followed, in labeling books by specific category or genre, which were to deliver predefined pleasures. Though readers may have dismissed specific claims of copywriters as exaggeration, the attitudes and inclinations that the ads suggested—the importance of a "good read" and of the immediate vicarious pleasure—may have stuck and developed expectations in terms that advertising devised.[72]

Publishers did have at their disposal one promotional technique that was almost effective in fostering a brand-name loyalty among readers. The promotion of an author's personality created an interest in his or her product that extended beyond the work itself. Stressing the glamour and the creativity of the author, publishers and editors were able to exploit interest in authorial lifestyle. Capitalizing on the ability of authors to embody certain desires and hopes of the readership, publishers, with the active connivance of authors, turned personalities into virtual commodities. The consumer of the novel received not only its contents but also a share of the unique and now marketable qualities of the author. By purchasing a text one could hope to soak up some of the qualities of the author. Even conservative houses understood the importance of transforming the author's name into an imprimatur. When Scribner's published Edith Wharton's *House of Mirth* in 1905, the firm devoted every effort to supplying newspapers and literary magazines with information about her life as a figure in New York society. Implied, but never stated, in the news accounts was that Wharton's firsthand observation of the underside of the "aristocracy" of Old New York would give the reader an authentic experience.[73]

Not all publicity was publisher-initiated advertising. Part of the new publicity system was increased coverage of literary affairs in the nation's press. Newspapers, which had hitherto generally defined news as political and commercial affairs, began covering authors as a matter of course. As newspapers became dependent upon paid advertising in the late nineteenth century, a number of papers created special literary supplements to accommodate the increased volume of book advertising. Devoted to book reviews, literary gossip, and an occasional essay, these literary supplements, of which the two most important were carried in the *New York Times* (beginning in 1893) and the *New York Tribune* (beginning in 1894), provided a new avenue for the presentation of new books and for the promotion of authors' personalities.[74] Nearly every general-circulation monthly likewise included enhanced literary news. Profiles of authors and best-seller lists were common features. In addition a new crop of specialized literary magazines proliferated during the late nineteenth century. Many of these, like *The Bookman*, had direct connections with book publishers.[75] Although some skeptics charged that literary magazines rewarded publishers' large advertising investments by serving up favorable reviews, publishers denied any unethical behavior, replying that the news columns were more crucial to promotion than the reviews, which few readers actually followed.[76]

Promotion of the author's life meant making the author's personality accessible. By sharing personal, though not the most intimate, details of the author's life, publicity could allow the reader a glimpse of an enviable life and hold out the promise that the reader could partake of it. At times it seemed that nothing went unexamined. The author's home, work habits, dress, and physiognomy became objects of intense scrutiny. The "author at home" books became a flourishing cottage industry in the late nineteenth century, bringing to the curious an examination of authorial life that Hawthorne most certainly would have labeled an indecorous invasion of the authorial self.[77] The well-informed knew all there was to know of Mark Twain's Tiffany decorations, William Dean Howells's cigars, and James Whitcomb Riley's porch and rocking chair. In effect, an author's life became public property, exchanged and circulated in neatly defined packages.

Given the importance of personality, the number of pseudonyms and anonymous novels declined during the period. Except for reasons of circumspection (as in the case of John Hay's controversial *Breadwinners*) or lark (as with Henry Adams's *Democracy*), the traditional modesty about authorship vanished. Respected journals, which during the antebellum period had automatically withheld authors' names, adopted a policy of bylines. Authors had long agitated for such a change, and they reacted favorably. Edward Bok took note of the change in the publishing environment, writing in 1890 that authors "were realizing more and more that with two names they had two reputations to make; writers were daily becoming more convinced that the strength of one's personality in his work was an essential of success; and publishers were more reluctant to place pseudonyms on books than they were fifteen years ago."[78]

Rather than resenting the workings of the publicity machine as unwarranted intrusions, a good many writers embraced promotion and publicity. They sat patiently for personal interviews, a much-heralded feature of the "new" journalism of the late nineteenth century. Howells, for instance, was a particularly responsive subject and was the first to sit for *McClure's* column of interviews, "Real Conversations." He even incorporated the technique in his fiction. Readers of *The Rise of Silas Lapham* will recall that Howells began the novel with Bartley Hubbard, the protagonist of *A Modern Instance*, interviewing the mineral-paint king. Authors rushed to endorse various collections of memorabilia and marginalia in an effort to keep their names before the public. Edward Payson Roe and Dodd and Mead put out an E. P. Roe datebook for 1882 that featured an inspirational saying culled from his novels for each day of the year. Mark Twain showed no reluctance to use his literary name in such frankly money-making schemes as *The Mark Twain Scrapbook*.[79]

The personal lives of previous generations of authors had not been subject to the same level of scrutiny. For all the personal calumny aimed at authors, the insults and slander tended to have their basis in professional disputes rather than the personal lives of the disputants. Had Poe not been so scurrilous in print, it is entirely possible that his behavior would have prompted fewer remarks. Hawthorne too had received his share of coverage in the nation's newspapers, but his notoriety stemmed primarily from political concerns. His removal from the Salem Customs House prompted a political brouhaha because of the continual patronage disputes between the Democrats and the Whigs. Neither his political enemies nor his readers had any special interest in his personal or marital life, except as it could be used to discredit his political standing. Although Michael Gilmore has written on Hawthorne's fears about a new standard of criticism that treated the literary text as an index of the author's personality, symptomatic reading, as it was called, used the text, not newspaper reports and biographies, as its primary evidence.[80] Furthermore, it should be remembered that the techniques of information gathering of the antebellum period paled beside those of its postbellum counterpart. Without the glare that Howells, James, and Norris faced, Hawthorne had just enough space to construct his authorial persona of *The Scarlet Letter*. With the advent of a literary environment in which authors' lives were on display in the same manner as commodities, the authorial persona was no longer presented solely in the text. Even the most unlikely candidates for admiration drew the attention of the publicity machines.

The case of Henry James is instructive. Often considered an artist's artist who toiled for the pure joy of artistic creation, James came under public inspection with surprising frequency. Rather than practicing his craft in isolation, and for all his distaste for publicity, he was prominently mentioned in all sorts of venues. The August 1889 *Writer*, for instance, included the following information: "Henry James is spending the dreary months of August and September in London, writing all the harder because he has a vacation from his more pressing social duties." This seemingly innocuous bit of gossip could hardly rival the bleatings of the Hearst press in 1903: according to newspaper accounts James had become infatuated with Emilie Grigsby, whose affair with Charles Yerkes had served as the model for Berenice Fleming's in Theodore Dreiser's *Titan*. He was said to be so taken with her charm that he had her sit for the portrait of Mildred Theale in *The Wings of the Dove*. The story was so pervasive that James's brother William wrote him to inquire if it were true that the confirmed bachelor had, as reported, proposed marriage.[81]

The fascination that James evoked among American readers was not confined to personal scandals. He had been an object of curiosity ever since his controversial *Daisy Miller* in 1879. His expatriatism and slightly exotic philosophy of art provoked constant comment. When he made his famous return journey to the United States in 1904–5, his comings and goings were the subject of a barrage of cartoons and commentary. President Theodore Roosevelt, who found James's work too delicate for his taste, nonetheless dined with the author.[82] Nor did James's critical reputation founder during his lifetime. As Henry Nash Smith has demonstrated, James was well regarded in his native land. A *Critic* poll of important authors in 1884 placed him thirteenth. In the same year a survey of Harvard graduates ranked him tenth in importance, ahead of William Dean Howells (fourteenth) and Mark Twain (twentieth). In 1899 *Literature*'s poll of its readers placed James, Howells, and Twain in the top ten, with Howells securely nestled in first.[83]

The public may have honored Henry James as the consummate author, but it did not read his books. His ranking far exceeded his sales. Honored more for his symbolic value than for his actual work, James demonstrates the ambiguous status of novelists as a class. Although denigrated as impractical and odd, they also stood above the commercial morass. Having none of the political liabilities of politicians, business magnates, and labor leaders in an era of intense political rivalries and class conflict, writers provided much useful material for the publicity machine. Not only the occasional cultivated eccentricity but also the symbolic import of writing made novelists perfect candidates for enshrinement. Independent intellectuals who somehow had a common touch, novelists were venerated for their seeming devotion to the heights of disinterested truth. Their supposed lack of interest in the open pursuit of wealth only increased their attractiveness. Nearly every "author-at-home" book contained a set piece in which the novelist greeted the journalist in a comfortable study and spent a wonderful afternoon conducting the visitor through the glories of his or her home and the uncharted pleasures of art. The publicity stressed not only the author's leisure time but the meaningful work the author accomplished, which was undisciplined by an external authority. Unlike many other Americans, writers set their own hours at a job that brought a personal satisfaction that other jobs did not always bring. In an age in which the time clock ruled working life, writers had the luxury of not "punching in." In this caricature of literary work beyond the mean struggle for existence, novelists exemplified the allure of nonalienated work. The joy with which literary publicity reported the novelist's attire (seemingly unbound by the dictates of standard fashion), home (personally decorated rather than prefabricated), ability to drop work when a visitor called (so different from most work routines), and devotion to the highest ideals (a marked contrast to the drudgery of most work) made the novelist created by publicity an embodiment of wishes.

James fit the bill well. For a nation that had long worried about its inability to produce an artist of the first rank, here was a man who could rightly claim the title. He wrote and spoke in a cultured tongue and seemed preoccupied with larger, aesthetic issues. His very demeanor, so unlike that of his fellow citizens, suggested that he was at home in the world of art. In rising above the acquisitiveness of American society through his self-proclaimed interest in the "luminous paradise of art," he validated that society. A nation that could produce a Henry James had much to say for it. Despite some carping about his self-chosen exile in Britain, many literate Americans did not hesitate to claim him as one of their own.

For writers who recognized the fragmentation of communication and dedicated themselves to overcoming obstacles to discourse, publicity presented significant drawbacks. It focused attention less on the novel than on the creator, challenged the uniqueness of the novel as a communication, and undercut realist precepts on "work" and observation. With the expansion of publicity, the attributes of the author's life, not the characteristics of the novel, engaged the increasing number of readers. Celebrity, not the essence of the work, dominated readers' perceptions. Mere personal presence in publicity campaigns bestowed upon the novelist an aura of worth beyond that of ordinary people. By calling attention to what would be mundane details in the life of another, the system of celebrity magnified those aspects of authorial life and invested them with special significance. Because the author, unlike the reader, was an object of attention, the author's status dwarfed the reader's. In such circumstances a dialogue of equals was difficult, if not impossible. To use Alan Trachtenberg's phrase, the more knowable the author became as a datum of information, the more remote and mysterious literary activity seemed as a possible experience.[84]

Publicity also deemphasized the importance of a single novel. Although not celebrities whose fame rested on their style of life or their invested glamour, novelists were known less for the particular books they wrote than for the fact that they wrote at all. The activity itself was more fascinating than the results. Readers came to know the writer through a screen of images that undermined the uniqueness of literary exchange. If the reader could find out about the author through alternative sources and engage with the author through publicity, there was less need to read the novel. Reading about both the book and its creator would suffice. The supersession of the novel as the meeting place between writer and reader limited the efficacy of the Hawthornian compromise. Whereas Hawthorne controlled the image of the author in order to facilitate communication under specific conditions of impersonality, the publicity-generated author only complicated the number of images that the reader had of the author and destroyed the uniqueness of the text.

Publicity also countered realists' hope that readers would regard writing as ordinary human endeavor. While authors argued for realist premises, publicity continually referred to romantic ones. It was not so much that the publicity was all taken in uncritically by readers. Much of it was not, especially the publicity that frankly did not ask for belief but presented itself as a knowing response to the criticisms of publicity. What publicity did was to convey attitudes and inclinations, and it was effective to the extent that it monopolized attention and denied other forms of response to the author and the work. Publicity, then, was less important in determining *what* to think than in setting the terms to think in. Investing the novel with mystery and glamour, publicity made the novelist part of the spectacle. The pose of the novel as neutral observer's report only partially hid its status as a performance.

Print lent a special authority to the work. It was not uncommon to find men and women who trusted the authority of the printed word over their own experience. During the Chicago World's Fair of 1893, thousands flocked to an exhibit that claimed to be the actual cabin that Uncle Tom had used during his stay in Louisiana. Rented to the fair by in-laws of the novelist Kate Chopin, the cabin was testimony to the inability of many to separate "fact" from "fiction." Howells reported a similar phenomenon. A tailor who had noted the similarity in names between a Howells character and a customer with an unsettled account, sent Howells the outstanding bill in hopes that he could help secure payment.[85] These two relatively minor episodes of misinterpretation were emblematic of the problems realists confronted in assuring that meaning was understood and recall the fears of early opponents of the novel that fiction would become intertwined with reality.

Realism Reconstructs the Literary Discourse

Realists greeted the glamour of publicity with marked ambivalence. On the positive side, naturally pleased to receive praise for their work, they welcomed their newfound celebrity. Aware that the expansion of the marketplace in literature had undermined the authority of the old literary elite that had dictated taste, they were gratified to have gained audience approval. Many embarked on lecture tours to promote themselves and to establish a rapport with this large, amorphous new audience. Twain was a well-known and admired public speaker, and he planned his effects carefully, including publicity. During a tour in 1884, for instance, he wrote to his agent, J. B. Pond: "You want to say nothing about original sketches written specially for this series, for that is too decided a confession of weakness. It confesses that we know we can't draw just on our *names* alone, but have got to *add* something extraordinary to persuade people to come. . . . I think it dangerous policy to let the public suppose we need any attraction but just our *names* alone."[86] Howells lacked Twain's skill on the platform and fretted about his abilities, but he too basked in the reflected glory of his audience. Writing boastfully to his wife during his 1899 trip to the Midwest, he noted the presence of the "elite" of Fort Wayne, Indiana, the twelve hundred privileged persons who received tickets by invitation only.[87]

To the extent that realists equated popularity with democratic choice, they saw publicity campaigns as part of the battle of realism against literary conservatism. A literature that held out democratic promise but had few adherents could be said to have failed. In Norris's view the people needed to be cultivated so as to improve their taste: "It is the people, after all, who 'make a literature.' If they read, the few, the 'illuminati,' will write. . . . The demand which he [the Great Writer] is to supply comes from the Plain People—from the masses and not from the classes."[88] Realists did not hesitate to lodge complaints about the inability of publishers to mount proper campaigns. Writing James in 1900, Howells admitted he was galled "that I should sell only as many thousands as the gilded youth of both sexes are selling hundred thousands." This showing, Howells concluded, was due to his publisher's reluctance to spend more on publicity.[89]

Despite the attractions of publicity realists harbored doubts about both its usefulness in composition and its ultimate effects on social life. Howells wrote savagely about the corrupting effects of advertising and the star system it fostered. Advertising, he maintained, had become the new, but inferior, criticism, rendering the text in clichés and trite terms. Infringing upon the "delicate and shrinking modesty which is the distinguishing ornament of the literary spirit," advertising drowned out the actual content with an "analytical warbling" that sounded sincere but lacked substance. Designed to convince readers that what was false was true, advertising resembled romanticism. The difference between utopia and advertising, Howells wrote, was that the former "legislates out the possibility of ugly things" whereas the latter exists to convince potential consumers "that such things are useful, beautiful, and pure." Should the values of advertising prevail, standards would inevitably erode, and "we shall none of us be able to criticize the others."[90]

Where Howells saw a social danger, James saw a threat to the writer. In his view the invasion of privacy from publicity eroded the author's "capital." With the author no longer assured of the Hawthornian privacy to construct a point of view, the very process of novel writing became problematic. When he stepped off the boat to begin his American tour, James reacted with horror at the atmosphere of publicity. He inhaled, he says in *The American Scene*, "the air of unmitigated publicity, publicity as a condition, as a doom, from which there could be no appeal." It was "as if the projection had been so completely outward that one could but find oneself almost uneasy about the mere perspective required for the common acts of personal life."[91] Howells may have granted a large number of interviews, but James resisted nearly every press inquiry, boasting of his escape from interviewers and publicity hounds during his American trip. The only interview that he did grant was to a woman armed with a letter of introduction from Scribner's—and that only on the condition that she send him no clippings.[92]

James's most damning criticism of the publicity-mad new journalism can be found in his novels. His works are populated with unpleasant, invading, and insincere newspaper people. Henrietta Stackpole of *The Portrait of a Lady* and Matthias Pardon of *The Bostonians*, to name just two unflattering portrayals, are both dissonant elements in their respective narratives. At nearly every step they frustrate the perceptions and the ideals of the characters about whom James is most concerned. Their brusque manner and insensitivity create a series of obstacles for the protagonists, Isabel Archer and Verena Tarrant. Pardon, who wants to share in the management of Verena with Olive Chancellor, is corruptly commercial. Pretending a concern for feminist principles but unable to comprehend their seriousness, he cares only for the spectacle and the public acclaim. Yearning to bask in the reflected glory, he can offer only the promise of eternal excitement—"a ten-year run"—for his patronage.

Publicity could also destroy and deform careers, as the case of Stephen Crane illustrates. Hailed throughout the country for *The Red Badge of Courage*, Crane found that the attention stifled his work and felt that the incessant revelation of his personal past was insulting and degrading. Writing to his editor, Ripley Hitchcock of Appleton, Crane confessed that celebrity in New York had "made a gibbering idiot out of me. I shall stick to my hills." Worried that his adulators would demand new and better things from him, he wondered if the note could be sustained: *Red Badge* was not "any great shakes, but . . . the very theme of it gives it an intensity that a writer can't reach every day."[93] Eventually he found the public interest in him more than he could bear. Writing Hitchcock about the dissection of his personality, he complained that "they are beginning to charge me with having played baseball. I am more proud of my baseball ability than some of my other things."[94] Half the things of which he was accused, he wrote to Harold Frederic, he never did.[95] This constant attention followed him throughout his remaining years, and he seems to have grown rebellious under the pressure. His defense of prostitutes rousted unfairly by New York policemen, his living quarters in the Art Students' League, and his common-law marriage made him a notorious writer and contributed to what some have seen as his constant desire to anticipate, rather than experience, life. Acting as if he had internalized the demand of publicity for sensation, he moved in his last years from confrontation to confrontation. Though celebrity never made Crane a "gibbering idiot," it is not farfetched to suggest that the intense glare of public scrutiny contributed to his inability to sustain the brilliance that he had achieved with *Red Badge* in other full-length novels.[96]

For some, like George Washington Cable, the solution to the problem of the decline of the discourse of consent was to organize and train the readership within the confines of formal organizations. As head of the Home Culture Clubs, Cable tried, among other things, to instruct the readership in the fundamentals of proper reading. After dabbling in various uplift schemes, he founded the clubs in 1886 in an effort to elevate "the masses." In its practice the club movement was catholic in its tastes. The reading list was left entirely in the hands of the local clubs. There was, however, an unwritten agenda that suggested Cable wanted very much to mold reading habits. Unable to reverse social fragmentation, Cable hoped for a new cultural unity. Aiming to substitute voluntary association for a social movement that was coercive and therefore, to Cable, counterproductive, the clubs prescribed reading, studying, and discussing in members' homes: "Without any disturbance of necessary social distinctions and divergencies, (and many are highly necessary,) we seek to establish between homes of contrary fortunes—and between homes and the homeless—relations which *something* must establish before either church, courthouse or school can give us very much better results." The purpose of this private interchange was to lay the groundwork for a common understanding. As Cable told an *Outlook* interviewer, Home Culture Clubs were designed for unanimity of response: "In the home culture idea the question of social affinity is not touched on in the least. There has to be affinity of some sort in order to make things work smoothly and successfully; but it is affinity of mind and aspiration, not likeness in wealth and rank."[97]

Other realists hoped to establish through the realist novel the affinity of mind and aspiration that Cable believed the Home Culture Clubs would promote. Aware of the diversity of their audience, they expected and to some extent encouraged a multiplicity of readings. Such was the import of Howells's contention that readers were the final arbiters of the truth of a novel, which they judged by their own fund of experiences.[98] No single, canonical meaning would arise; rather, each reader, engaging the text in a coherent fashion, would participate in the fashioning of a communal and shared meaning. Unlike narrators of previous genres, the realist narrator eschewed the undemocratic practice of dictating meaning to an audience, or at least so realist polemics argued. This sense that readers should have choice is why James scolded Flaubert and Zola for their seeming belief that readers must like types of novels: "He [Flaubert] passed his life in strange oblivion of the circumstance that, however incumbent it may be on most of us to do our duty, there is, in spite of a thousand narrow dogmatisms, nothing in the world that anyone is under the least obligation to *like*—not even (one braces one's self to risk the declaration), a particular kind of writing."[99] The belief that readers continually retest formulations and have expectations shattered and dicta challenged is why James could assert in "The New Novel" that "the simplest description of the cry of the novel when sincere . . . is as an appeal to us when we have read it once to read it yet again."[100]

Realists were not, however, prepared to accept so many different interpretations that the novel itself ceased to be important. The text itself remained as the centerpiece of any interpretation. Given the nature of both the actual readership and the readership that realists hoped to involve in the discourse, the form and content of the new novel would have to be reworked for those who were not trained in the literary niceties. The concept of "literature" itself needed to be jettisoned, because, as Howells explained, it had presented itself as "superfinely aloof, which makes it really unimportant to the great mass of mankind, without a message or a meaning for them."[101] What had been judged "literary" by previous generations had depended upon common consent of readers, albeit an elite and privileged group of them. Only the "common" or typical possessed the capacity to generate a new consensus. Likewise only a language that delivered reality as it actually was could aid this goal. It is not surprising, then, that realist language tended toward the neutral and the colorless so as not to interfere with the readers' response to the text. The goal of this new discourse was to provoke in readers a new sense of their commonality both as readers and as citizens and to stimulate an active participation in social life.

Realists encoded this theory of reading within the texts themselves. The six chapters of Howells's *Hazard of New Fortunes* in which he describes the tribulations of finding shelter in the nation's largest and most confusing city can be understood as a paradigm of realist reading. The manner in which the Marches learn to "read" New York corresponds to the way in which realist readers make their way through the text. By asking readers to judge the truth of a novel by its correspondence to their own life experience, Howells reckoned that they would emerge with a new sense of knowledge just as familiarity led the Marches to an understanding of New York. From initial confusion a renewed sense of security would emerge. What began as indeterminate and unclear would end as naturalized and understandable.

> At first all the New York streets looked to them ill-paved, dirty, and repulsive; the general infamy imparted itself in their casual impression to streets in no wise guilty. But they began to notice that some streets were quiet and clean, and though never so quiet and clean as Boston streets, that they wore an air of encouraging reform and suggested a future of greater and greater domesticity. Whole blocks of these downtown cross streets seemed to have been redeemed from decay, and even in the midst of squalor a dwelling here and there had been seized, painted a dull red as to its brick work and a glossy black as to its woodwork, and with a bright, brass bellpull and doorknob and a large brass plate for its keyhole escutcheon, had been endowed with an effect of purity and pride which removed its shabby neighborhood far from it.[102]

Some critics of realism have argued that the sheer materiality of the narrative and the translucent language operate to impose a reading on the audience. The attempt to mediate as little as possible, they charge, actually conceals a desire to manage the reader, to render him or her incapable of either contemplation or productivity. Gerald Lee, a turn-of-the-century critic, had a similar view. He thought that the fundamental characteristic of modern society was that it allowed only appeals to motion and mass. These appeals actually discouraged real thought. Lee's complaint was that modern men and women were inundated in a flood of information and consequently had lost touch with self and senses. Noting the immediacy upon which realism was based, Lee in effect postulated an identity between realism and publicity.[103] There is certainly some truth to the contention that realists attempted to "manage" the reading experience, particularly in their form of narration, their "commonsense" view of language as a vehicle that conveyed meaning without any mediation or distortion rather than an alterable system of signs, and their heavy reliance on material description; but the management was not linear or immediate. Realist reading was not quite the passive, directed endeavor that Christopher Wilson discerns in his "Rhetoric of Consumption." For many realists, particularly Howells and James, contemplation of the antebellum variety that Lee championed very easily resulted in a languid inactivity.

It was this inactivity that the major realists attempted to counteract. This point emerges in Howells's discussion of the Marches' actual reading habits. March did some writing, Howells tells the reader, "But for the most part, March was satisfied to read. He was proud of reading critically, and he kept in the current of literary interests and controversies. It all seemed to him, and to his wife at secondhand, very meritorious; and he could not help contrasting his life and its inner elegance with that of other men who had no such resources."[104] This attitude led to a certain smugness, untested by actual crisis: "They were very sympathetic; there was no good cause that they did not wish well; they had generous scorn of all kinds of narrow-heartedness; if it had ever come into their way to sacrifice themselves for others, they thought they would have done so, but they never asked why it had not come into their way."[105] In the same way that the firing of his mentor tests March, so too must the reader be generous and moral to traverse a Howells novel. By sympathetic reading the reader would become engaged with larger concerns, open to new thoughts, and willing to live in accordance with those uplifted sentiments.

Howells's liberal program to reconstruct an active discourse ran afoul of two limitations in his view that stymied its ability to make reading a transformative act. First, he presupposed precisely the type of reader that realist discourse was to create. Realist reading actually reconfirmed the tolerant reader that the reading process was to bring about. To make the process succeed, the ideal realist reader had to be open and flexible, able to know something other than his or her own mind, and alive to the limitations of personal prejudices. Otherwise the experience would be relatively fruitless. But openness and awareness were precisely the ends for which Howells aimed. An intolerant reader would end up like the magazine critics, whom Howells excoriated as thinking it "a virtue to be intolerant." The problem with critics, Howells maintained, was that they did not understand that "the same thing may be admirable at one time and deplorable at another."[106] Second, Howells required a reader who shared with him the same view of "reality." Making the text the source of meaning about which interpretations would fluctuate and presenting the text as an object that the flexible reader completed meant that the fulfillment rested upon similar beliefs. The multiplicity of readings that Howells sanctioned had a fairly limited breadth. As we shall see in chapter 6, realism was quite capable of handling some aspects of "reality" but troubled by others. In short, "truth" and "honesty" were something reader and writer shared prior to the reading.

Howells only complicated his problem when he insisted that the balanced seeing of realism was inherently moral. Linking truth and pleasure, he reassured American readers that a true picture was necessarily a moral one: "The light of civilization has already broken even upon the novel, and no conscientious man can now set about painting an image of life without perpetual question of the verity of his work and without feeling bound to distinguish so clearly that no reader of his may be misled, between what is right and what is wrong, what is noble and what is base, what is health and what is perdition, in the actions and the characters he portrays. . . . This truth, which necessarily includes the highest morality and the highest artistry—this truth given, the book cannot be wicked and cannot be weak."[107] In effect, Howellsian realism postulated the limits of reading. Designed to provoke a new reader awareness of custom and to transform beliefs brought to the text, Howellsian discourse knows its end.

This knowledge accounted for both the strengths and weaknesses of the realist conception of the discourse. It brought to literature a firm sense that readers were necessary not only to make the profession pay but also to complete the text. As Norris wrote in his essay "A Problem in Fiction," the purpose of writing is to convince a majority of intelligent people that what they have read has the ring of truth. Without such consent, no communication of anything vital could occur.[108] Realists understood that the diversity of the reading public meant that consensus could not be assumed but would have to be earned. Yet the terms of that consensus were limiting and predefined, and those who participated in it shared a common vision that put limits on what was observed and valued.

The empathetic reader whom Howells proposed as the ideal recipient of his novels proved difficult to attract. In a letter to Brander Matthews lamenting the poor reception of *The Kentons* (1902), Howells seems to have glimpsed the limitations of the ideal reconstruction that realism proposed: "I had hoped that

I was helping my people know themselves in the delicate beauty of their everyday lives and to find cause in the loveliness of an apparently homely average, but they don't want it. They bray at my flowers from the fruitful field of our common life, and turn aside among the thistles with keen appetites for the false and the impossible."[109] Rather than engaging with the novel and working with the author to perceive the typical in new ways, American readers turned to the romance, whose codes were more what they expected from a novel and whose conventions yielded different sorts of rewards.

Realists had hoped to pose the common and truthful as an alternative to the lies and exaggerations of publicity, but they misconstrued the way in which publicity was not a fraud but a reaffirmation of a way of experience. The realist thrust to display life as lived paralleled the advertiser's display of commodities. Instead of overcoming the logic of commercialization, realist reading tended to confirm it. Even as the Marches learned to interpret their new city, deciphering the morass of signs and consolidating the information contained in the streets and painted apartments, they became spectators of, not participants in, the city. "She now said that the night transit [on the El] was even more interesting than the day, and that the fleeting intimacy you formed with people in second- and third-floor interiors, while all the usual street life went on underneath, had a domestic intensity mixed with a perfect repose that was the last effect of good society with all its security and exclusiveness. He said it was better than the theater. . . . What suggestion! What drama! What infinite interest!"[110] The passage suggests a parallel to realist reading—what began as an anodyne to passivity so overwhelmed the reader that it led to a new spectatorship. The proliferation of display in the realist novel—the seemingly unbridled urge to "do" a subject in graphic plentitude—eventually distanced the reader from the very aspects of life under scrutiny. The train stations, department stores, and theaters of the realist novel yielded two contradictory responses that undercut the realists' dreams for a new discourse. Either the images seemed frozen and gave rise to a "conventional" response, thereby countering the project of animating a dialogue to "match the reader's truth with the author's"; or they became so overwhelming that readers withdrew, resigned to misunderstandings and confusions.

James was less sanguine than Howells about the possibilities of a renewed author-audience unity. Calling the American audience "dissolute," he believed as early as 1866 that "in every novel the work is divided between the writer and the reader; but the writer makes the reader very much as he makes his characters. When he makes him ill, that is, makes him indifferent, he does not work; the writer does all. When he makes him well, that is, makes him interested, then the reader does quite the labour." The early James had no answers but he did have faith. "I hold that there is a way. It is perhaps a secret; but until it is found out, I think that the art of story-telling cannot be said to have approached perfection."[111]

The later James was less optimistic about the task. In his 1908 preface to *The Portrait of a Lady* he held that the simplest forms of attention were all the writer could legitimately expect from his readers. Most readers cared only for plot developments. Because James regarded the plot as only one of many elements, he saw the discourse between the intelligent reader and the serious novelist as a protracted, almost negotiated affair, with each side struggling to come to terms with the other. The novelist "is entitled to nothing . . . that can come to him, from the reader, as a result of the latter's part of any act of reflexion or discrimination. He may *enjoy* this finer tribute—that is another affair . . . Against reflexion, against discrimination, in his interest, all earth and air conspire, wherefore it is that, as I say, he must in many a case have schooled himself, from the first, to work but for a 'living wage.' The living wage is the reader's grant of the least possible quantity of attention for con-sciousness of a spell." Believing that "the direct appeal to the intelligence might be legalized" was an "extravagance."[112]

In such conditions James took Howellsian discourse one step further. Delib-erately courting multiple interpretations, he required his readers to fill in their own readings. By single-mindedly hewing to textual complexity and resisting entertaining effects, he attempted to restore the discourse with a reader edu-cated to multiple and partial meanings. To prepare the reader for this process, James advocated the slightly outdated practice of reading aloud. Reading aloud called attention to "the finest and most numerous secrets," and gave them out "most gratefully, under the closest pressure." Only through difficulty in the text could passivity be shaken.[113]

Though Jamesian conceptions of discourse pointed to modernism and its anarchy of meaning, James himself never fully took the plunge. A reader who worked hard could discover stable meaning in a Jamesian text: "The *whole* of anything is never told; you can only take what groups together. What I have done has that unity—it groups together. It is complete in itself—and the rest may be taken up or not, later."[114] Although reader and writer stood isolated, this isolation could dissolve with an imaginative leap, an act of faith.

The anodyne is not the particular picture, it is our own act of surrender, and therefore most, for each reader, what he most surrenders to. This latter element would seem in turn to vary from case to case, were it not indeed that there are readers prepared, I believe, to limit their surrender in ad-vance. With some, we gather, it declines for instance to operate save on an exhibition of "high life." In others again it is proof against any solicitation but that of low. In many it vibrates only to "adventure"; in many only to Charlotte Bronte; in various groups, according to affinity, only to Jane Austen, to old Dumas, to Miss Corelli, to Dostoievsky or whomever it may be. For readers easiest to conceive, however, are probably those for whom in the whole impression, the note of sincerity in the artist is what most matters, what most reaches and touches.[115]

Realists were not protomodernists whose practice conflicted with theory. Modernist writers found nothing in common with their audience except a shared isolation; realists believed that some experiences were common to all and that perceptions were close enough that a reasonable dialogue could be established. Realists saw omniscient narration and common experience as the key to dialogue; modernists saw only reader construction and distorted and fragmented experience. Realists felt confident enough to use the ordinary language of the world; modernists entertained no such assurances. Yet even in their hope that a useful literature could be constructed from elements of commonality, realists found that the common was not the clear link that they had envisioned it to be. Forced by the rise of publicity and the reconstitution of the audience to address an ideal reader, rather than a known one, realists did not always see the limitations of their appeal. They assumed without much questioning an audience that was similar to themselves—open, flexible, non-ideological, sympathetic, and middle-class. The truth of the matter was that this ideal reader was as often absent as present. So Howells revealed when he articulated whom he thought read his books: "For my part, I like best to think of my stories, if they are so blest, as befriending outlying farms, small villages, and distant exiles."[116] In the conditional clause, Howells indicated that will and good intentions were not enough to secure discourse.

CHAPTER SIX

The Lure of Classlessness

The Antipolitics of Realism

I suppose I love America less because it won't let me love it more. I should hardly like to trust pen and ink with all the audacity of my social ideas; but after fifty years of optimistic content with "civilization" and its ability to come out all right in the end, I now abhor it, and feel that it is coming out all wrong in the end, unless it bases itself anew on a real equality.
—William Dean Howells to Henry James

The realist concern with repairing the fragmented communication between author and audience extended beyond the confines of literature. Drawing a parallel between the experience of reading and the conduct of social life, realists hoped that realism would also serve as a reminder to the nation of the possibilities of democracy in political and social life. They regarded their fiction as a form of political intervention designed to repair the fissures that had run through nearly every aspect of American life. In their analysis the United States lacked both solidarity among its people and a natural healing mechanism. As men like Howells and Norris envisioned it, by adhering to realist principles, the novel, which had become so crucial a part of modern living, could serve to knit together a conflict-ridden populace.

Realists felt that their social position as independent intellectuals uniquely qualified them to assume the mantle of reconciliator. Unlike their predecessors in the early republic, Gilded Age and Progressive writers as a group had no firm class identity. Antebellum writers had been members of the mercantile elite and the commercial gentry, but realists had no clear allegiance to either of the antagonistic new social poles: the industrial capitalists and the industrial working classes. Defined less by class position prior to the act of writing than by their specialized activity, realists found themselves standing alone, independent yet powerless. It was this situation that they hoped to remedy with their assertions that the realist novel had social and political relevance.

The Realist as Independent Intellectual

In the colonial and early republican periods writing was practically synonymous with elite status. Much writing took place under the auspices of coteries or with an eye toward the principles of polite and learned discourse that coteries embodied. Bearing such names as the Calliopean and the Aurelius, the literary clubs of the eastern seaboard provided the milieu in which composition and reading of essays and poems were undertaken. Group review and criticism enabled participants to learn and practice the art of elegant writing, belles-lettres. A review of the literary clubs of New York during the Revolution and the years immediately following indicates that the leading clubs boasted such influential men as Samuel Bard, one of the most prominent physicians in the city and one of the moving forces behind King's College (later Columbia), and Chancellor Kent, whose *Commentaries on American Law* was for many years a standard in the field. Bard and Kent were active in their clubs, not men who simply lent their names to the rosters. Belles-lettres was not confined to the local elites; such eminent revolutionaries as Thomas Jefferson and John Adams prided themselves on their mastery of the principles of elegant writing.[1]

Although belles-lettres was predominantly an activity of the elite, it was not exclusively so. Birth by itself prohibited no man or woman from joining the select. Hugh Brackenridge and Joel Barlow were both sons of yeomen, but their careers brought them into elite social relations. Both received college educations, Barlow at Yale and Brackenridge at Princeton, and both achieved later prominence, Brackenridge as a lawyer and Barlow as a political appointee and business agent.[2]

Brackenridge and Barlow were exceptions. The leisure to study literature and the financial resources necessary to accumulate a significant library generally restricted participation to the more privileged members of the new nation. Manual labor, which belletrists often reviled as uncivilized, rarely provided those who performed it with the credentials to enter the select circle or the chance to earn them. Belletrists themselves noticed the connection between wealth and culture. Writing in the Boston-based *Monthly Anthology*, James Savage argued that culture, the one attribute that separated man from beast, was inconceivable without commerce and the social division of labor: "If all are constrained to daily labour with their hands, there can be no cultivation of mind: and without intelligence there will be few delights of society and little interchange of benevolence. Man in such a state ceases to be sociable and becomes only gregarious. So that from gradual degradation to barbarism we shall be preserved by commerce."[3]

Savage's derision of manual labor and those who performed it as incapable of generating cultivation of mind went hand in hand with his belief that the purpose of belles-lettres was to insure the "delights of society." Although belles-lettres in the United States was predicated on a discourse among equals, its standards were rooted in beliefs and principles that justified continued political and social dominance by the cultivated. Belles-lettres venerated beauty, harmony, grandeur, and elegance of expression, which those who toiled did not possess.[4] Expressing the antagonisms of their class, belletrists saw the lives of ordinary people as mundane and not worthy of representation. Art, like the lives to which they aspired, should make contact with the ideal. Agrarians were more palatable as shepherds than as rough-hewn backwoodsmen and straining tillers of the soil. As Hugh Blair, whose *Lectures on Rhetoric and Belles-Lettres*, which was reprinted as late as 1870 in the United States, held, the sublime "must always be laid in the nature of the object described."[5]

Because of its political overtones, proper style was the basis of civilization and the rule of civilized men. Blair emphasized that belles-lettres served to extend men's knowledge and prepare those who had mastered its secrets for civic responsibility. When one rose to speak or put pen to paper (writing and speaking were not yet considered separate endeavors, and the assumed unity of the two was reflected in the title of Blair's book), one was defending not only a particular political position but the march of civilization. Belles-lettres, he contended, allowed men "to lay in a rich store of ideas relating to those subjects of which the occasions of life may call them to discourse or write. . . . Speech is the great instrument by which man becomes beneficial to man. . . . What we call human reason, is not the effect or the ability of one, so much as it is the result of many, arising from lights mutually communicated in consequence of discourse and writing." Emblematic of man's increased reliance on reasoning rather than force, elegant writing was "assumed as one mark of the progress of society towards its most improved period."[6]

Eager to safeguard writing from the intrusion of the mob, belletrists viewed the book market with disdain. Aware of the dangers that the book market posed to prestige and power of the literary elite, they campaigned against the excesses of the sale of literature and against what they regarded as its most degraded product, the novel.[7] As William Charvat has demonstrated, those who petitioned Congress in the 1780s and 1790s to protect the sanctity of literary property considered literature best protected when the price of books was high enough to render them an elite commodity.[8] Essayists and poets like Joseph Dennie condemned the literary pandering inherent in the market for literature as destructive of achievement. Dennie went so far as to reject the results of the Revolution because he saw in the victory at Yorktown the destruction of the patronage system and the end to the position of man of letters.[9]

Given these strictures, it is not surprising that American republicans considered elegant language and writing skills an essential qualification for leadership. Writing was both ideologically important in that it inculcated virtue in the masses and functional in that it eased the problems of ruling. Such at least was the opinion of those who wrote the circular soliciting funds for the Boston Atheneum in 1807: "In proportion as we increase in wealth, our obligations increase to guard against the pernicious effects of luxury by stimulating to a taste for intellectual enjoyment; the more we ought to perceive and urge the importance of maintaining the laws by manners, manners by opinion; and opinion by works, in which genius and taste unite to embellish truth."[10] American revolutionaries had felt similarly. Literacy, they insisted, was at the heart of liberty. A leader who could not express himself well was unworthy to lead, and a citizenry that was not well versed in literature could not long maintain its freedom. Nor was it accidental that the committees of correspondence, which formed one organizational unit of the revolutionary effort, developed so quickly. The classes that felt most acutely the domination of the British empire were the same classes that displayed the mastery of belleslettres as proof of their worth. Their skill in the written word followed naturally from their belief that proper expression was indispensable to state building.[11] Higher education, Thomas Jefferson argued in his plans for the University of Virginia, must insure that the informed citizenry at the center of American republicanism was a writing one. The university must "develop the reasoning faculties of our youth, enlarge their minds, cultivate their morals, and instill into them the precepts of virtue and order."[12] It was for this reason that rhetoric and belles-lettres, which Jefferson grouped in the same division of curriculum as ideology and ethics, remained central to education.

The early republicans discerned no absolute division between literary accomplishment and political activity. The former forwarded the latter, and the latter made possible the former. By the middle of the nineteenth century, this unity had been broken. The coteries that had formed the training grounds for belles-lettres no longer either generated the same enthusiasm or held the same importance. Where once literary clubs had been the province of the elite, now they were prevalent among the middle classes of the hinterland. Their function had changed as well. The literary clubs of the mid- and later nineteenth century replaced the older emphasis on original writing with organized discussions of published novels and poems and literary gossip. The limitations of such organizations are apparent in Sinclair Lewis's *Main Street*, in which Thanatopsis, modeled on his mother's Gradatim Club, proves incapable of anything but trite literary talk.[13]

Much of the responsibility for this change belongs to the increasingly powerful literary marketplace, which obliterated the hegemony of authors from elite family background and opened careers to talent. As the monetary rewards available through literary work grew, creating a professional class of writers whose social backgrounds were quite diverse rather than generally uniform, the importance of belletrist ideals faded. As men and women like Walt Whitman and Harriet Beecher Stowe joined the profession, the elite nature of the profession began to erode. Writers became specialists whose role was defined by their activity rather than by their preexisting social position. Where once writing had been part and parcel of membership in the mercantile and professional classes of the Eastern Seaboard and had been undertaken as a matter of course, by the middle of the nineteenth century it had become an individual career choice. In the process the purposes for writing became individual instead of social. Advancing a career, attaining fame, and personal expression all vied with articulating social values and with class defense as goals for writing. And at the same time that new vigor of the marketplace made possible a more disparate corps of authors, politicians began to assume a specialized role in which they became less interested in elegant expression than in popular appeal.[14] The increasing distance between political and literary life meant that authorship assumed a new status as an independent profession.

The connection between authorship and politics did not immediately vanish, lasting well into the mid-nineteenth century. Many authors turned to government patronage, which differed from the aristocratic form in that its recipients performed administrative rather than direct literary duties. Hawthorne received his famous position at the Salem Customs House through the intercession of George Bancroft, the distinguished historian who supervised the placement of Democratic literati. Melville came to Washington in 1861 to secure an appointment as consul in Florence and eventually settled in the New York Customs House, which a Cincinnati paper labeled a rest home for tired scribblers.[15] William Charvat estimates that two-thirds of American writers held or sought office during the antebellum period.[16]

Nonetheless the difference between early republican and Jacksonian authors is striking. Timothy Dwight (a Hartford wit and president of Yale), Barlow,

Dennie, and their confreres were political men by virtue of the milieu in which they wrote, the acknowledged purposes for writing that their milieu engendered, and the class alliances in which they found themselves. They and their readers accepted from the start the political nature of their art. Authors like Emerson, Thoreau, Hawthorne, and Poe, by contrast, certainly commented on political affairs and interjected themselves into political life, but their interjection was a conscious effort to overcome newly erected barriers. Because no natural and expected political role fell to these authors and to their craft, their decision to involve themselves in political affairs required effort.

As their political power began to wane and writers realized the marginality of letters to social life, they increasingly envisioned the author as existing in conflict with society. Concerned with the life of the mind and spirit, the writer stood apart from self-seeking conduct and cold rationality. Literature no longer complemented political life but instead acted as a silent comment on it. By remaining aloof from the fray in which they no longer participated, writers staked out a claim to a higher realm. Emerson's American Scholar, who penetrated to the facts amidst appearances, represented the epitome of the romantic vision of the author: "For the ease and pleasure of trading the old road, accepting the fashions, the education, the religion of society, he [the scholar] takes the cross of making his own, and, of course, the self-accusation, the faint heart, the frequent uncertainty and loss of time, which are the nettles and tangling vines in the way of the self-relying and self-directed; and the state of virtual hostility in which he seems to stand to society, and especially to educated society."[17]

Thomas Wentworth Higginson, writer, clergyman, discoverer of Emily Dickinson, and member of the Secret Six who funded John Brown, exemplifies the contradictory pressures that this stance embodied. Coming of age in the 1840s, Higginson faced the problem of building a career—a series of related life positions that involved specialized activities that he consciously chose. Alienated by the commercial motives expressed in the law, he resolved upon his graduation from Harvard to embark on a literary career. Looking back on his life, Higginson expressed a reluctance typical of many romantics to engage in commercial activities. "For myself," he wrote, "I have always been very grateful, first for not being rich, since wealth is a condition giving not merely new temptations, but new cares and responsibilities such as a student should not be called upon to undertake; and secondly, for having always had the health and habits which enabled me to earn an honest living by literature, and this without actual drudgery."[18] In this view, so different from that of Savage's generation, wealth and literature were incompatible. Savage had lauded the practice of literature because it was decidedly superior to manual labor but perfectly complementary to commerce; Higginson, on the other hand, saw writing as a type of spiritual fulfillment. Indeed, he saw writing as a complement to his other career choice, of the ministry.[19] The responsibilities that he explicitly shunned would have been cheerfully assumed by a confident and assured elite. Although the hostility between businessmen and intellectuals had not yet fully developed in the mid-nineteenth century, Higginson's prose indicates that the tension was smoldering.

While rejecting the pursuit of wealth as inappropriate, Higginson did not forgo social action. Running for Congress on the Free Soil ticket, organizing schools for textile workers, and commanding a Union regiment of free blacks, he was at the heart of every important reform movement of his time. Still historically close enough to the ideals of the coterie to take them seriously, he had yet to attain that alienated or free-floating state that was to become an identifying characteristic of twentieth-century men and women of letters. Though he decried many of the social arrangements of antebellum America, he had not rejected its official culture and its inheritance of literary service from the republicans. An intimate of James Russell Lowell and Oliver Wendell Holmes, he never severed his connections with the self-conscious literary elect of Boston nor did he presage the position of the rebels of the early twentieth century who refused to truck with a thoroughly philistine American culture.[20] Where he perceived an essential moral flaw that needed urgent repair, Higginson simply took his duty as a man of letters to mean active social engagement.[21] Oscillating between withdrawal and involvement, he embodied a new conflict: how to perform literary service in the absence of a clear connection to a particular stratum without falling prey to the dangers of the marketplace.

Not all writers who were unhappy with the new commercial and professional status of the author adopted Higginson's mix of social action and literary reflection. Some in the late nineteenth century enshrined leisure as the prime attribute of authorship and formed clubs and societies to preserve their version of literary values divorced from the vagaries of social action. Finding the struggle for market success offensive, many New York writers drew solace from a vision of the writer in neo-aristocratic repose. As concerned for the status and respect accorded the author as for the conditions and quality of literary work, writers like E. C. Stedman, R. H. Stoddard, and R. W. Gilder contrasted the success of antebellum Boston authors with the public disregard for postbellum New York authors and concluded that authors themselves had brought down the scorn of the nation by their own actions. In a self-pitying essay, "The Literary Disadvantages of Being Born Too Late," George Cary

Eggleston complained that craftless and inferior writers had taken charge, and ideas, once the proud currency of American writers, had become mere trivialities in an age of million-sellers.[22]

In a review of the literary situation in New York for *Harper's* in 1886, George Parsons Lathrop, a New York novelist and Hawthorne's son-in-law, put the case of authorial decline explicitly. He recalled with envy that even those who did not read antebellum Boston authors accorded them respect. In contrast, New York writers were either ignored or derided. Great art seemed a matter of supreme indifference to New York, for such things were unconnected to the essential pursuit of commerce and finance. Having no inherent importance, New York authors constantly struggled for existence. "There is something about local conditions in New York," wrote Lathrop, "which has led writers since the time of Irving and Cooper to divide their allegiance and attach themselves in part to some other occupation, often uncongenial. . . . Literary New York has no well-defined position as compared with the other activities of the city. The cost of living is high; and on both these accounts, authors find it well to fortify themselves with support furnished by commercial and editorial connections."[23] Lathrop's solution, however, was not a call for authors to take up the plight of a society in turmoil but a plea to men of power to respect authors.

It is interesting to note that Howells, who often rejected self-pity and had warned of the political dangers of literary centers, drew similar conclusions. For Howells the contrast was stark. New York was a vast literary mart where men and women came to strike their publishing deals and to establish their connections but did not stay to establish a disinterested literary program. Howells regarded Boston, on the other hand, as a precapitalist paradise where authors set the entire social tone. Discounting the validity of such an assessment (and given the activities of Boston financiers during this period it is probably incorrect), what is noteworthy is that Howells's fantasy constructs a past in which men and women did live by literature.[24] Unlike the politicians of the coteries, writers in antebellum Boston were not inherently political; political power bowed to literary power. "I do not believe," wrote Howells, "that since the capitalistic era began there was ever a community in which money counted for less. . . . The instincts which governed it were not such as can arise from the sordid competition of interests; they flowed from a devotion to letters and from a self-sacrifice in material things which I can give no better notion of than by saying the outlay of the richest college magnate seemed to be graduate to the income of the poorest. . . . Everybody had written a book, or an article, or a poem, or was in the process or expectation of doing it."[25]

Those who feared for New York literary life also turned their anger on a new group of pretenders for literary prominence, the bohemians. Antebellum bohemianism connoted not only asocial and outlandish behavior but also Grub Street, the congregation of ink-stained wretches who wrote "hack" pieces on assigned topics for a mere pittance. Despite their contempt for conventionality, bohemians were the original wage slaves of the writing profession, whom necessity compelled to write tripe in order to secure a living through letters. Bohemians did manage to found their own organ, however, the *Saturday Press*, and in the process emerged as a counterculture threat to the literary establishment.[26] Even the usually sympathetic Howells found much to deride in antebellum bohemianism: "It was clever and full of wit that tries its teeth upon everything. It attacked all literary shams but its own, and it made itself felt and feared." Bohemian society gathered in an underground beer cellar on lower Broadway, where "Bohemian nights were smoked and quaffed away." The talk was not so good as Howells had heard in Boston, and its participants were always recovering from a "fearful debauch," their "locks still damp from wet towels," their eyes "frenzied."[27]

Although actually a peripheral member of this bohemia, Walt Whitman represented to the worshipers of Boston the epitome of New York literary life. While the respectable members of the literary fraternity, who traced their lineage to the old literary standards, admired the formal aspects of his poetry, they found the content and his celebration of the common too earthy for genteel tastes.[28] Regarded as disreputable for his behavior, especially in the matter of obtaining Emerson's endorsement for *Leaves of Grass*, Whitman personified the irresponsible artist.

One senses in the complaints about misbehavior of the bohemians the implication that their immoral and scandalous behavior had alienated the opinion of good society against the class of writers as a whole. The point is not that the literary establishment of the immediate postbellum period was inaccurate in evaluating the literary potential of bohemianism or that in its concern for high principles it crushed a promising literary movement, but rather that bohemians drew the fire of a group of authors well aware that society no longer regarded authorship with the same sense of reverence that it once had.

Self-declared bohemians were few in number, but the Grub Street mentality permeated the literary life of the city. New York may have had its share of great writers (though Norris, who yearned for his native San Francisco, denied that it had produced a single one), but it was the city's commercial conditions, genteel authors felt, that created competitive chaos and destroyed the influence of writers. Contemporaries noted with great regret the internecine quarrels, the sneering of men like E. L. Godkin, and the scatological attacks of Edgar Fawcett, whose vituperation earned him the nickname "Leaky." Even the hardiest of the tribe felt the pressure. Norris, who was more at ease than most with the postwar conditions, complained that New York literary life was not true competition but simple scrambling.[29] True competition would exist if two or more writers worked on the same story. That condition was unthinkable. Instead, writers elbowed each other aside in the contest for attention and in the process managed only the most conventional or the most bizarre prose in an all-consuming effort to win the literary race.[30]

From its inception in 1882 the Authors Club of New York City aimed at reconstructing the exalted status of the writer. The seven men who founded the club—the dramatist and novelist Brander Matthews; the poet and critic E. C. Stedman; the editor and poet Richard Watson Gilder; the critic and dramatist Laurence Hutton; the popular Hoosier novelist and historian Edward Eggleston; the novelist and literary critic Charles DeKay; and the travel writer and historian Noah Brooks—all were born in the 1830s and 1840s and all had come to literary maturity at the beginning of the rapid surge in mass publishing. For the ills of rampant commercialism and the degradation of the prewar poet into the acquisitive and craftless "hack," the gentleman of the Authors Club prescribed the remedy of mutual acquaintance. Convinced that the glory of social clubs was the opportunities they afforded to cement social alliances, the founders sought to foster an environment in which associated producers could restore the American author to an honored position by stressing the leisure and dignity of literary life. Professional demeanor, not literary merit, was the basis of the club's membership. Abolishing the market was clearly beyond its power, but banishing bohemianism through an insistence on decorum was not.[31] In the words of George Cary Eggleston, the club aimed "at the better kind of bohemianism, the bohemianism which disregards all meaningless formalities, but respects the decencies and courtesies of social intercourse."[32]

Responding to criticism of the generally undistinguished character of the membership, Authors Club officers contended that the purpose of authors' associating with each other was to elevate the tone of literary life among all practitioners.[33] Although the club insisted that members be authors of "published books that voice creditable aspiration, and, at least, creditable attainment," its true standard was that members be gentlemen "who have always maintained in their work the best ethics of the craft."[34] Journalists and technical writers were expressly barred because they could not measure up to the club's vision of disinterested and contemplative men who communed with their imaginations in the quiet of club quarters.[35] It was with a sense of pride that Brander Matthews acknowledged his lack of best-seller status, for it demonstrated his commitment to literary hospitality, which he considered the best literary tradition. Stedman was full of praise for those "Squires of Poesy" who followed their art "because they adored it, quite as much as for what it did for them."[36] Writers should associate with the "best men," and for that reason the club elected Andrew Carnegie and Seth Low, the mayor of Brooklyn and president of Columbia from 1890 to 1901, during its transition from college to university.[37]

The gentleman author that the founders hoped to resurrect was, despite their efforts, in his dying days. The sociology of literature in the late nineteenth century gave no reason to believe that his health could be restored. Attempting to cure the symptom and not the cause, the leaders of the Authors Club did not recognize the extent to which the new literary conditions had forced the divorce of class and authorship. The gentlemen author had prevailed in literary life in the days in which gentlemen had controlled the writing profession. When writing had been part and parcel of class position, maintaining the existence of a gentleman author presented few problems. While the audience had remained homogeneous and deferential and while the purpose of writing had been the expression of the collective values of this group, such conditions as they had hoped for were unproblematic. Authors Club leaders tacitly admitted the utopian aspects of their quest when they began lobbying for the International Copyright Act in the 1890s. Authorship, they implicitly understood, had separate interests of its own that needed protection. Even though the Authors Club spun off the American Copyright League to remove the club from suspicion of ungentlemanly agitation, this direct involvement indicated that the club's conception of the author as man of repose was more an ideal than a possibility.[38]

It was more than the invasion of commercial relations into a privileged sphere that had devalued the author. Writers also had to confront the implications of the segregation of literature. Even the educated and well-read regarded literature an activity unto itself. In its former condition writing had been firmly integrated into a series of social activities and needed no special justification for its practice. But by the late nineteenth century writing had become a less "natural" act and had to struggle to define its social purpose. By entitling his book of essays *Literature and Life*, Howells indicated the divorce between the two realms. Though these realms could be brought together, Howells understood that this required concerted effort, for they were not necessarily part of the same field.

The struggle for a social place for writers is apparent in the changing reputation of the profession. Despite numerous complaints about the disregard in which Americans of the early republican period held their authors, the opposite was just as likely to be true. Many considered authors creators and wondered when American genius in practical matters and in the science of government would make itself felt in literature. Reviewers were often lavish in their praise. Edward Everett, for instance, believed that Washington Irving's "ease, simplicity, and elegance" compared quite favorably with that of the renowned Addison. He saw in Irving's initial triumph the dawning of American literary greatness. "We believe," he wrote, "that our republican princes are beginning to understand, that of all sordid things sordid affluence is the meanest; and that the portion of their riches, which will bring in the most exuberant return of pleasure to their possessors, is the portion devoted a generous and discriminating patronage."[39] That patronage never came, but the attitude of awe toward writers continued on after the Civil War. And if some of the deference toward creative artists was no doubt hypocritical and forced, much was truly reverential. Howells told with much relish the story of James Garfield's calling his neighbors to come to his porch to hear Howells tell stories of Lowell and Longfellow.[40]

Howells's story is a salutary reminder against the automatic assumption of American philistinism. Yet the fears of the members of the Authors Club were not without basis. In the 1880s a new image of the writer began to gain currency and competed with the image of creativity that Garfield and his neighbors held. In many ways this new version of the author was a caricature of antebellum Romanticism. In an age that prided itself on its practical, hardheaded nature the artist was considered eccentric, slightly effeminate, and impractical. *The Writer*, the journal devoted to professional advice to aspiring authors, caught this note in its admonition to avoid the eccentricities of Byron and to work at a steady, workmanlike pace. The repose that the Authors Club cultivated only reinforced the image of the author as impractical and out of touch with the pace and quality of American life in the late nineteenth century. Even realists noted this tendency among authors and artists. The character of Angus Beaton in Howells's *Hazard of New Fortunes* fleshes out the view of the typical artist: vain, self-centered, distant, finicky. Because Beaton is unable to meet others on social or human terms, his artistry degenerates into cleverness.

If writers held a socially ambiguous role in the late nineteenth century, their product, literature, was even more problematic. Though many Americans continued to pay homage in rhetoric to the glories and worth of literature, few felt it had any practical advantages. Richard Hofstadter has observed that the more thoroughly business dominated American life, the less need businessmen had to justify their existence and practices by references outside their domain.[41] Although he was referring to the Progressive Era, the point has some relevance for the late nineteenth century. A number of businessmen viewed literature as unproductive and wasteful. Combining the characteristic view of the early bourgeoisie, that art was a sign of aristocratic vice and luxury, with an emphasis on the virile activity of men of business, some considered writers opponents or misguided dreamers. Jay Gould, for whom the editor and journalist Edward Bok worked as a stenographer, was bemused by his young charge's literary interests and advised the lad to concentrate on the main chance.[42] Although, as Edward Kirkland has pointed out, the legend of the uncultured man of money is by no means entirely accurate, there are plenty of nineteenth-century examples of foul-mouthed, poorly read parvenus with which to build a prima facie case.[43]

The case of Andrew Carnegie would at first seem to run counter to the view that men of business viewed literature as an alien entity. Carnegie asserted that "liberal education gives a man who really absorbs it higher tastes and aims than the acquisition of wealth, and a world to enjoy, into which a mere millionaire cannot enter; to find therefore that it is not the best training for business is to prove its claim to a higher domain."[44] His career as a literary philanthropist and accomplished author lends credence to the argument that the opposition between authors and businessmen flourished as much in the imaginations of disenchanted and rejected authors as it did in fact. Certainly his accomplishments alert us to the dangers of making too much of the Babbittry of the Fiskes and Fords.

Yet closer examination reveals that Carnegie shared the common assumption that the practical and the intellectual were two separate realms. For him, as for the romantic and genteel writers, the glory of literature was its impracticality. Literature was sealed off from the world of action and from the normal, everyday practices of social life. (In the less frequently quoted sentence that follows his praise of the "higher domain," Carnegie acknowledges that no successful businessman ever graduated from a college literary or liberal arts program.) And if Carnegie valued literature and Jay Gould did not, both viewed literary and commercial practices as fragmented and divorced from each other. In holding that literature gives a "world to enjoy, into which a mere millionaire cannot enter," Carnegie saw literature as a distant repository of universal values preserved from, but unconnected to, the turbulent present.

This preservation of the separate realm of literature left novelists with neither firm social location nor defined class interests. In his essay "The Man of Letters as a Man of Business" Howells took a stab at definition.[45] Asserting that the writer was a worker who fashioned something that had not existed before, Howells argued that common status implied solidarity. Unless also an owner of a publishing firm, the author was "allied to the great mass of wage-workers who are paid for the labor they have put into the thing done or the thing made; who live by doing or making a thing, and not by marketing a thing after some other man has done it or made it." Contending that it was to their glory and not their shame that writers worked, Howells proclaimed that they "ought to feel the tie that binds us to all the toilers of the shop and field, not as a galling chain, but as a mystic bond also uniting us to Him who works hitherto and evermore." Most distinctly, the artist was not of the classes. "Except in our work, they have no use for us; if now and then they fancy qualifying their material splendor or their spiritual dullness with some artistic presence, the attempt is always a failure that bruises and abashes."

Howells did admit, however, that his classification of the writer as worker was more hope than sober analysis. For all his yearning to be one with "the people," he understood that the actual situation of authors was quite different. In truth, the writer existed between classes.

> I think that he [the writer] will do well to regard himself as in a transition state. He is really of the masses, but they do not know it, and what is worse, they do not know him; as yet the common people do not hear him gladly or hear him at all. He is apparently of the classes; they know him, and they listen to him; he often amuses them very much; but he is not quite at ease among them; whether they know it or not, he knows that he is not of their kind. Perhaps he will never be at home anywhere in the world as long as there are masses whom he ought to consort with, and classes whom he cannot consort with. The prospect is not brilliant for any artist now living, but perhaps the artist of the future will see in the flesh the accomplishment of that human equality of which the instinct has been divinely planted in the human soul.

The transition state that Howells described was not a psychological feeling of complete separation. The "homelessness" of the writer was more a professional uncertainty than a pervasive sense of personal disconnectedness or alienation. Whatever internal divisions and existential doubts the realists had, they never elevated those feelings into a badge of artistic worth.[46] Unlike later generations of modernists, realists were not "abroad at home." For all their occasional bitterness, none declared a personal war on the bourgeoisie. Their dilemma of establishing a social context for writing did not, Mark Twain's later pessimistic essays notwithstanding, escalate into radical rejection. As individuals, a number of realists were moderately comfortable. Although skill in writing no longer granted the same access to councils of government or levers of power that it once had, they were hardly a disenfranchised group.[47] Mark Twain associated with Henry Rogers, who was an important partner of J. P. Morgan, and William Dean Howells, who was a cousin of Rutherford B.

Hayes, served as a consul in Venice, earning his position in the time-honored manner of writing a campaign biography. Howells also occupied the prestigious "Editor's Study" in *Harper's*, which afforded him the most important platform of the day. For all his carping about his uselessness in the modern age, Henry Adams, whose methodology in his histories and memoirs has often caused him to be grouped with the realists, was not without influence in Washington salons.

Friendship and family ties aside, writers had to discover or forge for themselves a social context for their activities. Securing a place for a literature that was no longer guaranteed a "natural" home required a definition of the writer's role that was firmly established in relation to other social groups. Novelists began this search at the very moment at which the "social problem" had become a violent struggle. Investigators reported an alarming increase in class animosities among workmen. In the aftermath of the Commune and the Great Strikes of 1877, the urban landscape was dotted with armories. Harvard students drilled in anticipation of putting down domestic disturbances. The story from the factories, rail yards, and mines was no different. Four years after the Great Strikes raised the possibility of violent upheaval, 130,000 workers were involved in 477 work stoppages. In 1886 there were 1,572 strikes or walkouts involving 610,000. In that year in Boston, where Howells had just finished presiding over the *Atlantic*, some 500 businesses were closed at one time or another as a result of labor difficulties. Only once in the remainder of the century did the number of strikes fall below 1,000.[48]

Like many Americans, realists talked in terms of conflict and division. Howells did note that the "cheerful average" was more typically American, but he was quick to add that class polarization, once "almost inappreciable," was "changing for the worse."[49] A few years later he contended that the pursuit of material prosperity had had baneful effects on American life: "If it would at all help to put an end to that struggle for material prosperity which has eventuated with us in so many millionaires and so many tramps, I should be glad to believe that it was driving our literary men out of the country."[50]

Whatever their personal interest in the "social problem," realists also had a professional concern. Their literary commitment to mapping the history of their moment compelled them to take notice of the tensions and conflicts of the period. Their belief that literature needed to be relevant in the broadest sense and that it could not be confined to the studio invariably led them to depict a fundamental condition of American life. Yet the "social problem" had implications for realism of which the realists were only vaguely conscious. Howells and James in particular considered both the world and the art upon which it was based as fundamentally organic and complete. The organic and balanced form of the novel, which especially for Howells mirrored reality, rendered a solid, orderly universe that approached, if not always achieved, a kind of naturalness. The sheer materiality of realism, which provoked storms of controversy, held within it the implication of permanence. Social conflict, on the other hand, raised in sometimes obscured ways the possibility that the world was historical and transient, and not susceptible to a realist treatment predicated on observation of the "simple, natural, and honest."[51]

This difficulty only became apparent to realists at the end of the century. During the turbulent 1880s and 1890s, realists were quite politically involved, though on terms different from those of their predecessors. No longer firmly attached to any specific social group or bound by tradition or function to a particular ideology, realists possessed the freedom to engage in a thorough criticism of existing social arrangements. Almost unanimously they directed harsh criticism at the current state of affairs.[52] Hamlin Garland transformed a number of his stories in his first collection, *Main-Travelled Roads*, into literary defenses of Midwestern populism. The best known of these, "Under the Lion's Paw," was designed to illustrate in human terms Henry George's thesis of the unearned increment. Although the despair and hopelessness of the story render any solution to the farm problem a nostalgic pipe dream, Garland's story raised the ire of conservatives. Upton Sinclair and Jack London, whose work was peripherally realist, actually joined the Socialist party and wrote a number of undistinguished novels and a few classics—*The Jungle* and *The Iron Heel*— to illustrate their political opposition.[53]

Major realists were a bit more circumspect, but they too addressed the political and social crisis. In replying to a correspondent who, aware that he was writing a book on trusts, had asked him to praise them, Norris replied that as the title of *The Octopus* indicated he thought them neither legitimate nor tolerable. Stephen Crane earned a dismissal from the *New York Tribune* for his satiric coverage of a labor parade, which compared the workers to Roman slaves parading for their masters. Mark Twain publicly criticized American imperialism and occasionally supported unionization efforts, even though he saw one of the advantages of his printing press as its inability to go on strike. Moved by his discussions with union leaders, Twain presented testimony on the international copyright that accorded more with the unions' position than with the organized authors'. Even Henry James offered to shelter Emile Zola when the French author fled from his native land during the Dreyfus affair.[54]

Of all the realists Howells struck the most consistent political notes. An antiimperialist like Twain, he excoriated the annexation of the Philippines as a war for coaling stations and movingly covered the plight of Spanish prisoners during the war with the United States.[55] An original founder of the National

Association for the Advancement of Colored People, he wondered how black men and women could be so quiescent in the face of repression. Writing James in 1888, he confessed an inability to believe that all would come out right. "I suppose," he declared in a statement that separated him from later modernists, "I love it [the United States] less because it won't let me love it more."[56]

His early years gave no indication of later activism. Although his father had toyed with various utopian schemes, particularly Owenite socialism, Howells had been a staunch Republican prior to 1886 and rejected, at least consciously, much of his father's idealist thought.[57] In 1884 he resisted the urging of his colleague Twain to join the mugwumps in supporting Cleveland. Despite admitting that (however reprehensible his sexual escapades) Cleveland's public character was superior to his opponent Blaine's, Howells, standing firm for party loyalty, argued that the nation was safer with the party of Lincoln and abolition.[58] For all his later interest in the condition of labor, his letters barely register the Great Strikes of 1877.

The 1880s found Howells receiving an education in the issues of industrial social justice. In 1885, at the suggestion of Roswell Smith, the publisher of *The Century*, Howells went to Lowell, Massachusetts, to investigate factory conditions and developed his findings in *Annie Kilburn*. In May 1886 his involvement in the social question took a quantum leap to activism. On 4 May a bomb thrown by an unidentified assailant into a contingent of policemen in the process of dispersing demonstrators punctuated a rally in the Haymarket called to protest police brutality in the McCormick Reaper Works strike in Chicago. Although no direct evidence linking the accused to the crime was found, eight professed anarchists were arrested and convicted for the crime on the grounds that their advocacy had prompted the bomb. The trial had a galvanizing effect on the country and on Howells. While most men of letters leaped to the defense of the state, Howells embraced the cause of the defendants. When the convictions came down, he immediately wrote the defense counsel and offered his services. A few months later, Howells went public with his outrage. In a letter to the *New York Tribune* in the aftermath of the Supreme Court's denial of appeal on 2 November, Howells charged that the entire affair was a legal lynching and that the eight had been punished not for their deeds but their unpopular opinions.

Howells's letter drew immediate and concentrated fire. Concluding that "happily, it doesn't much matter what Mr. Howells believes," the *Tribune* urged Americans to avoid the error of cowardice. Despite the rebukes of nearly the entire press, Howells continued his campaign. No act of radical chic, his defense of the anarchists risked both condemnation and complete excommunication. Unlike the writers who rallied around Sacco and Vanzetti, the Scottsboro Boys, Alger Hiss, and the second Chicago Eight, Howells acted without the benefit of a tradition of intellectual opposition. Those later writers drew strength from the sense that they were acting in accordance with the intellectual's duty; Howells, so at odds with the prevailing opinion of American intellectuals, had no such resources.[59]

Much of the published reaction to Howells's intervention charged him with ignoring his proper role. An author of domestic novels, the argument went, had no right to insert himself into a legal matter. His province was literature, not politics. In reply Howells linked his fight in the Haymarket case to the struggle for literary realism. In an unpublished letter to the *Tribune* written after the executions he contended that the imaginative gifts of the prosecutor were better suited to a romantic novelist than to a public servant. Reviewing the evidence that had convicted men who at the time of the bombing were playing cards with their families, Howells charged that the state's attorney, Julius Grinnell, had exploited already heated passions in the manner of a romantic novelist: "He was, throughout, the expression of the worst passions of the better classes, their fear, their hate, their resentment." No better indication of the blindness of the romance could be found than Grinnell's making Anarchism the author of the crime and portraying legal injustice as the "Savior of Society." In a conception remarkably similar to that he used about the novel, Howells demanded that the newspapers cease to lie about the dead. "They were no vulgar or selfish murderers. However they came by their craze against society it was not through hate of the rich so much as the love of the poor. Let both poor and rich remember this, and do them this piece of justice at least."[60]

Realist political criticism received literary expression in realists' conscious choice to give representation to those classes previously denied serious consideration in literary work. Believing that the "typical" or "common" that realism pledged to portray was embodied in the middle or lower classes, realists rejected the high culture disdain for "low" or "ungrammatical" characters and placed them at or near the center of their work.[61] In giving expression to voices seldom heard in "high" literature, realists conferred upon the unrepresented a new seriousness, which they hoped would aid in the democratization of literature and in dampening real social tensions. James branded the English author Walter Besant's injunction to neophytes—to write only about the class to which they belonged—"chilling" because it instructed people to stay in their place.[62] Norris continually asserted that the material of literature was to be found in the streets among the lower and middle classes. Literature, he argued, "will not, will not, will not flourish indoors. Dependent solely upon fidelity to life for existence, it must be practiced in the very heart's heart of life, on the street corner, in the market-place, not in the studios."[63] Such was not idle talk.

Realists granted literary worth to a whole range of new characters from James's bookbinder, Hyacinth Robinson, to Crane's "girl of the streets," Maggie.

This new experimentation was not always greeted favorably. Some saw in this maneuver the vulgarization that they claimed infested realism. In a poem entitled "Realism," Thomas Bailey Aldrich compared the realist project to vivisection.

Romance beside his unstrung lute,
    Lies stricken mute,
The old-time fire, the antique grace,
You will not find them anywhere.
Today we breathe a commonplace,
    Polemic, scientific air:
We strip Illusion of her veil;
We vivisect the nightingale
To probe the secret of his note
The Muse in alien ways remote
    Goes wandering.

Realists returned the hostility in kind. Norris sneered at the upper classes, claiming that "they belong to a class whose whole scheme of life is concerned solely with an aim to avoid the unpleasant."[64] Such utterances hardly settled the knotty question of the social allegiance of the author or the problem of the purposes of fiction. Carping at the excesses of the upper classes may have soothed bruised feelings, but it did not set forth a program of what was to be done. Yet such talk indicated one option realists briefly considered in the 1880s: rejecting the "classes" and embracing the "masses." For a brief moment they envisioned a conscious declaration of unity with and the firm commitment to write to and for "the people" as the solution to their equivocal social role.

The Realist as Literary "Populist"

The growing tension between the two polar classes made the realist struggle for social place even more pressing. As class conflict intensified, many realists imagined "the people" as more reliable and attractive partners than the rich and powerful. It was a short step from Howells's belief that writers and workers shared a common condition to one holding that writers should employ their talents in political and social service to the common cause. Though resistant to becoming propagandists, realists did conceive of their social role as tribunes for the democratic elements. Some, like Howells, hoped that this new departure would increase the self-confidence of the common man and destroy habits of deference. "The mass of common men," he wrote, "have been afraid to apply their own simplicity, naturalness, and honesty to the appreciation of the beautiful. They have always cast about for the instruction of some one who professed to know better, and who browbeat wholesome commonsense into the self-distrust that ends in sophistication."[65]

Howells was not the only realist who felt that the place of the writer was with the distressed and not the comfortable. Norris's literary politics are infused with references to the needs and judgments of the masses. "Time was when the author was an aristocrat, living in seclusion, unspotted from the world," he wrote. "But the Revolution of which there is question here has meted out to him the fate the Revolutions usually prepare for Aristocrats, and his successor is, must be, *must* be—if he is to voice the spirit of the times aright, if he is to interpret his fellows justly—the Man of the People, the Good Citizen."[66]

The realist conception of the writer as the voice of the plebians developed in small and halting steps. Given the personal backgrounds and temperaments of the major realists and the lack of familiarity with literature and, in some cases at least, the English language on the part of large segments of industrial working class, the idea of obtaining a firm social anchor and definitive social position through an appeal to "low" elements worked itself out through echoes and traces rather than manifestos and ringing declarations. Although the logic of the realist authors' position as independent professionals and the breakdown of the links between writers and the "classes" dictated a search for new audiences, many realists balked at anything approaching an alliance. Some, like James, maintained a critical distance, put off by the crudity and near illiteracy of their prospective partners and by the class tensions that those who spoke in the name of workers and farmers seemed to provoke. Severe reservations remained uppermost in the minds of even the most enthusiastic "proponents." Howells, who unhesitatingly labeled himself a "socialist," demurred at joining any party. At pains to distinguish his Tolstoyan ethical variety from the materialist versions of DeLeon and Debs, he dissented from more politically active socialisms. Defining socialism as the goal of a society in which the common ethic of cooperation ruled life and eschewing the more radical calls for worker seizure of power, Howells limited his participation to public commentary.[67]

The prospects for such an alliance were far from brilliant. Few realists had begun their careers with any real knowledge of the lives and aspirations of industrial workers. Although Howells's father was a printer, he had at various times owned his own shop. James's father was an intellectual who moved the family between Boston and New York on his inheritance. Norris's father was a prosperous jeweler in Chicago and San Francisco. Crane's father was an itinerant minister. Henry Blake Fuller's father was active in Chicago real estate. Frederic's mother ran a sewing shop (his father had died when Frederic was young). Only Dreiser's and Garland's fathers qualify as bona fide factory workers and farmers, and their experience only succeeded in convincing their sons to avoid any manual labor. Further complicating any understanding were the different ethnic backgrounds of realists and workers. With the exception of Dreiser, the realists were to a man and woman Protestants, whereas an increasing number of workers were foreign-born Catholics and Jews.[68] Despite their attempts at understanding and their empathy, many realists found the ethnic traditions and character of the work force distasteful. Still regarding Catholicism as a religion of superstition, they were impatient with worker loyalties and sympathies. Given this background, it is not surprising that realists found political alliance difficult to contemplate, at least initially. Although family origins by no means indelibly stamp one's politics, they did bequeath to the realists an obstacle that few overcame completely. As it was, most of the politically involved realists limited their sympathy to an emotional reaction to perceived injustices and an intellectual declaration of concern, rather than full commitment to labor's cause.

It was more than simple curiosity that sparked the realists' concern with workers. Howells was not alone in imagining that a common condition—"working"—existed between writers and workers. Taking a cue from workers, a sizable number of writers saw in the labor union a model that could be adapted to their efforts to secure a better bargain with publishers. Beginning in 1890 and extending through the next two and a half decades, a spate of leagues and unions sprang up to define and extend the use of literary property by authors. The Authors' Protective Union, founded in Brooklyn in 1890, preceded by a year the American Society of Authors. The next year saw three new organizations: the American Authors' Society, which aimed at "a clear understanding of the position and rights of authors in literary property," furnishing "information to authors as to copyright laws, methods of publishing and forms of contracts," and assisting authors "in gaining the true value of their production, and when necessary, to secure the value"; the Association of American Authors, whose call for meeting was signed by William Dean Howells, George Washington Cable, and Thomas Wentworth Higginson, among others; and the Syndicate of Associated Authors, among whom numbered Richard Harding Davis and Thomas Nelson Page, which strove to replace literary syndicates and agents.[69] The scant evidence that does exist about these ventures indicates that the famous names who called the meetings soon lost interest, and the less renowned who might have benefited from them were incapable of sustaining the effort. The quick demise of these and subsequent organizations suggests that the cacophony of complaints about royalty payments, publishers' neglect, inferior advertising, and inadequate book distribution could not be met in the same fashion that railway workers met their problems.

Despite the failure of authors' organizations, calls for them continued, sometimes from unlikely sources. The publisher George Putnam, for example, believed that such organizations could stabilize the literary marketplace.

> The Author ought to secure the fullest and most specific information concerning the average market value of his work, and he ought to be able to feel assured that for this work he obtains the fullest net returns that are practicable under the existing literary and publishing conditions. . . . If the old personal publishing obligation relation, with its many attractions and with its various disadvantages, is to disappear, and if this system of purchase and sale, of contracts arrived at under the varying conditions of the market, and of publishing agreements requiring in the case of each book the service of brokers and solicitors [is to replace it], there ought to be the final advantage of a clearly specified business relation in which each party should accept definite obligations, and in which there should be some means of enforcing for each party the due fulfillment of such obligation.[70]

Putnam's call for an authors' union was part of the general drive to rationalize the book industry. In line with his progressive sympathies, his vision of using the collective strength of authors included the union's representing aggrieved or accused members in a series of hearings that the authors' organization chaired jointly with a proposed publishers'.

The Authors' League of America, established in 1912, met Putnam's requirements for an authors' organization, and he actually served as one of its officers. Claiming that "the writer, owing to his temperament, his lack of business training, and his frequent isolation from other members of his profession, is especially unfitted to drive a good bargain with those who buy his manuscripts," the league moved to protect those interests. From advising authors on the Treasury Department's ruling on the tax status of royalties to agitating for an industry-wide standard contract that limited publishers' control of the growing number of subsidiary rights, the league acted like a trade organization for independent producers. Though the membership may have sanctioned actions that improved the welfare of the average author, it did not necessarily expand its horizons and identify with laborers, as Howells had called for in the first decade of the twentieth century. A motion in favor of affiliating the league with the American Federation of Labor was defeated in 1916. *Publishers Weekly* reported that had it been passed, 40 percent of the league's 1,400 members would have resigned.[71]

Although Howells made no public comment on the Authors' League action, it seems unlikely that the league's inability to become more than a trade association would have surprised him. Having long since broached the subject of the unionization of authors, he expected that the jealousies of the authorial community would prevent fruition of any grand plans. In his essay "A Painful Subject" (1904) Howells had taken note of what he called the "feminine" temperament of the author. In his editorial column for *Harper's* he had commented in 1906 that the author-publisher relation was more akin to a love affair than an industrial dispute. The new publishing system, he said, violated authorial innocence. Expecting sincere regard, the author received cheap and deceptive flattery, which resulted from the publisher's need to negotiate anew for each book. Although each switched partners, the author still "cherished the illusion of the personal tenderness" of the publisher. The author was not totally mistaken in this belief, Howells concluded. Publishers had been capable of true acts of generosity, had possessed motivations other than money, and were forced to bear the sole cost of losses.[72] Describing literary relations as a primarily emotional affair was a far cry from the labor metaphor that Howells had used in the 1890s.

Howells's own ideas of a union for authors more closely resembled earlier producers' associations than the new industrial labor organizations. Believing that the natural market was distorted, he concentrated his agenda on the needs of more established and skilled authors. In his view stable net prices for novels severed the price of the artifact from its inherent quality. Price (and hence return to the author) did not reflect the worth of the item. Thus the major task for an author's union was to insure that major writers received major "wages." By pricing all novels at $1.50, the publisher allowed the buyer to get the book of a "writer of established fame and unquestionable quality for exactly the same cost that he gets the book of a perfectly unknown and unproven writer." In literature, unlike all other arts, the artist received payment on a case-by-case basis; the established painter or sculptor received payment on the basis of his or her reputation for quality. The solution that Howells proposed was a guild solution: a writers' cooperative that would at first bargain for the pay scale and then carry on publishing with union labor.[73] This suggestion did not come to fruition in part because Howells did not take into account the crucial difference between literary and other artistic property. In buying a painting and sculpture, the consumer purchased a commodity that was the exact one that the artist produced. In literature the manuscript, the actual production, did not reach the actual consumer. The transformation of the "raw material" introduced a new player into the game, the publisher, who oversaw and profited from the mechanical reproduction of the artist's work. In the process the aura and uniqueness of the production were drained away. So too was some of the force of Howells's claim.

Unionization efforts and stirring essays aside, authors were not part of the working class. Despite their problems with publishers, their work lives, interests, and culture were not identical with those of the working class. First of all, their work conditions varied considerably. Writers worked essentially alone; the completion of each manuscript depended entirely upon the individual writer. The sense of unity developed in work that had made unionization possible in heavy industry was virtually nonexistent among writers. Furthermore, writers were not supervised in the course of the production of their manuscripts, nor were they apt to feel the sense of immediate opposition to management that workers developed in the course of day-to-day relations in the workplace. Third, the royalty that writers received for their work was their share of the returns, not a wage. They sold a product and not their labor. For a period of time during the production cycle they controlled the product and thus maintained a far more independent status than did workers. Finally, the product was individual and only rarely interchangeable. For their own purposes publishers resisted turning the book business into one based on employee-employer relationships.

Occasionally reports of something akin to the proletarianization of writing did surface. Edward Bok discovered a "fiction factory" in Boston in which young women unearthed possible stories from newspapers and a board of editors farmed them out as assignments with explicit directions on treatment, plot, and vocabulary to writers who wrote in exchange for wages. But these remained the exception, not the rule.[74] When a young woman offered to write on salary for George Putnam, the publisher declined the request with the explanation that the uncertainty of the literary market made such arrangements impossible: "The supply of fiction is now greater than the demand and it is essential to consider each book for itself and apart from any continuing arrangement with the author. It is not likely that we should be able, even if the first book secured a satisfactory circulation to encourage the publication of books as rapidly as the author might be able to produce them."[75]

Consequently writers as a group found it difficult to sustain both unions for writers and a complete identification with the interests of industrial workers.

There was, of course, another problem with the proposed alliance. Despite the rhetoric there is no evidence that the American working class saw in authors a prospective ally. The image of the writer as an upper-class dilettante was strong and blocked any overtures from laborers. For reasons of education, leisure, and income most American workers were not consistent readers of the mainline fiction available in bookstores. Able to afford mostly story-papers and "cheap" fiction, most workers tended to prefer romances and older models of fiction. Howells himself noted this phenomenon and attributed it to the laborer's need to escape the drudgery of work: "As for the people who are still sunk in the life of toil, they know enough of it already, and far more than literature could ever tell them. They know that in a nation which honors toil, the toiler is socially nothing, and that he is going from bad to worse quite as if the body politic had no interest in him. What they would like would be some heroic workman who superhumanly triumphs over his environment and marries the boss's daughter, and lives idle and respected ever after."[76]

The degree to which romantic motifs permeated working-class taste can be most clearly seen in the radical political fiction of the late nineteenth century. In his study of the radical novel Walter Rideout has documented that the increasing number of books concerned with the "social problem" in the late nineteenth century, including a number by authors from working-class backgrounds, rarely broke new formal ground. In general these proletarian novels reproduced the conventions of an older literature, and their language was more stilted and formal than that of realist novels. For all their references to the heartlessness of employers and the valor of workers, the vast majority of these books clung to the narrative devices of sentimentality and melodrama. Their descriptions of the work process are scanty and stereotypic. In most texts the heroic workman not only leads the union but often, as Howells predicted, marries the boss's daughter.[77]

In a recent work Michael Denning has challenged the dismissal of working-class fiction in dime novels and story-papers as escapist and excessively emotional. It speaks, he explains, in "mechanic accents" and reveals a labor-republican ideology that honored the honest toiler and virtuous working girls. These tropes stand in contrast to middle-class fiction that dealt with the self-made entrepreneur and the domestic household: "These [diverse] narratives are the dream-work of the social, condensing (compressing a number of dream-thoughts into one image) and displacing (transferring energies invested in one image to another) the wishes, anxieties, and intractable antinomies of social life in a class society. Each of these formulas has its moment of success, when it is able to offer convincing symbolic resolutions to social contradictions, and its historical limits, when the pressure of the real reveals its plots and resolutions to be merely imaginary." Crucial to his argument is Denning's interpretation of the element of disguise that appears with great regularity in fiction read by the working class. He contends that different reading modes—allegorical among the working class, realistic ("novelistic") among the middle class—led readers toward different interpretations of fiction. Read differently, the revelation that a mechanic is a born nobleman does not negate his identity as a mechanic; for the allegorical reader, the character is both simultaneously. This condensation furthers the fable of the nobility of labor that is at the·heart of literature intended for the working class. As a consequence, working-class and middle-class readers held different views of what constituted a worthwhile story. Drawing from actual accounts of working-class reading experiences in the nineteenth century, Denning concludes that working-class readers desired a contemporary time and knowable landscape but required a plot with extraordinary happenings.[78] Such tastes would have made dialogue with realists difficult, if not impossible.

Howells was certainly aware of the indifference with which both workers and writers regarded each other. Yet he could still assert that a common ground existed, because he, like many social thinkers who came to maturity in the aftermath of the Civil War, thought of society in what can be called populist terms. Populist thought characteristically identified the fundamental division within society as the one between those who worked and those who sold what was produced. The fissure that counted was between "the people" or the "masses" on the one hand and the "classes" or "exploiters" on the other.[79] It barely credited those analyses that located the essential separation between those who employed labor and owned the product and those who took wages in exchange for performing labor. Although an increasingly more permanent condition in the years following 1877, wage taking was still not seen as an end, but as a stage through which one traveled and hence not determinant in the construction of society. As Eric Foner and David Montgomery have both pointed out, this "free labor" ideology posited affinity on the basis of a common position in the circulation, not the production, process and often resulted in the inclusion of small entrepreneurs, even if they were employers of labor, in the producing class.[80] Howells made this valorization of the "honest toiler" the centerpiece of his analysis of the writer as a species of worker. In the famous "smiling aspects" passage of *Criticism and Fiction* he argued that the United States had averted through "honest work and unselfish behavior" most of the ills that had darkened the annals of mankind.[81] Writers and workers therefore shared more than they lacked, for both engaged in honest work and unselfish behavior.

The ills of society stemmed, Howells and other like-minded social thinkers believed, from a lost unity and a decline in fraternal feeling. For them, what had kept cohesion within society was the acceptance of commonality. "Men," Howells concluded in *Criticism and Fiction*, "are more alike than unlike one another."[82] In the 1880s and 1890s, however, Americans had rejected their commonality and had set out on a path of material gain and individual distinction. The task of realism, Howells felt, was to defend "the people" against its adversaries. The realist, he wrote, "feels in every nerve the equality of things and the unity of men."[83] Howells's defense of the portrayal of the typical was designed to counter views that associated the average with the degraded and to widen the bonds of commonality: "Such beauty and such grandeur as we have is common beauty, common grandeur, or the beauty and grandeur in which the quality of solidarity so prevails that neither distinguishes itself to the disadvantage of anything else."[84] Realists thus set out to picture "the people," chronicling their diversity but taking care not to reach the point where the concept of commonality disintegrated and called attention to its inability to be truly totalizing or unifying. The "equality of things and the unity of man" could not sustain a representation of opposition and struggle that indicated otherwise.

The centrality of the concept of "the people" did not guarantee that realists unambiguously valued the people per se. For his part Howells endorsed their principles and aspirations and embraced their condition. From the very first pages of his *Criticism and Fiction* "the people" constitute the source of value. James, on the other hand, consistently fled. His notes about his return voyage to the United States reveal a suspicion of the people and their ways. Norris's reaction was more complex: he simultaneously celebrated the people and recoiled at their characteristics. He was quite capable of exclaiming that "the People pronounce the final judgment. . . . despised of the artist, hooted, caricatured and vilified, [they] are, after all, and in the main, the real seekers after Truth"—and then, a few pages later, of disparaging their judgment.[85]

Despite these mixed feelings realists clung to the concept of "the people" as the element that gave unity to social life. They rejected as particularistic and divisive those ideologies that stressed differences and inherent conflicts among the people. When confronted with characters who rent the unity of the people by staking out the claims of class, the fiction of both Howells and Norris underwent a severe strain. In two significant instances in which radicals were involved, both authors broke with the realist principle of neutral and uninvolved narration and asserted a moral that was not portrayed. In both *A Hazard of New Fortunes* and *The Octopus* Howells and Norris deliberately intervene to deride those who possess a class, or quasi-class, rather than populist orientation.[86] The consistency with which this is done and the break from normal realist practice should alert us to some disturbance or conflict that the authors were trying to resolve.

In *The Octopus* Norris singles out the radical saloonkeeper, Caraher, as responsible for the novel's central tragedy.

> He [Presley, the poet whose experience forms the narrating consciousness of the novel] did not stop at Caraher's saloon, for the heat of his rage had long since begun to cool, and dispassionately he saw things in their true light. For all the tragedy of his wife's death, Caraher was nonetheless an evil influence among the ranchers, an influence that worked only to the inciting of crime. Unwilling to venture himself, to risk his own life, that anarchist saloonkeeper had goaded Dyke and Presley both to murder; a bad man, a plague spot in the world of the ranchers, poisoning farmers' bodies with alcohol and their minds with discontent.[87]

There are a number of objections to Norris's contention that the destructive envy of the have-nots for the haves was responsible for the carnage and sadness. First, the conclusion is not well justified in the text, whatever view one might hold of the actions and responsibilities of anarchism in the political turmoil of late nineteenth-century America. Caraher plays a relatively small role in the entire sweep of the narrative. Though he does harangue Dyke (the engineer who loses his livelihood and goes on a rampage that ends with his death), insisting that the railroad only understands dynamite, the logic of the narrative suggests that Presley and especially Dyke, whose entire life was destroyed by the arbitrary actions of an unyielding railroad, actually have no other recourse to redress their grievances. The escalation between the railroad and its opponents would seem to need little encouragement from the saloonkeeper. Yet after detailing the crimes of the railroad at length, the narration suddenly blames an individual agitator as if the characters would have acted differently without his provocation. Caraher's responsibility is recognized in the text only in retrospect. At the time that he makes his speeches, neither the characters nor the narration takes much notice. Even if it were contended that Caraher was the specific agent of a more general force, a ploy that naturalists like Norris often used, the skimpiness of the treatment of Caraher's actions or the force that he supposedly represented would negate that view.

Second, and more intriguing, this explanation conflicts with the well-known climax of the book, in which Presley concludes that what happened followed ineluctably from forces greater than men.

Men—motes in the sunshine—perished, were shot down in the very noon of life; hearts were broken; little children started in life lamentably handicapped; young girls were brought to a life of shame; old women died in the heart of life for lack of food. In that little, isolated group of human insects, misery, death, and anguish spun like a wheel on fire.

But the WHEAT *remained.* Untouched, unassailable, undefiled, that mighty world force, that nourisher of nations, wrapped in Nirvanic calm, indifferent to the human swarm, gigantic, resistless, moved onward in its appointed grooves. Through the welter of blood at the irrigation ditch, through the sham charity and shallow philanthropy of famine relief committees, the great harvest of Los Muertos rolled like a flood from the Sierras to the Himalayas to feed thousands of starving scarecrows on the barren plains of India.[88]

Norris has given us two contrasting endings. On the one hand, the venality of the agent provocateur Caraher, his whiskey, and his bad words point toward his culpability. Individuals remain responsible for their actions. On the other hand, in asserting that "the mighty world force" was "indifferent to the human swarm," the narrator diminishes any individual's guilt or responsibility. These two contrasting endings suggest the difficulty in maintaining a stance of radical determinism. Denying individual responsibility in favor of the power of impersonal forces ran counter to deeply ingrained American traditions of self-determination. Religious and political thought long placed upon individuals the burden of making one's self, and for all his naturalism Norris was not immune to prevailing ideological currents. These two endings may also be seen as a measure of Norris's desire to retain the organizing principle of "the people" in the face of potentially destructive conflict. In order to arrive at the view that "injustice and oppression in the end of everything fade and vanish away," Norris must assert that the "People" retain coherence ("the individual suffers but the race goes on"). He accomplishes this end by simultaneously postulating an outsider who introduces foreign elements and by arbitrarily asserting their ultimate survival. In blaming Caraher he is able to conclude that the people are in the final analysis sound and unified. Yet this maneuver is not without its problems. Forced to concede some success on the part of the agitator in order to make him a viable threat, the first solution uncomfortably reveals the pressures and divisions among the populace. Only by demonstrating real complaints and tensions can the agitator make inroads that require ultimate banishment. The second solution vitiates the populist concept by transforming the people into an abstraction. In the process Norris drains their potential for meaningful action. The people persevere only because it is fated that they should do so, but they cease to be a lived experience or organic unity. Unable to integrate the notion of popular determination with the fact of powerlessness, the author swings between the two solutions, favoring one and then the other in an attempt to center the novel. Norris may have registered doubts about the masses, but he could not posit an alternative.

Faced with a similar problem in *A Hazard of New Fortunes*, Howells, whose sympathy for radicals was greater than Norris's, nonetheless judged the radical instead of merely presenting him. The verdict, delivered by a character rather than the narrator, does not square precisely with the presentation of events. During a dinner conversation with his family Basil March, who witnessed the event, confirms his son's opinion that the anarchist Lindau, whose clash with a police officer had led to his own death and that of his defender, Conrad Dryfoos, had died in a bad cause. Lindau, March opined, died in "the cause of disorder; he was trying to obstruct the law. No doubt there was a wrong there, an inconsistency and an injustice that he felt keenly, but it could not be reached in his way without greater wrong . . . men like Lindau who renounce the American means as hopeless and let their love of justice hurry them into sympathy with violence, yes, they are wrong."[89]

Howells's text does not show what March concludes:

One of the officers rushed up toward the corner where Conrad stood, and then he saw at his side a tall old man with a long white beard. He was calling out at the policeman: "Ah yes! Glup the strikerss-git it to them! Why don't you co and glup the bresidents that insoalt your lawss, and gick your Boart of Arpidration out of toors? Glup the strikerss—they cot no friendts! They cot no money to pribe you, to dreat you!"

The officer whirled his club, and the old man threw his left arm up to shield his head. Conrad recognized Lindau. . . . He heard a shot in that turmoil beside the car, and something strike him in the breast. . . . The policeman stood there; he saw his face; it was not bad, not cruel; it was like the face of a statue, fixed, perdurable, a mere image of irresponsible and involuntary authority.[90]

Though it might be argued that March is not a stand-in for the narrator and that the purpose of his dinner conversation was to cast an ironic light on his failure once again to engage in what Howells called "complicity," the text does not really countenance such an interpretation. Though Lindau's death is deplored and March is now unable to distance himself from the event, the dinner conversation is presented in a starkly realistic fashion. The narrator gives no clues to counter March's judgment about the cause in which Lindau died. Both

Conrad's and Lindau's deaths occurred in the pursuit of restraining police violence, but it is the death of Conrad and his Christian socialist cause that animates the discussion and that brings March to a realization of the meaning of involvement. Lindau's anarchism colors March's judgment of the meaning of Lindau's death.

Although it is often an error to conflate biographical information about an author with the views expressed by the author's characters, March's argument reproduces contentions that Howells made elsewhere. In a letter of praise to John Hay, whose *Breadwinners* had portrayed the perfidy of "walking delegates" who led honest toilers into the paths of violence and anarchy, Howells declared that "workingmen *as* workingmen [are] no better or wiser than the rich *as* rich and are quite likely to be false and foolish."[91] His sympathy, most clearly revealed in his utopian romances, went to those "free fighters that are left to get ground to pieces between organized labor and organized capital."[92] Although he wrote the literary critic T. S. Perry that he would vote for a labor party if one existed, this pledge was not an endorsement of collective industrial action. Strikes, he wrote, were no remedy, they were simply a symptom. In a letter to his father about the Homestead strike of 6 July 1892, in which Pinkerton agents and strikers battled along the Monongahela near Pittsburgh, Howells contended that "it is hard, in our sympathy with the working class, to remember that the men are playing a lawless part, and that they must be made to give up the Carnegie property. . . . I come back to my old conviction that every drop of blood shed for a good cause helps make a bad cause. How much better if the Homesteaders could have suffered the Pinkertons to shoot them down unarmed. Then they would have had the power of martyrs in the world."[93]

Howells was not a systematic political thinker, and it is unfair to tax him with inconsistency. Yet his "Are We a Plutocracy?" (1894) reveals the same ambiguity of attraction and repulsion toward the expressed aspirations of the working class, and a similar diagnosis and remedy for the "social problem," as his novels of the same period.[94] Writing at the height of the worst depression of the century, Howells stressed both the ideational causes for the breakdown of prior social unity and the hope that reconciliation could be achieved through a return to a common code of conduct. He began by distinguishing between earning a living and making money: earning a living was a matter of working to support a family in a comfortable manner; making money involved receiving value beyond the worth of the work performed. Although he searched for an objective measure of the difference between the two, he continually returned in the course of the essay to a subjective one: the actor's motives and desires. Making money was not merely the search for profit; Howells regarded capitalists as entitled to a return on their investment for the work that their money did. What separated parasitic employers who lived off others' work and those who did not was less the amount of profit gained than the craving for money for its own sake. Those who were dominated by the search for riches at any cost and who consequently dealt unfairly with their workers were the true "plutocrats." Their attitudes, not their class position or social role, constituted the antisocial element in their makeup. Given these premises and his refusal to acknowledge that capitalists by the very nature of their competition with others must search for more profit or face extinction, Howells's argument tended to be a plea for more humane treatment of others rather than a prescription for social reconstruction.

"Plutocratic" attitudes were not limited to the owners and managers. On the contrary, in Howells's view, workers qualified as plutocrats because they often demanded wages beyond the value of the thing produced and hence cut into the value of the property of the capitalist. Further, as a group they had not renounced "making money." Because both capitalists and workers "approve of the gain of money which is not earned and agree to the sole arrangement by which the great fortunes are won or the worship of wealth perpetuated," neither won Howells's sympathy. This view of the question saved him from "much intense feeling concerning strikes, which I might otherwise wish to see carried by the wage takers." They were "themselves ready to go over to the enemy as soon as they have money enough." The class position of workers—the growing permanence of wage taking—did not enter into the argument. Until strikers struck against the plutocratic principle, Howells reserved commitment.

Having established to his own satisfaction the nature of the problem, Howells devoted the majority of his essay to tracing the damage the plutocratic principle accomplished. It was responsible for ripping apart American society, preventing employers from treating their employees with dignity, and obscuring employees' recognition of their common interest with employers. The problem was "not so much, or so merely, the rule of the moneyed class, as it is the political embodiment of the money-making ideal; and the mass who have no money at all may cling as fondly and worship as fully as the classes who have millions of money."[95] The solution to this predicament was to be found in the ballot box. If Americans so chose, Howells wrote in the vein of Basil March, they could easily rid themselves of plutocrats and plutocratic principles. Echoing the firmly entrenched sentiments of village democracy, Howells contended that the average American was responsible for his own fate: "For slowly or swiftly, it is he who ultimately makes and unmakes the laws by political methods, which, if still somewhat clumsy, he can promptly improve. It is time, in fine, that he should leave off railing at the rich, who are no more to blame than he, who are perhaps not so much to blame, since they are infinitely fewer than the poor, and have but a vote apiece, unless the poor sell them more. If we have a plutocracy, it may be partly because the rich want it, but it is infinitely more because the poor want it or allow it."[96] What separated Howells from radicals like DeLeon and Debs was that he saw the drive for possession as the primary ill; they saw it as a secondary effect. Howells located the malaise of the United States in ideological distortion, they in the structural conflicts of a class system.

Howells once labeled himself and his friend Mark Twain "theoretical socialists and practical aristocrats." Ostensibly the comment signified the contrast between their sympathies and their comfortable lives and possessions. Howells meant to castigate both for personal reticence, lack of commitment, and failure to live up to the Tolstoyan ideal of self-sacrifice. Putting aside the displaced contrast of socialism and aristocracy, his comment underscores the conflicts that greeted independent intellectuals. With no obvious or formal class ties, writers vacillated between attraction to and repulsion from both polar classes. What was novel about literary realists was the degree to which they were attracted to the dispossessed for both emotional and literary reasons. No previous group of classical American writers had felt such a kinship with the "common people" as they did. Realists alone made the conscious decision to speak to the masses in the language of the people. Others may have written for the people; realists tried to write from them. No other writers, with the possible exception of Melville, went as far in elevating the unrepresented to literary significance.

There were, however, limits to the realist approach. At times realists seemed incapable of penetrating fully into the lives of their subjects. Much as Howells pointed up the foreignness of Lindau's speech through spellings that overemphasized mispronunciations ("lawss"), realists marked out some of "the people" as inferior or as distant. There were some aspects of their lives that realists could not apprehend. This timidity was not a matter of bad faith, nor simply the politics that emerged from their generally petty-bourgeois backgrounds. Rather their literary and political commitment to the concept of "the people" made the concept difficult to use at a historical juncture when the conflicts that the process of proletarianization had engendered undermined the unity of the formation. Their "populism" could not admit the depth of the struggle and still maintain its categories of analysis. As "the people" began to act in "class" ways, the unity and naturalness of social life, which formed the first postulate of realist thought, began to erode. When the crisis matured in the late 1880s and early 1890s and sober men talked of the possibility of revolution, realists found themselves isolated. In response they defined the crisis as primarily an ideological one and created for themselves a new social role. As writers they were uniquely equipped to address the decline of faith and to supply a new set of beliefs.

Literature above Politics: The Realist as Social Conciliator

In an essay on the author in politics Howells took note of the increasingly rigid specialization of American life. Americans, he observed, regarded these divisions as fixed. The writer was assigned the literary sphere, and any attempt to overstep its boundaries was subject to immediate criticism, as he himself knew from personal experience. "Business to the business man, law to the lawyer, medicine to the physician, politics to the politician, and letters to the literary man; that is the rule. One is not expected to transcend his function, and commonly one does not. We keep each to his last, as if there were not human interests, civic interests, which had a higher claim than the last upon our thinking and feeling."[97] Americans, Howells seemed to be saying, were unable to see the divisiveness of specialization. Consequently they lacked a unifying picture of their common life.

It was this absence of community feeling that realists proposed to remedy. Where aesthetes gloried in the "uselessness" of art, realists trumpeted its ultimate usefulness. In a modern society afflicted by isolation and atomization, the mass-circulated novel held out the promise of a new common currency that would promote a new unity. Howells saw the function of the novel in overtly political terms. A new sense of literary service would aid in the rejuvenation of democracy. Addressing his fellow novelists, Howells exclaimed, "Let us make them know one another better, that they may be all humbled and strengthened with a sense of their fraternity." Indeed, this service was the ultimate justification for the novel that Howells offered in *Criticism and Fiction.* "Except as they [novelists] do this office they are idle."[98] James did not phrase his conception of the social use of the novel in such explicitly political terms, but his rationale for writing contained a similar notion of the novel as a creator of a new ideological community. "The great thing to say for them [novelists] is surely that at any given moment they offer us another world, another consciousness, an experience that . . . , by helping us to an interval, tides us over and makes us face, in the return to the inevitable, a combination that may at least have changed."[99]

The literary service that realists proposed differed from the type that early republican authors had assumed as a matter of course. Earlier generations of writers, who were clearly identified with and hailed from a distinct social group, regarded their task as instructing the populace in the values and virtues of civilization. Realists, less anchored to a definitive class, saw themselves as conciliators, revealing to contending parties their shared characteristics. Because of their ostensible neutrality and burgeoning professionalism, realists felt themselves admirably suited for the task. This task was not a natural one but one that the writer had to choose. Though society had lost its ability to correct itself, writers had the capacity to step into the breech. The instruction they offered was not in the prevailing standards of either group but in the democratic lessons of the American republic.

With the choice came responsibility. Norris argued in true realist fashion that it was "*not* right that they [the people] be exploited and deceived with false views of life, false characters, false morality, false history, false philosophy, false emotions, false heroism or self-sacrifice, false views of religion, of duty, of conduct, and of manners," but he saw that in providing the truth to those who did not have it, the novelist was constrained to keep a certain distance.[100] The novelist could not adopt the people's causes personally but must instead ruthlessly and unemotionally fictionalize them. Using the example of Thomas Hardy, whom he believed had successfully mastered the problems of writing a social novel, Norris reflected that

> If he is to remain an artist, if he is to write his novel successfully, [he] will, as a novelist, care very little about the iniquitous labor system of the Welsh coal-mines. It will be as impersonal a thing as the key is to the composer of a sonata. As a man Hardy may or may not be vitally concerned in the Welsh coal-miner. That is quite unessential. But as a novelist, as an artist, their sufferings must be for him a matter of the mildest interest. They are important for they constitute his keynote. They are *not* interesting for the reason that the working out of his *story*, its people, episodes, scenes, and pictures is for the moment the most interesting thing in all the world to him, exclusive of everything else.[101]

Norris asserted that the novelist with a social purpose was constrained for the sake of successful realization of the work to remain personally aloof and distant: "The moment, however, that the writer becomes really and vitally interested in his purpose the novel fails." In converting the stuff of life to fiction, the novelist needed to study the world dispassionately, as if it were under a microscope. Understanding that the only way to avoid the danger of becoming a polemicist was to regard living human beings as the means to writing fiction, the novelist whom Norris detailed must not so much interact with the world as halt it. Despite Norris's explicit disavowal of such an intention, his strictures to the novelist result in viewing the world as a series of fixed and foreign abstractions. Writing became an algebra problem in which both people and society "must be combined and manipulated to evolve the purpose—to find the value of x."[102] This authorial stance toward actual social problems was mirrored in many of Norris's novels. In the wheat in *The Octopus* and the gold in *McTeague* Norris fastened upon symbols that presented the world in just the same manner that he recommended the social-purpose novelist approach it. Such was the consequence of the novelist's own social position as an unattached observer.

Just as realists tried to carve out for themselves a sphere of influence that they could dominate, so too did their novels exist as a separate or new form of discourse. Realists envisioned their novels as an alternative or competitor to politics rather than a companion. As practiced, political life in the United States was often dirty and egoistic, prompting Henry James to apologize to Grace Norton for being so "beastly" in mentioning it.[103] Howells thought it only natural that an author should abstain from a political life that featured the spectacle of elections and the decline of moral purpose: "If any one were to ask me why then American authors were not active in American politics, as they once were, I should feel a certain diffidence in replying that the question of other people's accession to office was, however emotional, unimportant to them as compared with literary questions."[104] Frederic's Theron Ware, who in the novel that bears his name, *The Damnation of Theron Ware*, migrates to the West to pursue a political career after his disgrace as a Methodist minister in upstate New York, captures this sense of decline. Though the title has an ironic meaning and Frederic held politics in higher regard than James did, the book ends with the sense of Ware's fall from innocence.

It was not solely politics in its organized and electoral meaning that bothered authors. The deployment of power to organize and direct social life received surprisingly little coverage in their texts. The mechanisms of social power were often less emphasized than their effect as "input" in individual lives. In line with their diagnosis that the causes of turmoil were ideological and not material, realists converted the political into the personal, a position James had favored in the 1870s when he criticized Charles Nordhoff's *Communistic Societies of the United States from Personal Visit and Observation* for its effacement of the private.[105] Howells argued that in the successful social-problem novel the "wonders of the outer-world can be related to the miracles of the inner world. Fiction can deal with the facts of finance and industry and inventions only as the expression of character; otherwise these things are wholly dead. Nobody really lives in them, though for the most part we live among them, in the toils of the day and the dreams of the night."[106] Hence

Howells, who could rail against capitalist behavior in the aggregate, was more kindly disposed toward individual capitalists. What concerned Howells about Silas Lapham and Jacob Dryfoos, his two major portraits of capitalists in the 1880s, was the way in which their rise in position (from small entrepreneur and farmer, respectively) brought about a tragic retreat from their sturdy village ethics. When the pursuit of money became an end, they both faltered. When they sacrificed gain and returned to their anchorage, they both rose. The social problem was thus rewritten as a moral one.

In the aftermath of the Haymarket executions Howells devoted a series of three novels to the "social problem." In *The Minister's Charge, Annie Kilburn*, and *A Hazard of New Fortunes* he attempted to work out the nature of the social bonds that required strengthening in the present crisis. The social portraiture of the first two, especially in its depiction of working life, was a clear departure toward that goal. In *Annie Kilburn* Howells mixed form and content to achieve many of the representational goals upon which realism prided itself. For an audience who he suspected knew nothing of factory life, he captured the routine of the factory in striking detail.

> The tireless machines marched back and forth across the floor, and the men who watched them with suicidal intensity ran after them barefooted when they made off with a broken thread, spliced it, and then escaped from them to their stations again. In other rooms, where there was a stunning whir of spindles, girls and women were at work. . . . She [Annie Kilburn, the society-connected heroine, who has become interested in social reform] tried to understand the machinery that wrought and seemed to live before her eyes. But her mind wandered to the men and women who were operating it, and who seemed no more a voluntary part of it than all the rest.[107]

In its confusions of pronoun reference and its adaptation of industrial rhythms in its prose, the passage aims at evoking in its readers a sense of the dehumanizing atmosphere of the factory and the development of what Howells had called, in his previous novel *A Minister's Charge*, "complicity." There the term is employed by the minister, David Sewell, to describe the bonds of human solidarity that entwine all men and women in each others' fates. As Sewell's charge, Lem Barker, suffers a series of social horrors, Sewell comes to a new awareness of the deficiency of community feeling: " 'No man,' he said, 'sinned or suffered alone, his error and his pain darkened and afflicted men who never heard his name. If a community was corrupt, if an age was immoral, it was not because of the vicious, but the virtuous who fancied themselves indifferent spectators. Only those who had the care of others laid upon them lived usefully, fruitfully.' "[108] As Kenneth Lynn reminds us, Howells's effort to erect a new web of complicity was only partially successful. Annie Kilburn's attempt to establish the Social Union meets with complete failure, and the tensions in the town only grow more fierce.[109]

Annie Kilburn represents the dilemma of the realists' "nonpolitical" approach to social problems. At pains to distinguish his concept from philanthropy, Howells confronted the deficiencies in such a project.[110] First, complicity, however defined, had no social agent and relied upon the exertion of individual will infused with religious conviction. And though this empathy ameliorated the sense of guilt (as Sewell hints) that plagues the privileged, its rewards for the exploited, defined as the "less fortunate," were not immediately apparent. No matter how sympathetic, individual action could not overcome systematic problems. Second, the need for extraordinary individual action only revealed the absence of a natural healing mechanism in society. The community upon which the realists and a generation of social scientists had placed their hopes was a diseased one.[111] If the "common man" had to become extraordinary to resolve the social conflict, then his sufficiency was in doubt. Either the social facts overwhelmed him, or he lost his defining characteristics. In translating the social problem into a moral or ideological one, Howells had arrived at the limits of his approach. Although he struggled to retain a social analysis that rested upon ideological factors, he was increasingly unable to manage the growing number of tensions that such an approach generated. As he entered the 1890s, Howells berated himself for his personal inability to meet the Tolstoyan ethic.

The three major realist political novels, Henry James's *Princess Casamassima* (1886), William Dean Howells's *Hazard of New Fortunes* (1890), and Frank Norris's *Octopus* (1900), rework the central tenets of the realist approach to politics.[112] All three shift emphasis from the outer world to the miracles of the inner, locate the source of tension in the disintegration of social bonds, and propose art as the soothing balm that has the potential to act as the healing or corrective measure that social life lacked. In each novel the class issue, which seems to be the center of the narrative, functions not as the object of study but as a frame for the picture that each author truly wants to draw. For all their representation of the concretely political, it is not their ultimate locus of concern. The conflicts portrayed—between the revolutionary anarchist conspiracy and aristocratic society, between capital and labor, and between the railroad and the ranchers—are gradually revealed to be ethical problems that shift the political problem to a different plane. Hyacinth Robinson's struggle with the meaning of freedom, Basil March's with complicity, and Presley's with personal peace form the center of these books. Distrusting the political as such and envisioning their task as offering an alternative to the divisive particularisms of politics, all three realist authors bracketed the class issue and assigned it a separate compartment as subtext. In all three novels class is not a condition that structures a way of life but a characteristic to be transcended.

Indeed, class as such does not appear in these novels. Howells, James, and Norris retain as their central category "the people" or, more precisely, the masses. The poor, the underprivileged, and "lower" strata of various sorts constitute a type of "other," whose basic quality is their facelessness. The dispossessed remain specimens for observation rather than active participants in the flow of the narrative. Despite their essential decency, Howells's Marches regard this segment of society as part of the panorama of the city. When the pair is struck by artistic fancy, they see the streets as "picturesque" and the city as a "spectacle." When they feel overwhelmed and withdraw, poverty appears disgusting and an affront. Entering the homes and the lives of the poor is a task that the narrator does not attempt.

Norris does not even build on Howellsian sympathy. Norris implicitly equates a priest's concern for his poor parishioners with his concern for animals, implying that the objects of concern are identical (p. 147). Even more telling is the evolution of Presley's attitude toward "the people." At the begin-ning of the novel, the poet, who functions as a partial narrator, observes that "These uncouth brutes of farmhands and petty ranchers, grimed with the soil they worked upon, were odious to him beyond words. Never could he feel in sympathy with them, nor with their lives, their ways, their marriages, deaths, bickerings, and the monotonous round of their existence" (pp. 10–11). By the end of the novel Presley has abandoned his clouded romantic notions and has written "The Toilers," modeled on Edwin Markham's "The Man with the Hoe." This new maturity, however, comes not through his encounter with the lives of the farmhands and petty ranchers whom he disparages in the early pages but through his alliance with the large ranchers. It is their fate that kindles his sympathy and propels his violence against the railroad.

If the poor exist as an object of investigation far removed from the essential workings of these novels, the figure of the artist is pivotal. The crisis of artistic sensibility displaces the political situation as a matter of concern. More "auto-biography" than objective exploration of a social whole, these three works rewrite the social problem as a trial of artistic relevance. All three are either set in the world of the artist or make the problem of art in the late nineteenth century the focus. Howells's book chronicles the world of a literary journal, *Every Other Week*, whose combination of modern management techniques and literary adventurousness has a special valence for realists. For all the scenes of

New York in the novel and the variety of identifiable social types who congregate around the journal, it is to the development of Basil March's "complicity" that Howells returns in the final seven chapters. James's novel follows the same course. *The Princess Casamassima* is populated with characters from the fringes of artistic life. "The people" or, to use James's term, "the democracy" is composed not of the actual working class, but of scions of urban bohemia: bookbinders (Hyacinth Robinson and Eustace Poupin), costumers (Robinson's guardian Pynnie) and violinists (Vetch). Not only is the novel a lived drama— "a public show"—in which characters treat their lives as if they were observers rather than participants (as James made clear in his notes for the New York edition), but it is the promise of art that prevents Robinson from carrying out the assassination pledge that he has made to the revolutionary conspirators. Like March and Robinson, Norris's Presley emerges from a large cast of characters to center the text. Unlike March, who "philosophizes" the action, and Robinson, who refrains from any, Presley acts: he bombs the house of S. Behrman, the powerful railroad agent whose machinations doom Presley's allies. In the end, however, he returns to a more typical artistic position, a chastened philosopher resigned to the impersonality of forces and to the belief that good "issued from this crisis, untouched, unassailable, undefiled."

In the world but not of it, March, Robinson, and Presley, like the novelists of the late nineteenth century, approach art as an alternative to the carnage and suffering of the world. Theirs, like their creators', is not an art of retreat in which the world is written off as so corrupted and debased as to be irredeemable. On the contrary, it is an art that takes a measure of social life and from its portrayal reveals an essential unity—the unity so absent in a fallen world in which society no longer seems capable of holding together. It is in the portrayal of the crisis of artistic sensibility that Howells, James, and Norris reveal their hopes for the new political function of literature and their doubts about the efficacy of their project.

James's Hyacinth Robinson sees both politics and art as ways to escape "the bad air" of the personal. His tendency, the product of his birth and his inclination, favors him toward art. The illegitimate son of an aristocratic father and a plebian mother, he resents his "exile" in poverty-stricken London and yearns to claim his birthright. He desires to "drive in every carriage, to mount every horse, to feel on his arm the hand of every pretty woman in the place" (p. 125). Feeling part of neither parental class, he practices an alienated politics more notable for its rage than its program. We are told that he was "absorbed in the struggles and sufferings of the millions whose life flowed in the same current as his, and who, though they constantly excited his disgust, and made him shrink and turn away, had the power to claim his sympathy, to make it glow to a kind of ecstasy, to convince him, for the time at least, that real success in the world would be to do something with them and for them" (p. 120). Robinson's sentiments are, however, divided. Despite his allegiance to the cause of revolution, he secretly enjoys, in "however a platonic a manner, a spectacle which rest[s] on a hideous social inequality" (p. 125). It is not the contradiction between the world's splendors and its miseries that drives and motivates Robinson throughout the novel, but rather his eagerness to store his perceptions and to live artistically. He finds his happiest moments in the British Museum and National Gallery (p. 214). He delights in the vistas of historic Europe and the gardens of the house that the princess rents. Faced with the barrenness of those who seek to level the props on which art rests, Robinson inwardly rebels at his commitment. As the narrator notes, "The sense of the wonderful, precious things it had produced, of the brilliant, impressive fabric it had raised overwhelmed him. That destruction was waiting for it there was forcible evidence, known to himself and others, to show; but since this truth had risen before him, in its magnitude he had become conscious of a transfer, partial, if not complete, of his sympathies; the same revulsion of which he had given a sign to the Princess in saying now he pitied the rich, those who were regarded as happy" (p. 365).

Robinson makes the transfer complete in a letter to the Princess in which he declares for the transcendental quality of art. Choosing art rather than conspiracy, he writes: " 'The monuments and treasures of art, the great palaces and properties, the conquests of learning, the general fabric of civilization as we know it, based, if you will, upon all the despotism, the cruelties, the exclusions, the monopolies and rapacities of the past, but thanks to which, all the same, the world is less impracticable and life more tolerable—our friend Hoffendahl [the archconspirator of the revolution] seems to me to hold them too cheap and to wish to substitute for them something in which I can't somehow believe as I do in things with which the aspiration and the tears of generations have been mixed' " (p. 380). By the end of his considerations Robinson no longer bears the rich any resentment at all and seems to recoil against the struggle. " 'Why equality?' " he asks his comrade Paul Muniment. " 'Somehow that word does not say so much to me as it used to. Inequality—Inequality! I don't know whether it's by the dint of repeating it over to myself, but *that* doesn't shock me as it used to' " (p. 433). It is not simply Robinson whom art delivers from the "torment of his present life, the perpetual laceration of the rebound"; it is the world that is "rescued and redeemed" by the "vast, vague, dazzling presence" of art (p. 434).

For Howells not only its appreciation, but the manner of its production, was a crucial issue in the ability of art to heal social wounds. When art is an

emblem of self-centeredness—as exemplified by *Every Other Week's* art direc-
tor, Angus Beaton—the result is mere commodities and worthless trifles. The
making of a productive, social art is not a natural phenomenon but a practiced
one. March characteristically responds to this challenge with an ironic disen-
gagement and must unlearn his stance in order to liberate art's potential.
Initially, an interest in literature is portrayed as a quiet conceit. The Marches
have "generous scorn for all kinds of narrow-heartedness" but have never
"asked themselves why it had not come their way" to sacrifice for others.
Living "a divided life," March sees in his literary interest "a high privilege, a
sacred refuge." Artistic interest gives him a sense of pride, "inner elegance"
(pp. 23–24) that functions as a screen for keeping others at a distance. March
"philosophizes"—devises concepts to remove himself from the immediacy of
life. His every curiosity is labeled "literary," from his explorations of New
York neighborhoods to his presence at the strike violence where Conrad loses
his life.

This pose prevents March from finishing the sketches for which his trip
around the city has provided material. Although the press of editing is the
supposed reason for this failure, Howells suggests that March's personal reserve and distance are at least partly responsible. When Conrad contends that
the "city itself is preaching the best sermon all the time," March does not
comprehend (p. 138). Nor does he fully concur when Conrad suggests that the
mission of *Every Other Week* should be to make comfortable people understand how the uncomfortable live. March agrees "from the surface only." For
him low life is immensely picturesque. Poverty becomes not a human fact but
a human artifact, an existence to be grasped as a philosophical problem.

There are points in the narrative in which March does glimpse the possibility that art could become a totalizing view that would comprehend the unity
of humankind. During a trip to 125th Street, subtle changes in his attitude
begin to appear.

> Their point of view was singularly unchanged, and their impressions of
> New York remained the same that they had been fifteen years before:
> huge, noisy, ugly, kindly, it seemed to them now as it seemed then. The
> main difference was that they saw it more now as a life, and then they re-
> garded it a spectacle; and March could not release himself from a sense of
> complicity with it, no matter what whimsical, or alien, or critical, attitude
> he took. A sense of the striving and the suffering deeply possessed him,
> and this grew more intense as he gained some knowledge of the forces at
> work—forces of pity, of destruction, of perdition, of salvation. (p. 265)

This sense of possession is asserted, not demonstrated. The strike puts him to the final test. An exchange with a humorless policeman made him "feel like populace, but he struggled with himself and regained his character of philosophical observer. In this character he remained in the car and let it carry him by the corner where he ought to have got out and gone home, and let it keep on with him to one of the furthermost tracks westward, where so much of the fighting was reported to have taken place" (p. 360). March remains the philosophical observer and not the participant, much the same way that the realist author, floating freely in society, took upon himself the role of observer. Nonetheless, March is clearly a changed observer. In rejecting Fulkerson's idea of a series of articles on the color of the strike, March ends his romance with the notion of spectacle. This conversion in attitude contrasts with a new role for him. When the elder Dryfoos sells the paper to March and Fulkerson, March, now the employer of labor, institutes "reforms," a euphemism for firings.

Norris too saw art as the ultimate conciliator. *The Octopus* begins with Presley's searching for the romance of the West, the unspoiled terrain that prompts grand visions. This search is rudely and suddenly interrupted by the telegraph wires, the lot of the inhabitants, and most importantly of all, the machinations of the octopus, the grasping railroad that has taken everything in its path. Yet Presley ends with a new artistic vision: a more refined art provides the answers to the big picture; by grasping totality, art instilled a "Nirvanic calm." A solution to the disease of politics, art is the healing mechanism society needs.

> What then was left? Was there no hope, no outlook for the future, no rift in the black curtain, no glimmer through the night? Was good to be thus overthrown? Was evil thus to be strong and prevail? Was nothing left?
>
> Then suddenly Vanamee's [a mystical shepherd who has the ability of mental telepathy] words came back to his [Presley's] mind. What was the larger view, what contributed the greatest good to the greatest numbers? What was the full round of the circle whose segment only he beheld? In the end, the ultimate, final end of all, what was left? Yes good issued from this crisis, untouched, unassailable, undefiled. (pp. 457–58)

This resignation mirrored the position at which realist authors had arrived by the end of the century. They had originally believed that their art was capable of providing a sense of complicity that would allow Americans to overcome the struggle and divisions that had marked their history. Realists had taken this chore upon themselves on the basis that they not only had the skills of observation and creation but also owed no firm allegiance to any of the contending social forces. They could therefore transcend the petty differences, peer into the true essence of things, and derive a series of bonds based on commonality of feeling. Holding firmly to the concept of "the people," realists rejected "class" for its particularistic and divisive claims. When the masses began to act in "class" ways, realists found their entire plan threatened, and they responded by resignation and deflection of the problem into the realm of belief and attitude. It was not their reluctance to carry high the banner of proletarian revolution that limited realists, but their insistence on defining the social problem as an artistic one to be resolved through voluntaristic means. Such a solution flowed from their position as in the world but not of it. Observing the world but not experiencing it, they replicated that position within their texts. Howells's own career after *A Hazard of New Fortunes* offers striking testimony to the limitations of realism in conceptualizing political problems. In the years that followed, Howells published *A World of Chance* and *The Coast of Bohemia*, both of which dealt with authors and publishers or artists and did not draw upon class conflicts as a backdrop. Even more striking was his publication of two utopian romances. For a writer who had based his career on the proposition that the novel must tell the truth of life, resorting to the romance was a tacit admission that to become political the writer needed to abandon realism for another form.

CHAPTER SEVEN

The Moment of Realism

American Literary Practice and the Nineteenth Century

To-day is the day of the novel. In no other day and by no other vehicle is contemporaneous life so adequately expressed; and the critics of the twenty-second century, reviewing our times, striving to reconstruct our civilization, will look not to the painters, not to the architects nor dramatists, but to the novelists to find our idiosyncrasy.
—Frank Norris

In numbers of readers and authors and in the centrality of its productions to the concerns of the late nineteenth century, the novel towered over other cultural forms of expression. This predominance gave the genre a new respectability. Fifty years before, the novel had been scorned as a plaything for women and girls. By the turn of the century the most prominent universities, led by such innovators as Lewis Gates at Harvard, Harry Thurston Peck at Columbia, and Fred Lewis Pattee at Pennsylvania State College, featured studies of the novel in their literature courses. Those who set the canon may have given short shrift to the novel, but like Barrett Wendell they could not ignore it.[1] Wendell's concessions were understandable. Poetry, which had once held the day, diminished in popularity, and modern poets seemed, at least to established tastes, arcane specialists. As one reviewer in *The Forum* noted in an essay on E. C. Stedman's *American Anthology*, the collection revealed the "inadequacy of poetic literature to sustain a large and vigorous modern national life."[2]

Not only academics but journalists paid homage to the novel. One is struck by the haste of muckrakers to turn their observations into novels. Writers like

David Graham Phillips, Theodore Dreiser, George Ade, and Will Payne all switched forms, if not necessarily jobs. Reporting put writers in touch with the heady events of the day and exposed them to aspects of American life that were previously unacknowledged. At the same time it frustrated them by placing limitations on what could be printed. As Lincoln Steffens noted, "What reporters know and don't report is news—not from the newspaper's point of view, but from the sociologists' and the novelists'."[3]

Although not the most popular form of late nineteenth-century fiction, realism was certainly the boldest. It alone declared that it was prepared to remake American literature. Realists envisioned their efforts as an attempt, not to change fashion, but to rewrite the rules and to remove, as Howells remarked, the dead hand of tradition. Realism aimed not just for a little more verisimilitude but for a new way of comprehending human activities and organization. Its practitioners may not have been systematic in their attempt to outline their basic principles nor consistent in their practice, but they did lay down a series of guidelines that covered the whole range of literary practices, from a new sense of craft to new relations with the readership. Making life as lived the central basis of their fictions, realists mapped for the first time the new industrial civilization and the rules by which it lived.

The tendency of realists to endow their fiction with the materials of their age has led historians and critics to label realism an industrial literature. Realism in this view emerged in the late nineteenth century as a protest against the rapid and harsh modernization of the period. Venerating a preindustrial past, novelists took to realism to inveigh against the decline of the village community and the heartless exploitation characteristic of capitalist development. Such was the view of Alfred Kazin in his pathbreaking *On Native Grounds* (1942), which was one of the first books to rediscover the contribution of William Dean Howells. Kazin rejected a simpleminded explanation for realism that perceived in it only imitation of European models. Whereas European realism and naturalism had grown from philosophical consistency, particularly positivism, and commitment to a belief in the necessity of literary movements, "realism in America grew out of the bewilderment, and thrived on the simple grimness, of a generation suddenly brought face to face with the pervasive materialism of industrial capitalism. . . . Realism in America, whatever it owed to contemporary skepticism and the influence of Darwinism, poured sullenly out of agrarian bitterness, the class hatreds of the eighties and nineties, the bleakness of small-town life, the mockery of the nouveaux riches, and the bitterness in the great new proletarian cities." The hurt and anger that the new order caused among literary men and women, Kazin hypothesized, prompted them to turn their backs on the literature of the past and forge a new one: "In a modern American literature that erupted suddenly into maturity, leaving so many basic problems untouched and unremembered behind it, the need of truth, the need to make manifest the divorce between the old bloodless ideas passed on to the new generation and the new world in which they had to live, came first." This assertion was one reason that Kazin could maintain that "the history of early American realism is a series of documents by men and women who were not artists but spokesmen."[4]

Kazin advanced the understanding of realism by looking beyond developments in scientific thought and mechanical reproduction, two factors that had often been hypothesized as the determinants of the genre. Influenced by the growing prestige of science and the ability to capture "reality" through such inventions as the camera and the phonograph, realists, the argument went, had aimed for similar effects in literature. Though no one would deny the influence of science on literary realism, thanks to Kazin modern critics have learned that care must be taken not to elevate the impact of the natural and social sciences to a self-evident determination. To be sure, realists and naturalists read Darwin and Spencer. Dreiser explicitly acknowledged their influence in his autobiography. Even more important may have been William James's *Principles of Psychology* (1891), which Henry James most certainly knew and William Dean Howells lauded in the July 1891 *Harper's Monthly*. William James's search for a unified physiological and philosophical theory that would explain human behavior paralleled the tension that many realist texts tried to mediate. Yet realist tracts and letters contain very few references to the natural and social sciences. This, of course, does not invalidate the claim, but it remains true that Howells, Henry James, and, to a lesser extent, Norris all rejected the signal attempt of Zola to use Claude Bernard's theories as the basis of a science of literature.[5] The scientific method is better thought of as a necessary rather than sufficient cause for the rise of realism. Writers could have responded to the presence of science by rejecting its claims as too automatic and oppressive. The same objection can be lodged against explanations that concentrate on technological developments in mechanical reproduction. Literature, like Impressionism in painting, could well have turned its back on the camera.

Kazin himself erred in underestimating the formal contributions of realism. It is certainly understandable that in an age of industrial transformation and class strife a literature of protest should arise. The changes were too jarring and the injustices too palpable for it to have been otherwise. There is, however, no necessary reason that the *form* of that protest should have been realism. Why should the "simple, natural, honest" have presented to writers understandably upset at the direction of a history in which they lived, a desirable method for lodging their objections? Why should the "truthful treat-

ment of material," to use Howells's second definition of realism, have been the
vehicle of the protest? Why, in other words, would someone write a realist
novel? Could not a romanticism invigorated with new ideals and conceptions
or a "modernism" that took for granted the fragmentation of life have done as
well? One need only to think of "Bartleby the Scrivener" or *The Great Gatsby*
to see that other genres were capable of registering a protest against capitalist
behavior and transformation.

Newer views of realism have challenged the liberating thrust that Kazin
identified as one of the hallmarks of realism. Realism becomes, in these
views, the literary counterpart to industrial modernization. Rather than opposing capitalism, realism was at one with it, translating its modes of operation
into literary texts. Some New Historicists have argued that realism recapitu-
lated the logic of other prevailing discourses. Walter Benn Michaels has
contended that rather than either opposing or embracing capitalism, realism
exemplifies it.[6] This also is the brunt of Eric Sundquist's contribution to *The
Columbia Literary History of the United States*: "If we instead judge realism
from the 1870s through the early 1900s as a developing series of responses to
the transformation of land into capital, of raw materials into products, of
agrarian values into urban values, and of private experience into public property, then the city appears as one region among others, part of the national
network of modernization actualized as much by ties of language and literature
as by new railroad lines and telegraph wires." Realism, Sundquist goes on to
say, at points often seems a means of middle-class regulation, rather than a
liberating force.[7]

The classic explanation of the relationship between history and literary form
is that of the Hungarian Marxist Georg Lukács's studies of European realism.
For Lukács the distinguishing mark of realism was its ability to inscribe its
historical period within the text. Realism has arisen at those critical historical
junctures in which human action can be seen as interrelated human stories and
in which things can be seen as products of human work, not contemplated as
things apart. In those moments when the capitalist order has not hardened and
projects itself as the natural order of things, realism can connect the present
with past and future. What distinguishes realism is its avoidance of symbolism
and reliance on typicality. For Lukács the symbolic mode is that method of
writing in which the writer, unable to discern from his own living the meanings
of objects, invents a new meaning. In Norris's *Octopus*, for instance, the
wheat assumes transcendental qualities and is experienced as a mighty world
force, a "Nirvanic calm." Realists do not portray static worlds; hence symbols
are unnecessary. By "typicality" Lukács means that in realism people and
things embody social forces in the process of evolution.[8]

Lukács's arguments are more applicable to European than to United States literature and to the difference between realism and naturalism. In his terms realism in the United States probably does not fully fall under the rubric of classic realism. The ability of Howells and the early James to embody social forces in the way that Lukács considers realistic is questionable. This inability may have had much to do with the relatively late appearance of realism in the United States, a fact that has led Richard Chase to argue that the romance is the characteristic mode of classical American literary expression.[9] Yet his view and those of Sundquist and Michaels call into question again the nature of the relationship between history and literary form. Though few today would deny that history and literature are linked (especially in the case of realism, which seems so evidently to be about history), neither type of explanation explicitly tells us *how* these two different entities are related. Written expression and historical development seem to remain apart until the text is completed. History seems to be a flow of events that shapes the material, creates the categories of observation, and provides the philosophical bent but not what happens to and in the writing process itself.

What is needed to complement these explanations of the importance of historical developments to the rise of realism is evidence for some "micro-foundation," some mechanism or series of activities that may tie writers to their history. Some method of specific transmission or experience by which "macro" developments make themselves felt would seem necessary to connect writers to a history in which they participated. Put another way, how did industrialism, urbanization, class conflict, and imperialism specifically reach and affect authorship? The postulate that they did seems plausible, but we need to explain by what ways they did so. In the preceding chapters of this book I have located that mechanism in the specific historical relationships that writers entered into in the practice of their profession. Each writer in the act of writing answers questions about the process by which facts, experience, and knowledge take literary shape, about the relationship between author and audience and the most appropriate address for that relationship, and about the social function of writing. It is questionable whether authors can simply invent these relationships. It is precisely in the process of discovering the possibilities and limits of these relationships that writers confront most directly their own historical moment.

The development of industrial capitalism in the late nineteenth century had implications for writers beyond the general transformation of the means of production and the social relations that structured life. Not only the basic industries but the literary profession as well felt the brunt of industrial capitalist transformation. The modernization of the book and the improved distribution system that was a direct result of the industrial boom of the late nineteenth century revolutionized the production of literary works. Now a literary entrepreneur regardless of individual feelings about the matter, the writer was separated in time and space far more than ever before from the audience. No longer did the face-to-face mode of belletrist discourse hold any viability for American authors. Gone was the connection of writers to a specific class that automatically defined the goals of writing. Meeting the audience through the marketplace, writers of the late nineteenth century had before them the task of redefining just what it was that an author did. This crucial development opened new space at the same time that it presented knotty problems. In the course of writing, realists defined writing as "work"; consumption of the resulting product depended upon the establishment of a common dialogue; and the writer's responsibility was to insure social cohesiveness.

Making these choices had profound implications for the types of texts that realists produced. These responses allowed realists to plunge for the first time into material that previous generations had considered unworthy of literary representation, to develop techniques that aimed at giving readers a direct impression of a confusing and jumbled life, and to present a plea for reform. Still close enough to their readers to share the rudiments of a discourse, realists were confident enough to assert that a novel meant what it said. In the process they were able to salvage from the dislocations of the marketplace a literature that presented the world as it appeared to many of their readers. When the historical moment upon which they thrived ended, the solutions that realists derived were no longer viable. Indeed, their solutions had never been as stable as their pronouncements had portended. Their definitions of the work process, the nature of literary consumption, and the social position of the author were assertions made in the face of contradictions. Following out their logic presented realists with the possibility that their material was not natural, that dialogue was flawed, and that realists could not serve as literary mediators.

When Colonel Harvey, whose tenure at the revamped House of Harper was nearing its end feted William Dean Howells at a newfangled promotional dinner in March 1912, the literary world in which Howells had created his fiction was in decline.[10] A younger generation had grown up to regard material reality, which realists had seen as liberating art from a tradition based on ethereal spirituality, as oppressive, stale, and common; stable characterization as unrealistic, and language as intended not to capture event but to celebrate language itself. New senses of time, psychology, and society pervaded this new work. Modernists like Faulkner and Hemingway in the United States and Kafka and Musil in Europe not only described a world that was different from that of the realists but one that they experienced differently as writers. The increasing complications of author-audience relationships, the perceived con-gealment of writing institutions, and the growing sense that the artist existed best sealed off from society provoked a new response to the task of writing. Relying primarily on the "little magazine" with its erudite audience, modern-ists had in mind a specific, self-consciously elite readership, not a general common one. The self-contained nature of their discourse promoted an inter-nal exploration of fiction. Embracing the notion that the novel was a human endeavor, modernists doubted the ability of the genre to extend beyond itself. Interested in what constituted a novel, authors became engaged in wordplay and literary conventions that described the construction of the novel, not of a stable world. In such circumstances writing was less "work" than "experimen-tation." Spurred by a growing sense of their own differences from both their predecessors and the mass audience and regarding their craft as special, modernists seemed to celebrate their alienation as a sign of their worth.

This is not to argue that the changes in the mode of literary production were sufficient causes for realism. A mass market in literature does in no way assure realist texts. Many Gilded Age writers responded to these conditions with all manner of romances, historical dramas, and bracing adventure tales. Nor is it necessarily to deny arguments that locate the source of realism in the charac-teristic ways of seeing that emerge as dominant at a given historical juncture. Rather it is to call attention to the ways in which the practical professional problem of how to write a novel has ramifications for the form that the novel assumes. It was through questions of practice as much as through prevailing ideology that realism exemplified its historical moment.

Notes

Abbreviations

ALS	autograph letter(s), signed
FN	Frank Norris
HJ	Henry James
MT	Mark Twain (Samuel L. Clemens)
PW	*Publishers Weekly*
TCS	typed copy, signed
TLS	typed letter(s), signed
Twain–Howells Correspondence	Smith and Gibson, *The Mark Twain– William Dean Howells Correspondence*
WDH	William Dean Howells

Chapter 1

1. The literature on realism is immense. The following books are only a sample of the work on the genre: Berthoff, *The Ferment of Realism*; Brooks, *The Confident Years*; Cady, *The Light of Common Day*; Chase, *The American Novel and Its Tradition*; Geismar, *Rebels and Ancestors*; Hicks, *The Great Tradition*; Kazin, *On Native Grounds*; Kolb, *The Illusion of Life*; Martin, *Harvests of Change*; Michaels, *The Gold Standard and the Logic of Naturalism*; Parrington, *The Beginnings of Critical Realism*; Pizer, *Realism and Naturalism*; Sundquist, *American Literary Realism*; and Trachtenberg, *The Incorporation of America*. Also to be consulted are treatments in Spiller et al., *The Literary History of the United States*, and Elliott et al., *The Columbia Literary History*. Relevant articles far too numerous to list.

2. Bailyn et al. *The Great Republic*.

3. Bender, "The Cultures of Intellectual Life," p. 185.

4. See Higham's introduction to *New Directions in American Intellectual History*, and Darnton, "Intellectual and Cultural History." Eagleton, *Literary Theory*, is a readable critique of the proliferation of literary theories since the turn of the century.

5. An elegant defense of this proposition is contained in Welter, "On Studying the National Mind." In Welter's view, locating a discourse in its historical framework does not explain its origins and impact. Context alone cannot reveal content. Nor does a view in which intellectuals are seen in discourse with each other suffice. Such an approach makes ideas solely talks between intellectuals rather than attempts to understand the world.

6. Mizruchi, *The Power of Historical Knowledge*, pp. 25–40, contains an excellent discussion of the issue. See also Rabinowitz, "Assertion and Assumption."

7. Denning, *Mechanic Accents*, chap. 5 and pp. 146–47, 152, presents a sustained argument about the uses to which fiction can be put. He goes on to suggest that different classes had different responses to narratives and implies that social and intellectual history can therefore be combined in new ways.

8. Parrington, *The Beginnings of Critical Realism*; Commager, *The American Mind*; and Hicks, *The Great Tradition* are the leading exemplars of this method. Though their specific progressive and Stalinist conclusions have long been rejected, their methodology still remains a forceful example for historians interested in literary texts.

9. Parrington, *The Beginnings of Critical Realism*, pp. 249–51. It should be noted that this book, the last of his trilogy on American thought, was unfinished at the time of his death. Although totally consistent with his theory of the conflict between the Jeffersonian (principles of democracy, freedom, and liberal thought) and the Hamiltonian (forces that pushed for centrality, control, and business ascendancy), much of the book comes from his lecture notes.

10. LaCapra, *History and Criticism*, pp. 125–26, has pointed out that such an approach has the effect of making literature an inferior source of history, for clearly a contemporary investigation of the slums of New York City is more "reliable" for most historians' purposes than Crane's *Maggie* is.

11. Parrington, *The Beginnings of Critical Realism*, p. 243.

12. Elliott et al., *The Columbia Literary History*, p. ix. Examples include the contributions to Sundquist, *American Literary Realism*; Bercovitch, *Reconstructing American Literary History*; and Bercovitch and Jehlen, *Ideology and Classic American Literature*.

13. See, for example, Michaels, "The Gold Standard and the Logic of Naturalism," which draws upon William James's *Principles of Psychology*, Simmel's *Philosophy of Money*, and Donnelly's populist speeches.

14. Ibid., pp. 18–20.

15. Williams, *Marxism and Literature* and *Writing in Society*.

16. Morgan, *American Writers in Rebellion*, p. vii.

17. See Cady, *The Light of Common Day*, chaps. 1–2, for the commonly accepted differences between the two variants.

18. See, for instance, Douglas, *The Feminization of American Culture*, and Tompkins, *Sensational Designs*, for two important and opposing views of the influence of gender. Race as a structural determinant is the focus of Baker, *The Journey Back*, and Stepto, *From behind the Veil*.

Chapter 2

The epigraph is taken from Howells, *Criticism and Fiction*, p. 15.

1. Among the surveys of the late nineteenth century are Garraty, *The New Commonwealth*; Hays, *The Response to Industrialism*; Jones, *The Age of Energy*; Keller, *Affairs of State*; Morgan, *The Gilded Age*; Weisberger, *The New Industrial Society*; and Wiebe, *The Search for Order*. The variety of dates in these titles indicates the problems of periodization of the industrial era.

2. The literature on the new social sciences of the late nineteenth century is plentiful. Among the most valuable are Bledstein, *The Culture of Professionalism*; Furner, *Advocacy and Objectivity*; Haskell, *The Emergence of Professional Social Science*; Kuklick, *The Rise of American Philosophy*; Miller, *American Thought*; Noble, *The Paradox of Progressive Thought*; Ross, "The Development of the Social Sciences"; and White, *Social Thought in America*. For two perspectives on similar trends in Europe see Hughes, *Consciousness and Society*; and Therbon, *Science, Class and Society*.

3. Mead, "Cooley's Contribution to American Social Thought," reprinted in Cooley, *Human Nature and the Social Order*, p. xxiv.

4. Howells, *Criticism and Fiction*, pp. 15–16.

5. Major realist tracts include: Dreiser, "True Art Speaks Plainly"; Howells, *Criticism and Fiction*; Howells, *Literature and Life*; Garland, *Crumbling Idols: Twelve Essays on Art and Literature*; James, "The Art of Fiction"; James, "The Future of the Novel"; James, *Partial Portraits*; James, *Notes on Novelists*; Norris, *The Responsibilities of the Novelist*; and Twain, "Fenimore Cooper's Literary Offenses."

6. Howells, "Novel-Writing and Novel-Reading," p. 6.

7. Norris, "Salt and Sincerity," p. 296.

8. Jones, *The Age of Energy*, pp. 216–58, who presents a measured and intelligible case for the Genteel Tradition in American letters, painstakingly constructs its aesthetic ideology and demonstrates convincingly that these writers were far from the no-account "old maids" that H. L. Mencken and Sinclair Lewis believed them to be. Jones does not deny, however, their considerable resistance to realism. For them realism represented art without technique, ideals, or purpose. In this charge they misunderstood realism. Tomsich, *A Genteel Endeavor*, also presents a systematic exploration of genteel literary and aesthetic principles.

9. Mabie, "A Typical Novel."

10. Thayer, "The New Storytellers"; Thompson, "The Analysts Analyzed." Wheeler, *Maurice Thompson*, pp. 58–92, contains a full discussion of Thompson's relations with Howells. See Cady, *The Realist at War*, chap. 2, for a fuller discussion of the "Realism War."

11. The term is that of Lee Mitchell, "Naturalism and the Languages of Determinism," p. 526.

12. *New York Times*, 13 December 1930, 12.

13. See Nochlin, *Realism*, chap. 1.

14. Mitchell, "Naturalism and the Languages of Determinism," pp. 530–31. Mitchell does note that many of the writers hitherto considered realists did flirt

with the problem of determinism and he does not draw the line as rigidly as Harold Kolb does in *The Illusion of Life* or Edwin Cady in *The Light of Common Day*.

15. Michaels, *The Gold Standard and the Logic of Naturalism*, pp. 26–27, 37–51.

16. Norris, "Salt and Sincerity," p. 309.

17. Norris, "An American School of Fiction?" p. 272.

18. Sundquist, "Realism and Regionalism," p. 523.

19. Jameson, *Marxism and Form*, pp. 182–205.

20. Smith, *Democracy and the Novel*, pp. 56–74.

21. Howells, *Criticism and Fiction*, pp. 144–45; Norris, "A Plea for Romantic Fiction," p. 281.

22. Sundquist, "In the Country of the Blue," p. 15.

23. See, for example, Michaels, "Corporate Fiction," and Seltzer, "The Naturalist Machine."

24. Twain, *Huckleberry Finn*, p. 1. In this note realism declares itself. Not only is the speech authentic, but the author vouchsafes it by his own personal observation. In addition, aware that his audience may not have shared his experience, the author hopes to ease the path of consumption, not unlike the brunt of realist representational technique.

25. Narration is a much belabored subject in literary studies. The nonspecialist who enters it begins one of the most ensnared paths imaginable. A word of definition: the term "omniscient narration" has a number of meanings. I have used it to designate a narrative strategy in which the narrator exists in the text as a knowing presence, even if that presence is not formally acknowledged and much of the narrative seems to be filtered through the vision of the characters. The narrative presence remains as an organizer of meaning. Although realists experimented with a narration that concentrated on how the individual character viewed the events, they mainly objected to what I term the intruding or omnipotent author who revealed himself as a puppeteer. The realist novelist was also a puppeteer, but took great pains to disguise such handiwork, sometimes presenting the text as from a central character's viewpoint. In this stance the realist differs from the modernist, who wondering if narration is indeed possible, takes point of view so far as seemingly to eliminate the narrator at all. So when Kolb calls classical American realism antiomniscient he is referring to what I term the intruding or omnipotent narrator. See McKay, *Narration and Discourse*, esp. p. 193, who follows Kolb in concluding that in realist prose the narrator must be unobtrusive but must remain. This is accomplished, McKay argues, through the narrator's "editing" process.

26. The transformation of literature into a commodity was an essential condition for the generalization of the printing press. The influence of the printing press is discussed in Hall, "Print and Collective Mentality." For European trends see Febvre, *The Coming of the Book*.

27. Benjamin Franklin to the *Pennsylvania Gazette*, quoted in Ruland, *The Native Muse*, p. 36.

28. Colonial and early republican writing is explored in Brooks, *Washington Irving*, pp. 39–40; Cowie, *The Rise of the American Novel*, pp. 3–5; Davidson, *The Revolution and the Word*; Sears, *American Literature in Its Colonial and National Periods*, pp. 171–75; Silverman, *A Cultural History of the American*

Revolution, p. 200; Scott, "Early Literary Clubs in New York City," pp. 3–16; Trent, *A History of American Literature*, p. 100; and Wurzbach, *The Novel in Letters*, pp. xxi–xxiii. The letter, of course, played an important role in the acceptance of the novel. Given moralists' fears that the novel amounted to an extended lie, the presentation of fiction as an epistle had not only narrative advantages but also social ones in that its very form signified authenticity.

29. WDH to Howard Pyle, 22 December 1890, in *Life in Letters*, 2:9–11. See Hauser, *The Social History of Art*, 4:73–85, for a European example in Flaubert.

30. Blair, *Lectures on Rhetoric and Belles-Lettres*, pp. 3–7. In the title Blair signals that he regarded speaking and writing as equivalent forms rather than different types of communication.

Chapter 3

The epigraph is taken from WDH to Charles Eliot Norton, 12 December 1891, in *Life in Letters*, 2:19.

1. Davidson, *The Revolution and the Word*, chap. 3, esp. pp. 49–50.

2. Because there exists a congruence between the formal elements of the novel and the tenets of the new philosophical currents that accompanied the political and social changes that began with the English Revolution, a number of writers have labeled the novel the preeminent middle-class form of literature. The classic works are Auerbach, *Mimesis*; Hauser, *The Social History of Art*, 3:103–206; Lukács, *Studies in European Realism*; Watt, *The Rise of the Novel*, chap. 1; and Williams, *The Idea of the Novel in Europe*.

3. For an inventory of private libraries see Kett and McClung, "Book Culture," pp. 97–147.

4. Quoted in Cowie, *The Rise of the American Novel*, p. 8. A general overview is contained in Bennet, "A Portrait of the Artist in Eighteenth-Century America," pp. 492–507, and Davidson, *The Revolution and the Word*, chap. 3.

5. Thomas Jefferson to Nathaniel Burwell, 15 March 1818, in *The Writings of Thomas Jefferson*, 15:166. Jefferson actually wavered on the effects of the novel. Some forty years earlier he had written to Robert Skipworth that the true value of the novel was not its portrayal of actualities, but its congruence with moral truths. "We are therefore wisely framed to be as warmly interested for a fictitious as for a real personage. The spacious field of imagination is thus laid open to our use, and lessons may be formed to illustrate and carry home to the mind every moral rule of life" (*The Papers of Thomas Jefferson*, 1:76–80).

6. Silverman, *A Cultural History of the American Revolution*, p. 490.

7. Quoted in Cowie, *The Rise of the American Novel*, p. 9. Tyler had another complaint: Americans were not reading native literature. His attack on English fiction had the additional purpose of protecting the home market. See also Brown, *The Sentimental Novel*, and Petter, *The Early American Novel*. As late as 1862 the same reasoning persisted. Isaac Ray, an alienist and asylum superintendent, gave belletrist charges a psychological twist in his *Mental Hygiene*, p. 243: "There can be no question that excessive indulgence in novel-reading necessarily enervates the mind and diminishes its power of endurance. In other departments of literature,

such as biology and history, the mental powers are more or less exercised by the ideas which they convey. . . . Of late years, a class of books has arisen, the sole object of which is to stir the feelings, not by ingenious plots, not by touching the finer chords of the heart and skillfully unfolding the springs of action, not by arousing our sympathies for unadulterated, unsophisticated goodness, truth and beauty, for that would assimilate them to the immortal productions of Shakespeare and Scott; but by the coarse exaggeration of every sentiment, by investing every scene in glaring colors, and in short, by every possible form of unnatural excitement. . . . The sickly sentimentality which craves this kind of stimulus is as different from the sensibility of a well-ordered mind, as the crimson flush of disease from the ruddy glow of high health."

8. For a demonstration of female readership see Mott, *Golden Multitudes*, and Pattee, *The Feminine Fifties*. Davidson, *The Revolution and the Word*; Douglas, *The Feminization of American Culture*; and Habegger, *Gender, Fantasy, and Realism*, are especially good at pointing out the cultural implications of female readership in different periods of the eighteenth and nineteenth centuries.

Female readership seemed to go hand in hand with the novel wherever it made headway. In both England and France the complaints were of a similar nature, although the English added in much more forceful tones the issue of class and the wasted leisure of the lower orders. As Ian Watt points out (*The Rise of the Novel*, chap. 2), these alarms were much exaggerated. The cost was most prohibitive, and the amount of leisure time available to the lower classes probably did not exist. But, Watt notes, the appearance of reading servants and apprentices could very well make it seem as if the novel-reading habit was spreading.

9. Though popular, the novel was not the premier literary form—at least in terms of books published in the United States. Religious works were still the most numerous of the productions that rolled off American presses before the Civil War.

10. Silverman, *A Cultural History of the American Revolution*, pp. 496–99, 589–91. Although he dates prior attempts, written earlier but published later, Silverman notes that the first novel advertised as "The First American Novel" was *The Power of Sympathy: Or, The Triumph in Nature Founded in Truth* (1789), written by William Hill Brown. It concerns a seducer who turns into a genuine lover, then kills himself when he learns that his love is incestuous. At his side when he ends his life is *The Sorrows of Young Werther*.

11. Goodrich, *Recollections*, 2:380–91.

12. Charvat, *Literary Publishing*; Charvat, *Authorship*, pp. 74–76; Madison, *Book Publishing*, pp. 1–47.

13. Davidson, *The Revolution and the Word*, chap. 2, contains a superb summary of the revolutionary-era book market. She further notes that few novelists took advantage of copyright protection.

14. Charvat, *Literary Publishing*, pp. 74–76.

15. Davidson, *The Revolution and the Word*, chap. 2. Madison, *From Irving to Irving*, pp. 1–9; Spiller et al., *The Literary History of the United States*, pp. 513–25.

16. Smith, *The Wealth of Nations*, p. 527.

17. Bourdieu, "La production de la croyance." Coser, Kadushin, and Powell,

Books, chap. 2, discuss the advantages and disadvantages of various orientations to the market.

18. Charvat, *Literary Publishing*, pp. 42–46.

19. Putnam, quoted in Stern, *Books and Book People*, p. 149.

20. Dampen, but not eliminate. Conflicts between authors and publishers did occur during the early nineteenth century. The way in which publishers could manipulate costs to make a profit was particularly galling to some authors. In fact publishers staged a ball and dinner for authors in The Crystal Palace in New York in an effort to defuse tensions.

21. Madison, *From Irving to Irving*, chaps. 4–5; Tebbel, *Book Publishing*, 1:passim; Wilson, *The Labor of Words*, chap. 1.

22. Hawthorne, *Notebooks*, p. 337.

23. Charvat, *Literary Publishing*, pp. 56–59. Charvat's explanation is incomplete and mechanical. It takes no note of the partially autonomous character of literary theory and limits historical explanation for theoretical positions to market determination alone.

24. Tocqueville, *Democracy in America*, 2:64.

25. Ibid., pp. 58–63.

26. W. O. Peabody quoted in Ruland, *The Native Muse*, pp. 231–34.

27. Willis's career is explored in Douglas, *The Feminization of American Culture*, pp. 282–87.

28. Hawthorne, *Notebooks*, pp. 236–37.

29. Brownson, "Address." By 1864 Brownson had changed his mind: a public of parvenus and businessmen "is not favorable to high literary culture, and it is no wonder that American literature is no great thing. In these days, when the public are the only literary patrons, literature of a high generous and ennobling character cannot be produced without a high, generous and cultivated literary public, that finds its amusement and relaxations from business or dissipation in literature, in works of taste, in creation of thought and imagination. . . . The literary man is not independent of his medium. He can never be formed by himself alone. . . . This 'mercantile spirit,' which turns even religion into speculation and coins genius into money—of which Barnum if a vulgar, is yet a real impersonation—is more rife in our country, and finds less to counteract or temper it than elsewhere" ("Literature, Love, and Marriage," pp. 500–501).

30. Brooks, *Melville and Whitman*, p. 114; Goodrich, *Recollections*, p. 278; Miller, *The Raven and the Whale*, p. 245.

31. Hawthorne did not completely reject the literary marketplace. At one point he suggested that the cover of *The Scarlet Letter* be emblazoned with a red *A*. See Charvat, *Literary Publishing*, pp. 56–62.

32. Gilmore's *American Romanticism and the Marketplace* is a masterful discussion of the ambiguous nature of the romantics' stance toward literary capitalism. He argues forcefully that the rejectionism inherent in Emerson's contention that commodity and excrement were one and the same, or in Melville's distinction between "the public" and "the people" in which the author swore "to hate the one and cleave to the other," also contained a significant element of acceptance and accommodation. "Traits of romantic art that arise out of antagonism toward the

market system prove upon closer inspection to replicate the very conditions against which they protest. Even on this more latent level, the relationship between literature and economic change is neither wholly disabling nor empowering but a complex combination of the two" (p. 12).

33. *Pierre, Or the Ambiguities*, p. 286. Melville's commercial failure in the 1850s can be traced in the contract books of Harper and Brothers. With *Omoo* (1847) he held the sole copyright, and the firm agreed to pay the entire cost of the plates and to split the returns evenly. For *Pierre* (1853) all expenses and risks were his (*Harper Contract Book*, 7:237–249). For Melville's financial status, see Spiller et al., *The Literary History of the United States*, p. 460. Care should be taken to avoid placing undue stress on the alienation of antebellum writers. Unrewarded in the marketplace, many simply stopped writing and did not advertise their separation. See Hofstader, *Anti-Intellectualism in American Life*, p. 406.

34. For the English example, twenty years prior to American developments, see Williams, *Culture and Society*, chap. 2.

35. Whipple, "Novels and Novelists." Whipple's definition followed up on an early one by Charles Brockden Brown of the "Rhapsodist" as one who "delivers the sentiment suggested by the movement in artless and unpremeditated language and transcribes the devious wonderings of a quick but thoughtful mind" (Charvat, *Authorship*, p. 24).

36. Emerson, "The American Scholar," p. 233.

37. Hawthorne, *The Scarlet Letter*, p. 25. Hawthorne was not the only fictionist to feel this way.

38. The reference here is to the production of certain types of literature. The consumption continued to flourish. Blair's *Lectures* were reprinted until the 1870s, and Emerson's essays proved even more popular in the 1890s than they had been in the 1830s.

39. Jones, *The Age of Energy*, p. 223; Tebbel, *Book Publishing*, 2:482–83. In the first issue of *Publishers Weekly* (24 January 1872) forty-five patents pertaining to the book trade were listed.

40. See Denning, *Mechanic Accents*, pp. 69–72, for a discussion of reading styles or modes that varied with class in the nineteenth century. The problems of judging the size of the readership are addressed below in chapter 5.

41. See Schudson, *Advertising*, chap. 5, for a discussion of similar trends in other forms of selling commodities.

42. Yard, *The Publisher*, pp. 45, 71. My discussion of the progressive marketplace has been influenced by two works: Wilson, *The Labor of Words*, and Lichtenstein, "Authorial Professionalism."

43. *PW* 1, no. 4 (14 February 1872): 128 (emphasis added).

44. Tebbel, *Book Publishing*, 2:23–31.

45. Mott, *Golden Multitudes*, pp. 55–180. See also Hackett, *Seventy Years of Best Sellers*.

46. Tebbel, *Book Publishing*, 2:28; *Harper Royalty Book*, 3:187.

47. Tebbel, *Book Publishing*, 2:259–60; Sheehan, *This Was Publishing*, pp. 125–65.

48. "William Dean Howells," *Harper Royalty Ledger*, 2:38–39.

49. The story of the "second" paperback revolution and the cheap foreign

imports is contained in Tebbel, *Book Publishing*, 2:435–508; Sheehan, *This Was Publishing*, pp. 66–94; Madison, *Book Publishing*, pp. 50–62; and Shove, *Cheap Book Production*.

50. Madison, *The Owl among the Colophons*, p. 35.

51. Tebbel, *Book Publishing*, 2:75–80; Sheehan, *This Was Publishing*, pp. 214–20; and Madison, *Publishing*, pp. 157-221, are standard. Wilson, *The Labor of Words*, pp. 22–28, puts great stress on the battle for the international copyright as a sign of trade consciousness and points to the changes in business practices that accompanied it. Wilson discusses the juridical status of property, not its actual status within production. Rudimentary planning actually preceded the International Copyright Law and stemmed from the economic crisis of the 1880s. The passage of the law most definitely ratified an existing situation, rather than, as Wilson seems to suggest, changed it. After all, American fiction had copyright protection long before 1891 (and hence status as legal literary property) and foreign competition had little effect on either E. P. Roe or Lew Wallace, whose best-seller status predated the act. Two further points need to be made. As early as 1889 American pirates turned to American fiction, which required royalties. This suggests that overproduction involved more than foreign competition. See Shove, *Cheap Book Production*, p. 35. Second, the Lovell Trust, the consolidation of the pirates, haunted American publishing for years after its official demise. With each new bankruptcy, creditors were paid in stock and plates, which they threw onto the market at cheap rates. In 1893, some 7 million to 8 million copies were dumped on the market. Tebbel, *Book Publishing*, 2:507–8.

52. *PW*, 26 October 1901, 348. Complaints of overproduction can be found in every year after the passage of the act. An 1894 *PW* editorial noted that "The tendency of modern publishing, as in other trades, has been towards overproduction, without regard for capacity for consumption. This has brought about a congestion that has entailed unnumbered hardship upon the bookseller, has rendered the public apathetic, and is beginning to react on the publisher. So, for instance, during the past season, the publishers have had no trouble in disposing of new books—the fads of the hour—while their best books of previous seasons rested idly in their bins. There is no overlooking the fact that books require leisure to read, and that the publisher who markets a few books will in the end fare better than one who indifferently fumbles many into the market" (3 March 1894). In 1911 the New York Public Library declared 15 million volumes out of date and useless. As late as 1930 Alfred McIntyre, head of Little, Brown, complained of "too many books" (*PW*, 4 January 1930).

53. *Harper Royalty Account Book*, vol. 2. The fractions of successes (defined as a sale of 1,000 books) to total fiction are: 1886—39/174; 1887—58/194; 1888—88/239; 1889—36/218; 1890—31/114; 1891—27/118; 1892—44/147; 1893—45/220; 1894—34/126. The justification for 1,000 books as the break-even point is in Miller, *The Book Industry*, and is borne out by publishers' accounts of costs. Walter Hines Page in his *A Publisher's Confession*, pp. 6–7, 139–44, put the number required for success at 50 percent to 75 percent higher. Harper figures indicate that some firms did make a concerted effort to keep down the number of novels released.

54. *PW*, 12 October 1901, 815; Sheehan, *This Was Publishing*, pp. 22–26.

55. Publishing was a classic example of a sector of a monopolizing economy that was prone to easy entrance and a low rate of profit. It is interesting in this light to review the failure of the two largest firms, Harper and Appleton, in the space of two years around the turn of the century. Though the proximate events that led to these failures were clear miscalculation—Harper sold its textbooks to the American Book Company a year before the 1893 depression, depriving the house of backlist income; Appleton tied up too much of its capital in an installment-buying plan—both firms had turned to these schemes to shore up declining profit margins. Overproduction gave book firms little room to operate. In both cases large capital infusions came to the rescue—the House of Morgan in Harper's case and a syndicate led by First National in Appleton's. The effect of these failures sent shivers through the authorial community. William Dean Howells said that he felt as if someone had told him that the government of the United States was bankrupt. Considering the constant surplus the government ran in the nineteenth century, that statement says a great deal. Tebbel, *Book Publishing*, 2:194–210; Exman, *The House of Harper*, pp. 175–91; and Harper, *The House of Harper*, all detail Harper's problems. Appleton's situation is described in Tebbel, 2:213–16, and Chews, *Fruit among the Leaves*.

56. Watson, *Newspaper Syndicates*, is standard. For magazines see Ziff, *The American 1890s*, chap. 6; Wilson, *The Labor of Words*, chap. 2; Allen, *American Magazines*; and Alden, *Magazine Writing and New Literature*. Individual literary entrepreneurs of the 1890s are detailed in Bacheller, *From Stores of Memory*; Bok, *Americanization*; Lyon, *Success Story*; and McClure, *Autobiography*. By the 1890s a number of dissident intellectuals regarded the ten-cent magazines and literary syndicates as fully integrated in the prevailing literary system and pressed for an alternative. The art house (Stone and Kimball) and the "small" magazines (such as *M'lle New York*, *The Wave*, and *The Lark*) drew upon a self-conscious elite audience and an avant-garde approach to art to break the perceived logjam. A tentative movement that foreshadowed Greenwich Village cultural radicalism, 1890s aestheticism did not last the century. Although Frederic published with Stone, and Norris had editorial connections with *The Wave*, the 1890s movement was not the true vehicle by which realism made itself known.

57. McClure, *Autobiography*, p. 225.

58. Overton, *Portrait of a Publisher*, pp. 23. As early as 1890 Harper, which owned its printing plant, had nearly 800 employees and an annual payroll of a half a million dollars (Tebbel, *Book Publishing*, 2:192–93).

59. Burlingame, *Of Making Many Books*, pp. 25, 33–34.

60. Putnam and Putnam, *Authors and Publishers*, pp. 26–27.

61. McClure, *Autobiography*, pp. 234–36.

62. Stallman, *Stephen Crane*, p. 600.

63. Speed, "Confessions of a Literary Hack," pp. 629–40; Daniel Ammen to S. S. McClure, TLS, 11 November 1891, McClure Papers; WDH to Henry Mills Alden, TLS, 28 March 1890, *Harper Correspondence Book*. Speed was no obscure writer. He was an editor of the American edition of the poet Keats and the grandson of Keats's younger brother.

64. See Page, *A Publisher's Confession*, esp. pp. 61–77, 172–76. (A number of

the essays that were included in the hardcover version had first appeared in the *Boston Transcript* in 1905.) Holt's reply was "The Commercialization of Literature." Holt's acceptance criteria are noted in Madison, *The Owl among the Colophons*, p. 47.

According to common usage, "progressive" publishers were those who began active work in the mid-1890s and who were responsible for the rationalization of the book market. They began to organize markets aggressively and to eliminate many of the gentlemanly and leisurely aspects of publishing. Though there is some truth in this distinction, it is also true that the Gilded Age publishers, whom the progressives disparaged as stodgy, began many of the same practices for which the progressives have received credit: royalties, advances, interventionist editing, and a close eye on the bottom line. Rhetoric aside, the Gilded Age publishers in their business practices had more in common with the progressives than they had with their antebellum predecessors.

65. McClure, *Autobiography*, pp. 204, 233; Lyon, *Success Story*, pp. 67–70.

66. Page, *A Publisher's Confession*, pp. 82–88, discusses the mechanics of editorial reading.

67. Putnam, *Authors and Publishers*, p. 37.

68. Gross, *Publishers*, pp. 104–11, 295; Doran, *Chronicles of Barabbas*, pp. 70–95.

69. Page, *A Publisher's Confession*, pp. 27–41. Such comments suggest that Page was not always the literary patron that he claimed to be and that his historians have portrayed. What is striking is not his opinion of Henry James (James was and is a difficult writer) but the glee he takes in dismissing James as insignificant because his sales were poor.

70. McClure, *Autobiography*, p. 236.

71. Putnam, *Authors and Publishers*, p. 39; Bok, *Americanization*, pp. 293, 379; Madison, *The Owl among the Colophons*, p. 89.

72. Ripley Hitchcock to William Colles, ALS, 17 February 1903, Hitchcock Papers.

73. McClure, *Autobiography*, p. 244; Britt, *Forty Years, Forty Millions*, p. 98.

74. Norris, "The Volunteer Manuscript." E. P. Roe to S. S. McClure, ALS, 7 September 1886, 3 February 1887, E. P. Roe Papers.

75. Page, "The Writer and the University." John Milton Cooper, Page's biographer, points to this proposal as proof of Page's hope to devise institutions that would transcend "commercialism" by making writing a profession. Cooper believes this proposal is in line with Page's constant attacks on "literary drummers" and shortsighted readers who forced publishers into "speculation." Allowing for the particular nineteenth-century rhetoric that conjoined workers and businessmen as producers and set this bloc against the parasitic financiers and speculators, Page's suggestions were designed to make the market in books more efficient, not to overturn it. Page's belief that professional standards for writers would bridge the gap between scholars and the rest of the community has its roots in the commercial fear that too many books were not reaching their audience. Page most certainly wanted to shear away the more grotesque characteristics of commercialization in order to allow publishers to assume a service role. This role, as he pointed out

many times, required the financial stability of the publisher. Profitability was the precondition of commercialization and therefore its end. See Cooper, *Walter Hines Page*, p. 192.

76. Madison, *The Owl among the Colophons*, p. 109; Doran, *Chronicles*, p. 124; Bok, *Americanization*, p. 293; Sheehan, *This Was Publishing*, pp. 138–43; Norris, "Salt and Sincerity," p. 297.

77. Wheeler, *Maurice Thompson*, p. 27.

78. Burlingame, *Making Books*, pp. 8–10; Berg, *Maxwell Perkins*, p. 50.

79. Page, *A Publisher's Confession*, pp. 92–96; 131–44, 179–95.

80. Bok, *Americanization*, p. 382; *Pocket Magazine* 1 (June 1894): 153–54. For antebellum conditions see Howells, *Literary Friends and Acquaintances*, pp. 138–39.

81. Bok, *Americanization*, pp. 113, 382; Sheehan, *This Was Publishing*, p. 137; McClure, *Autobiography*, pp. 184–86, 196.

82. Brooks, *Melville and Whitman*, p. 285. "Slash away, with entire freedom," Twain wrote Howells, "and the more you slash, the better I shall like it and the more I shall be cordially obliged to you" (15 October 1881, in *Twain–Howells Correspondence*, p. 284).

83. Madison, *The Owl among the Colophons*, pp. 41–45; Sheehan, *This Was Publishing*, pp. 137–38.

84. Madison, *From Irving to Irving*, p. 118.

85. Spiller et al., *The Literary History of the United States*, p. 964.

86. Tebbel, *Book Publishing*, 2:135; Exman, *The House of Harper*, pp. 194–95.

87. Gross, *Publishers*, p. 296; Page, *A Publisher's Confession*, pp. 35–38; Putnam, *Authors and Publishers*, pp. 86–92; Madison, *The Owl among the Colophons*, p. 94.

88. Swanberg, *Theodore Dreiser*, pp. 90–93; Wilson, *Literary Apprenticeship*, p. 271; Madison, *From Irving to Irving*, p. 96; Cooper, *Walter Hines Page*, p. 184; and Brenan, "The Publication of *Sister Carrie*." Swanberg includes the fascinating tidbit that the trip Doubleday was taking when Page originally accepted *Carrie* was to secure American rights for Zola, whom no one has accused of prissiness. Mrs. Doubleday, whom Dreiser appointed villainess of the piece, was assisting. The persistence of Dreiser's version, despite countless historical attempts to refute it, is testimony to his power as an author, a willingness to believe ill of Victorian women, and a conviction that publishers were disreputable.

89. Theodore Dreiser to Ripley Hitchcock, ALS, 27 February, 2 March 1903, Hitchcock Papers.

90. WDH to Ripley Hitchcock, ALS, 13 July 1896, Hitchcock Papers. Hitchcock was a fascinating minor literary figure. A genteel throwback, he had connections with some of the more eccentric and daring naturalists. He made his fortune by discovering Edward Westcott, whose *David Harum* had been rejected by a number of houses but went on to be a best-seller of the highest order. Hitchcock collaborated with Westcott on the highly successful play version of *David Harum* and was his literary heir. The Westcott story was a late nineteenth-century publishing nightmare, which prompted publishers to make sure their preliminary readers

looked at everything. See Page, *A Publisher's Confession*, pp. 27–31, 79–81.

91. *Harper Contract Book*, 5:280 (6 October 1885).

92. WDH to Ripley Hitchcock, ALS, 14 July 1901, Hitchcock Papers. Also WDH to Henry Mills Alden, ALS, 12 May 1890, *Harper Contract Book*, 6:616, 623.

93. Quoted in Stallman, *Stephen Crane*, p. 317.

94. Norris, "Fiction Writing as a Business," pp. 255–58. The celebration among authors with the advent of the Sunday supplement is apparent in the claim by one John Young that it liberated writing: "It has lifted the man of letters out of the slough of despondency and given him a chance in the struggle for existence. It has eliminated Grub Street and has enabled genius to market its wares at a figure somewhat commensurate with their real value. The author of merit no longer burns the midnight oil in a garret; . . . otherwise he revels in a blaze of electricity and lives in marble halls, because he is able to reach a world of readers through the Sunday magazine. That he can do so is due in large part to the development of the syndicate" (quoted in Watson, *Newspaper Syndicates*, pp. 48–49). As a panacea, however, syndicates were short-lived. By the end of the 1890s they were not the payday for the average author that they once had been.

95. *Harper Royalty Ledger Book*, 2:65, 128.

96. *PW*, no. 73 (7 June 1873): 554.

97. The popularity of writing as a profession can be seen in Norris, Speed, and the countless jottings in magazines about joining the profession. Howells, "The Man of Letters as a Man of Business."

98. Richard Harding Davis, the original dashing man of the 1890s, can be found on p. 29 of *Harper Royalty Ledger Book*, no. 2; Henry James on p. 455; Henry Blake Fuller, the author of the important *Cliff Dwellers*, p. 408; Ellen Glasgow, p. 403.

99. *Harper Royalty Ledger Book*, nos. 1–4, passim.

100. Sheehan, *This Was Publishing*, pp. 91–98. For a discussion of the "crazy period" see Yard, *Publisher*, pp. 58–65.

101. Harold Frederic to S. S. McClure, ALS, 14 March 1894, in *The Correspondence of Harold Frederic*, pp. 361–62.

102. Norris, "Fiction Writing as a Business," p. 255.

103. Mott, *American Magazines*, p. 139. The Harper collection at Columbia reveals the disparity of contract terms.

104. *Harper Contract Books*, nos. 1–5.

105. Hepburn, *The Author's Empty Purse*.

106. Cooper, *Walter Hines Page*, p. 164; McClure, *Autobiography*, p. 233; Sheehan, *This Was Publishing*, p. 58; Tebbel, *Book Publishing*, 2:337–38.

107. Madison, *The Owl among the Colophons*, p. 123.

108. Page, *A Publisher's Confession*, pp. 9–14, 45–58.

109. Cady, *The Realist at War*; Tebbel, *Book Publishing*, 2:269.

110. Stallman, *Stephen Crane*, p. 204.

111. Sheehan, *This Was Publishing*, pp. 95–96.

112. Putnam, *Authors and Publishers*, pp. 86–88, 185–90. The consensus among publishers was that publishers and authors were partners and should not

begin reaping profits until expenses had been paid. Both parties should begin earning at the same time. Authors disagreed, questioning why partnership extended only to the division of the returns; they saw royalties as payments for use of the manuscript.

113. Sheehan, *This Was Publishing*, pp. 94–95; Doran, *Chronicles*, p. 91.

114. Norris, "Fiction Writing as a Business," pp. 255–58.

115. Reynolds, *Middle Man*, pp. 3–10.

116. Hepburn, *The Author's Empty Purse*, pp. 72–74; Reynolds, *Middle Man*, pp. 13–17.

117. *Journal*, 1905, in Paul Revere Reynolds Papers.

118. Correspondence files, Reynolds Papers. Crane and James used J. B. Pinker in England.

119. *Ledger*, Reynolds Papers.

120. Richard Harding Davis file, Reynolds Papers. See particularly 6 January 1906, in which Reynolds explains to Davis that with the fee that an agent charged, the agent had to deliver a higher rate to keep the business. A similar response was no doubt given to Hamlin Garland (see below). See also Reynolds to Richard Harding Davis, TCS, 24 August 1910, 4 March 1911.

121. Hamlin Garland to Paul Revere Reynolds, ALS, 1 March n.y., 25 November 1898, Hamlin Garland file, Reynolds Papers.

122. Theodore Dreiser to Paul Revere Reynolds, ALS, 19 October 1912, Reynolds Papers. It was for this reason that publishers who initially excoriated the agent came to trust him. At first agents were blamed for driving the royalty rates ridiculously high. See Yard, *The Publisher*, pp. 79–80. In addition they were seen as the destroyers of publisher-author relations for having injected financial considerations into the relationship. Soon, however, publishers saw that in the long term not only did agents bring authors more than the cost of commission in elevated rates, but also that agents served as scouts for the publisher and saved the publisher the costs of readers by ploughing through the piles of unsolicited manuscripts. See Doran, *Chronicles*, p. 95. In addition agents secured manuscripts from those who were famous and acted as "marriage brokers," guiding the author to the proper venue. Reynolds occasionally received complaints from magazines that contended he did not properly perform his function of matching material with vehicle and was simply passing on every manuscript that he could not immediately place. See Arthur W. Little to Paul Revere Reynolds, ALS, 30 August 1907, and Francis Warner to Reynolds, TLS, 7 December 1907, Reynolds Papers. Doran added another advantage: protecting the publisher from charges of unfairness. Through his knowledge of the established conditions of the trade, the agent shielded the author from unfair practices and was often able to explain satisfactorily some technical point in question.

123. Theodore Dreiser to Paul Revere Reynolds, ALS, 19 October 1912, Reynolds Papers.

124. "A Chat with A. P. Watt," *The Bookman* 1 (March 1895): 131–32.

125. Stallman, *Stephen Crane*, p. 317.

126. *Harper Contract Book*, no. 7, reveals in great depth the tough bargaining position Howells took with the firm. He understood nuances of delivery, obligation, and rights and was not above "forgetting" them when it served his interests.

127. Writing to Richard Harding Davis, Reynolds noted that "the market for your wares seems to me to grow keener and keener. I believe in the case of some of the stocks down on Wall Street the price seems to go up although no sales are reported. Everybody keeps telling me what they can do if they had a story of yours. . . . If I knew beforehand that I was to have a story of yours I should take advantage of this keenness by raising the price" (TCS, 15 October 1912, Davis file, Reynolds Papers). It would be wrong to think of Reynolds as a philistine. He loved literature and cared for writers, as his correspondence with Willa Cather testifies. He believed he was doing them a service, which he was. The point is that, in doing so, Reynolds reinforced the very conditions of writing that bothered his clients—the commodification of literature.

128. Putnam, *Authors and Publishers*, pp. 116–18.

129. Harold Frederic to Walter Hines Page, ALS, 27 January 1897, in *The Correspondence of Harold Frederic*, p. 434.

130. James, "The Future of the Novel," p. 338.

131. Howells, "New Historical Romances," p. 306. A sampling of realist complaints about popular literature can be found in Howells, *Criticism and Fiction*, "Neo-romanticism, Imperialism, and Taste," and "Of Originality and Imitation"; James, "Art of Fiction" and "The Future of the Novel"; and Norris, *The Responsibilities of the Novelist*.

132. Relevant works of mass-culture theorists include Horkheimer, "Art and Mass Culture"; Macdonald, "A Theory of Popular Culture"; Horkheimer and Adorno, "The Culture Industry"; Macdonald, *Against the American Grain*; and Lowenthal, *Literature, Popular Culture, and Society*. See also Lasch, "Mass Culture Reconsidered."

133. Williams's *Keywords* is an invaluable source of historical semantics.

134. Crawford, *The Novel*, pp. 11, 50.

135. Schudson, *Advertising*, pp. 28–31. There are, of course, limitations in the definitions of wants that marketers use. Primary among these is that when they refer to wants, marketers mean commercially viable wants—commodities that can be sold in large enough quantities to reap profits.

136. Crawford's essential psychological bent was in direct contrast with Edgar Allan Poe's insistence upon universal moral standards. "That a criticism 'now' should be different in spirit . . . from a criticism at any previous period, is to insinuate a charge of variability in laws that cannot vary—the laws of man's heart and intellect—for these are the sole basis on which the true critical art is established. . . . Criticism is thus no 'test of opinion.' For this test, the work, divested of its pretensions as an *art-product*, is turned over for discussion to the world at large" (Poe, *Complete Poems and Stories with Selection from His Critical Writings*, 2:932–33).

137. Hamilton, *Material and Methods of Fiction*, esp. p. 4; Lathrop, "The Novel and Its Future"; Matthews, *Aspects of Fiction*; Overton, *The Philosophy of Fiction*; Perry, *A Study of Prose Fiction*, esp. p. 256; Thompson, *The Philosophy of Fiction*; Wilson, *Mere Literature*, esp. p. 9. Three excellent reviews of criticism of the period are Jones, *The Theory of American Literature*; McMahon, *Criticism of Fiction*; and Rathbun and Clark, *American Literary Criticism*.

138. Norris, "Novelists of the Future," p. 277. In "Salt and Sincerity," pp. 300–

301, Norris opines that he can imagine no more wasted effort than that of the Yale winner of the Townsend Prize: "Nine years—think of it—the best, most important of a boy's life given to devoted study!—not of Men, not of Life, not of Realities, but of the books of Other People, mere fatuous, unreasoned, pig-headed absorption of ideas at second hand. . . . The United States . . . does not want and does not need Scholars, but Men."

139. Howells, *Criticism and Fiction*, p. 146; see also pp. 9, 14, 100.

140. Ibid., pp. 65–68; 128–31; Howells, "Fears Realists Must Wait."

141. Howells, "The What and The How in Art," p. 288.

142. Howells, *Criticism and Fiction*, pp. 108–11.

143. Howells, "The New Historical Romances," p. 303.

144. James, "The Art of Fiction," pp. 33, 35.

145. James, "The Future of the Novel," pp. 336–44.

146. James, "The Art of Fiction," pp. 32–33.

147. Howells, "The What and the How in Art," p. 288.

148. James, "The Future of the Novel," p. 337.

149. James, "The Art of Fiction," pp. 38–39.

150. Howells, "The Man of Letters as a Man of Business," p. 3.

151. Ibid., p. 31.

152. Ibid., pp. 34–35.

153. Howells, "The What and the How in Art," pp. 284–89.

154. Howells, "The Easy Chair," *Harper's Monthly*, February 1906, 473–74.

Chapter 4

The epigraph is taken from Norris, "The Mechanics of Fiction," p. 254.

1. Roe, "The Element of Life in Fiction," p. 229–33.

2. It is interesting to note that Marx relied on the image of the writer as worker to designate work under unalienated conditions. In a passage in *The Grundrisse* he excoriated Fourier's view of work as play as the pipedream of a naive shop girl. "Really free work, such as composing, is at the same time the most grimly serious, the most intense exertion" (*Grundrisse*, p. 611). For a view of the middle-class version of the work ethic, see Rodgers, *The Work Ethic*.

3. Gilmore, *American Romanticism and the Marketplace*.

4. Ibid., chap. 3.

5. Emerson, "The Poet," p. 310.

6. Gilmore, *American Romanticism and the Marketplace*, p. 80.

7. Hawthorne, *The Scarlet Letter*, p. 25; Hawthorne, *Notebooks*, p. 236.

8. Quoted in Brooks, *Washington Irving*, p. 343.

9. Howells, "The Man of Letters as a Man of Business," pp. 33–35.

10. Norris, "Novelists to Order—While You Wait," p. 246; "Story-Tellers vs. Novelists," pp. 209–10; "Novelists of the Future," p. 277; and "The Mechanics of Fiction," p. 254.

11. Howells, *Criticism and Fiction*, pp. 88–91, esp. p. 91, where his political cast comes through: "Or is 'genius' the indefinable, preternatural quality, sacred to

the musicians, the painters, the sculptors, the actors, and above all, the poets? Or is it that the poets, having the most of the say in this world, abuse it to shameless self-flattery, and would persuade the inarticulate classes that they are on peculiar terms of confidence with the deity?" See also Norris, "Novelists to Order," pp. 244–47.

12. Edel, *Henry James*, vols. 3–4.

13. Cowley, "A Natural History of American Naturalism," pp. 440–42.

14. FN to Isaac Marcosson, in *The Letters of Frank Norris*, pp. 22–23.

15. Cowley, "A Natural History of American Naturalism," pp. 441.

16. MT to WDH, 20 July 1883, *Twain–Howells Correspondence*, pp. 435–36.

17. MT to WDH, 22 August 1883, *Twain–Howells Correspondence*, pp. 438–39.

18. Lynn, *Howells*, p. 253.

19. Trollope not only set himself a daily requirement but also began a new work if he finished a novel before the allotted limit for the day had been reached.

20. Edel, *Henry James*, 5:27.

21. Lynn, *Howells*, pp. 252–67. In the appendix to the Penguin edition of the novel Edwin Cady, who originally hypothesized a nervous breakdown during the writing, introduces medical evidence that contradicts his original hypothesis. Urethral blockage, Cady argues, is the most likely cause of the symptoms that Howells reported at the time of writing the most climactic scenes in November 1881. Whatever the cause, Howells's discomfort was by no means the result of a spontaneously generated conflict in the heat of composition.

22. Cady, *The Realist at War*, p. 64; Stallman, *Stephen Crane*, pp. 204–10, 218–36; Franchere and O'Donnell, *Harold Frederic*, pp. 45–49, 73–89; Edel, *Henry James*, 3:147–48.

23. Perry, *The Study of Prose Fiction*, p. 89.

24. James, "Honoré de Balzac," p. 822; *New Orleans Times-Democrat*, quoted in *The Critic*, 9 August 1890, pp. 74–75.

25. Norris, "Salt and Sincerity," pp. 298–302. For James's revisions see Anesko, *Friction with the Market*. The Twain–Howells editing relationship is handled in Brooks, *The Ordeal of Mark Twain*, and Smith, *Mark Twain*. Romantics, of course, revised too. Melville, for instance, was so bogged down in revisions during the writing of *Moby Dick* that he requested an advance from his publishers, which was denied. The difference between realists and their predecessors is that earlier writers neither called attention to their reworkings nor considered it an intrinsic part of the process.

26. The relevant letters in *Twain–Howells Correspondence* are MT to WDH, 9 December 1874 (p. 51), 4 April 1891 (pp. 641–42); WDH to MT, 19 October (p. 106), 5 November 1875 (p. 109), 11 December 1874 (p. 51–52).

27. Spiller et al., *The Literary History of the United States*, p. 803.

28. Madison, *From Irving to Irving*, p. 216.

29. Bosanquet, *Henry James at Work*.

30. HJ to Mrs. Cadwalader Jones, 23 October 1902, *Letters of Henry James*, 1:401–3; Edel, *Henry James*, 4:174–83. For a different view of James's relation to industrial and consumer capitalism see Agnew, "The Consuming Vision of Henry James."

31. WDH to MT, 23 October 1898, *Twain–Howells Correspondence*, pp. 679–82.

32. Norris, "Salt and Sincerity," pp. 315–16.

33. James, *Notebooks*, p. 11 (22 October 1891); Lynn, *Howells*, pp. 306–7; MT to WDH, 22 September 1889, *Twain–Howells Correspondence*, p. 613.

34. Mabie, "A Typical Novel," p. 423.

35. Thayer, "The New Storytellers."

36. Norris, "Simplicity in Art," pp. 291–92.

37. Page, *A Publisher's Confession*, p. 43; George Haven Putnam Papers.

38. Norris, "The Volunteer Manuscript," p. 260.

39. Porter, *Books and Reading*, chap. 8.

40. Smith, *Democracy and the Novel*, pp. 1–20, argues in favor of the existence of a tripartite system of taste levels. Though such a system no doubt existed, it was not rigidly segregated into distinct journals. The borrowings were many, and from the late 1850s to the mid-1870s the offerings of the "high-brow" sector were scanty.

41. MacMahon, *Criticism of Fiction*, pp. 3–65.

42. James, "The Future of the Novel," pp. 335–41.

43. One sign of the subtle shift in the meaning of "literature" in the late nineteenth century to designate creative, fictional work was the elevation of Hawthorne at the expense of Emerson.

44. Denning, *Mechanic Accents*, chap. 3; Davidson, *The Revolution and the Word*, chaps. 1 and 4. Both these authors and Jane Tompkins (*Sensational Designs*) have advanced arguments designed to show the value in noncanonical literatures. The arguments are persuasive in demonstrating the intellectual value of dime novels and sentimental fiction, two of the literatures that realists aimed to overcome and weaned away readers. What was at stake for realists was how to establish criteria that would make literature more than commodities, which is one of the things that they meant when they referred to sentimental and popular novels as mediocre.

45. Arnold, *Civilization in the United States*, pp. 180–94; Steevens, *The Land of the Dollar*, pp. 48–62; Bryce, *The American Commonwealth*, 2:175–78; Hamsun, *The Cultural Life of Modern America*, pp. 1–25. Hamsun's complaint had a personal component. Believing that he himself was worthy of more attention than he received, he returned to Norway where he did his best work.

46. Jefferson, *Notes on the State of Virginia*, p. 64.

47. Freneau, "Literary Importation," p. 303.

48. DeForest, "The Great American Novel," pp. 27–29.

49. Perry, "American Novels." By defining realism as the portrayal of truth, critics were able to combine two antithetical principles: literature as the portrayal of ideal forms and literature as description of what is at hand.

50. Boyesen, "Why We Have No Great Novelists."

51. Hackett, *Seventy-Five Years of Best Sellers*; Hart, *The Popular Book*; Madison, *Book Publishing*; Mott, *Golden Multitudes*; Nye, *The Unembarrassed Muse*.

52. Howells, *Criticism and Fiction*, pp. 163–82. Howells did produce an annual Christmas farce for *Harper's Monthly*, although not quite of the variety he excoriated.

53. "The Cash Author," pp. 36–37; "The Star System in Literature."

54. Gilmore, *American Romanticism*, p. 14 and chap. 2. For a slightly less classical formulation of the same goals see Higginson, *Cheerful Yesterdays*, pp. 77, 87–89, 358–59, and Lichtenstein, "Authorial Professionalism."

55. Howells, "The Editor's Study," *Harper's Monthly*, March 1890, 642–47.

56. Edgar Saltus to John Brisbane Walker, 12 March n.y., Walker Papers.

57. Crawford, *The Novel*, pp. 12–13.

58. The writing apprenticeship in the late nineteenth century is covered in Wilson, *The Labor of Words*, and Ziff, *The American 1890s*, chaps. 5–6.

59. Details on Roe's life are contained in Roe, *Reminiscences*; Roe, " 'A Native Author Called Roe' "; and "Interview with E. P. Roe."

60. Roe, "The Element of Life in Fiction," pp. 235.

61. "Interview with E. P. Roe."

62. The claim that God wrote nineteenth-century texts was quite common. In addition to Stowe and Phelps, Mary Baker Eddy, the leading light of Christian Science, made a similar claim, which prompted Mark Twain to allow that it was possible but he was surprised that the Almighty had such poor grammar.

63. E. P. Roe to Dr. Hugo Erikson, 2 December 1884, Roe Papers.

64. E. P. Roe to *Youth's Companion*, 21 October 1884, Roe Papers.

65. Ibid.

66. See, among others, Ballard, "Successful Authorship"; Garnett, "How to Write Short Stories"; Hanscom, "Method Needed in Literary Work"; Winslip, "The Literary Focus"; Fowie, "How to Get in Print"; and Luce, "Three Pointers for Novices."

67. Winslip, "The Literary Focus," p. 8; Hanscom, "Method Needed," p. 85. Hanscom's exclamation has another function besides the declaration of independence from the romantic. In its lampoon of the romantic author Hanscom's work hopes to free the professional writer from the sexual stereotyping that had become prevalent. As Hanscom presents the writer, he (and the emphasis is on "he") is clearly a business *man*. Hanscom's warnings against long hair, open collars, and delirium tremens are attempts to undo what he sees as the unfortunate association of novel writing with femininity. So too is the surreptitious bragging about long hours.

The instructors of *The Writer* were not the only guides who preached routine as the solution to writing problems. Henry James's famous essay "The Art of Fiction" was a response to Walter Besant's essay of the same name which, to James's mind, had insisted that successful literature had a simple formula. Besant's eleven steps read like a more literate synopsis of an article in *The Writer*. Besant offered advice that was as commonplace as it was free from specifics: (1) Practice writing something original every day. (2) Cultivate the habit of observation. (3) Work regularly at certain hours. (4) Read no rubbish. (5) Aim at the formation of style. (6) Endeavor to be dramatic. (7) A great element of dramatic skill is selection. (8) Avoid the sin of writing about a character. (9) Never attempt to describe any kind of life except that with which you are familiar. (10) Learn as much as you can about men and women. (11) For the sake of forming a good and natural style and acquiring a command of language, write poetry.

68. Ford, *The Literary Shop*, pp. 173–74.

69. Perhaps only Jack London took the *Writer* model to heart. For London's relationship with literary success magazines see Wilson, *The Labor of Words*, chaps. 4–5.

70. For letters of resentment and envy of the sales of "hacks" and incompetent scribblers, see HJ to WDH, 21 February 1884, 22 January 1895, in *The Letters of Henry James*, 1:27–29, 230. In the first, James complains of Francis Marion Crawford's success and asks "what's the use of trying to write anything decent or serious for a public so absolutely idiotic? . . . work so shamelessly bad seems to me to dishonour the novelist's art to a degree that is absolutely not to be forgiven." Howells had similar moments in which he complained about the phenomenal success of the gilded and callow youth. Jacobson, *James and the Mass Market*, treats the problem as an attempt at imitation on the part of James. Drawing upon the "context" of writing, she concludes that James was aware of various popular novels and while trying to reproduce their conventions ended up upgrading them and turning them against themselves. In Jacobson's version, James was divided against himself. In his "Art of Fiction" phase he suppressed his popular or mass side. Jacobson is most certainly correct to indicate that no absolute division between "popular" and "high" culture exists and that James's 1880s are best seen as spent in an attempt to separate art from commodity, while aiming for a popular audience. See also Anesko, *Friction with the Market*.

71. Howells, "Editor's Study," *Harper's Monthly*, March 1890, 644.

72. Anesko, *Friction with the Market*, passim, esp. pp. 120–30 and Appendix II; Edel, *Henry James*, 2:160, 3:264.

73. Carter, *Howells and the Age of Realism*, p. 50.

74. Howells, *Criticism and Fiction*, pp. 105–14. By the 1890s Howells was less sure of the eventual redemption of taste. In an 1894 interview with Stephen Crane, Howells declared poignantly that realists would have to wait for their eventual triumph and cited the sudden success of the "New Romances" (Howells, "Fears Realists Must Wait").

75. James, "London Notes," p. 754.

76. Norris, "The Responsibilities of the Novelist," p. 196.

77. Howells, *Criticism and Fiction*, p. 155.

78. Norris, "The True Reward of the Novelist," pp. 198, 202. At the same time, Norris believed that the people were capable of discerning the difference between quality and pretension. Adopting the tenets of populism, he believed that when presented with the truth, the populace would flock to it. Although doubtful about the ability of readers to discriminate, he found distasteful and disheartening the supplication of American novelists to the "Prince of Fashion." In such essays as "Retail Bookseller: Literary Dictator" and "The American Public and 'Popular' Fiction," he proclaimed the ability of the reading public to throw the literary rascals out: "The sham novelist who is in literature . . . 'for his own pocket every time' sooner or later meets the wave of reaction that he can not stem nor turn and under which he and his shame are conclusively . . . buried. . . . He fools himself all of the time, he fools the publisher three times, he fools the retail dealer twice, and he fools the Great American Public just exactly once" ("Retail Bookseller," p. 269).

79. James, "Alphonse Daudet," pp. 227–28.

80. James, "Charles de Bernard and Gustave Flaubert," p. 225.

81. James, "The Art of Fiction," p. 43.

82. See Boris, *Art and Labor*, and Lears, *No Place of Grace*, chap. 2, for a discussion of American uses and misuses of Ruskin and William Morris. Rodgers, *The Work Ethic*, chap. 3, deals with a similar topic.

83. Howells, *Criticism and Fiction*, p. 184.

84. Howells, "The Editor's Relations with the Young Contributor," pp. 74–75.

85. HJ to WDH, 17 May 1890, in *Henry James Letters*, 3:282–83.

86. Howells, "The Editor's Relations with the Young Contributor," pp. 74–75.

87. James, "The Art of Fiction," pp. 39, 38. See also James, "The Future of the Novel," p. 394, in which he asserts that "the form of novel that is stupid on the general question of its freedom is the single form that may, a priori, be unhesitatingly pronounced wrong."

88. Howells, "Novel-Writing and Novel-Reading," pp. 5–6.

89. James, "The Art of Fiction," p. 39.

90. The scholarly discussions on narration are extensive. My purpose here, as should become clear, is not to enter into the various debates about the actual versus implied narrators and readers or the narrative or authorial audiences. Rather, it is to present the problem as realists themselves argued it and to demonstrate that the pristine nature of their assertions led to contradictions that undermined their efforts to bring about their stated goals and to overcome the effects of commodification. I have, however, been much influenced by two recent works: Warhol, "Toward a Theory of the Engaging Narrator," and Rabinowitz, "Assertion and Assumption."

91. James, "Ivan Turgenieff," p. 298, and "Anthony Trollope," pp. 116–17.

92. Howells, "Novel-Writing and Novel-Reading," pp. 5, 7, 9, 15, 21–24.

93. James, "William Dean Howells," pp. 394–95.

94. Howells, "Novel-Writing and Novel-Reading," pp. 15–16.

95. Norris, "A Problem in Fiction," pp. 204, 206.

96. Howells, "Fears Realists Must Wait."

97. Howells, "Emile Zola."

98. HJ to WDH, 17 May 1890, in *Henry James Letters*, 3:280–85; to WDH, 19 February 1912, in *The Letters of Henry James*, 2:221–26.

99. Howells, *Criticism and Fiction*, pp. 11–2.

100. Howells, "Novel-Writing and Novel-Reading," p. 24.

101. James, "Gustave Flaubert."

102. Carolyn Porter makes a similar point in a slightly different way. She argues that the central problem of reification for literature is that the observer is simultaneously mediating the world as he or she is observing it. Observing is itself an act that renders the stable world unstable. One problem of bourgeois thought is that in including the object it loses the subject. For most theories of the world, the making of it, the indeterminacy of the apparently stable and given, is absent. See Porter, "Reification and American Literature." The problem is apropos to realist narrative theory, which swings between a supreme objectivism (in which the narrator is denied) and a subjectivism, but which does not fully achieve a synthesis of the two moments.

103. Howells, *The Rise of Silas Lapham*, pp. 173–74.

104. Agnew, "The Consuming Vision of Henry James"; Gilmore, *American Romanticism and the Marketplace*; Jameson, *The Political Unconscious*; Porter, "Reification and American Literature"; Sundquist, "In the Country of the Blue."

Chapter 5

The epigraph is taken from James, "The Novels of George Eliot," p. 485.

1. It is, of course, quite difficult to describe the reading process one hundred years after the fact with anything approaching the precision that one would like. What follows is surmise. We do have evidence of considerable concern about the change in the reading process. See Abbott, ed., *Hints for Home Reading*; Crothers, "The Gentle Reader"; Lee, *The Lost Art of Reading*; Matthews, *Aspects of Fiction*; Perry, "On Reading the *Atlantic* Cheerfully"; and Porter, *Books and Reading*. Important secondary works are Schulte-Sasse, "Toward a 'Culture' for the Masses"; Habegger, *Gender, Fantasy, and Realism*; Jameson, "Reification and Utopia"; Wilson, "The Rhetoric of Consumption"; and Denning, *Mechanic Accents*, chap. 5.

2. The problems of author-audience relations before the Civil War are handled masterfully in Gilmore, *American Romanticism and the Marketplace*.

3. Crèvecoeur, *Letters from an American Farmer*; Chevalier, *Society, Manners, and Politics*; Arnold, *Civilization in the United States*; and Bennett, quoted in Ruland, *This Storied Land*, pp. 193–99.

4. *Historical Statistics of the United States*, p. 214. Literacy statistics are notoriously slippery. First of all a problem of definition always haunts such studies. Some use signing one's name rather than making a mark as proof. While such a skill should not be dismissed, it hardly prepares the possessor for the intricacies of Jamesian prose. Because literacy measures included those fluent in their native languages, the estimated 1 million citizens who could read or speak no English represented a pool that realists could not feasibly tap. Others rely on actual tests.

Book reading also is difficult to measure. Most studies have found that people continually overestimate by about 100 percent the amount of reading they do. See Cole and Gold, *Reading*, and Berelson, "Who Reads What Books and Why?" Reading revolutions seem to have been declared nearly every generation and nearly every generation not come to pass. Book publishers, whom one would expect to be the beneficiaries of such a revolution, have met each generation with a new excuse for the failed takeoff. Bicycles, radio, movies, and television have all been blamed as competition. With the recent spate of studies of illiteracy in the 1980s, perhaps advocates of the reading revolution have given up or reversed themselves.

5. Soltow and Stevens, *Literacy and the Common School*, pp. 50–52.

6. Spiller et al., *The Literary History of the United States*, p. 955.

7. *PW*, 27 January 1894, 163–65.

8. Mott, *American Magazines*, 3:73–77.

9. Lyon, *Success Story*, p. 251.

10. Spiller et al., *The Literary History of the United States*, pp. 803–6, 955–56.

The distribution of these facilities was remarkably skewed. As late as the 1930s large parts of the United States still lacked adequate access to books, periodicals, and libraries. See Wilson, *The Geography of Reading*.

11. Carrier, *Fiction in the Public Libraries*; Garrison, *The Apostles of Culture*.

12. *Historical Statistics of the United States*, p. 217.

13. Warner, *Streetcar Suburbs*, pp. 46–152.

14. The hopes labor put in the eight-hour day are reported in Rodgers, *The Work Ethic*, pp. 34, 42, 90–91, 156–60. Sometimes the slogan substituted "eight hours for our own use" for "eight hours for study."

15. Jacobsen, *American Marriage and Divorce*, pp. 21, 90.

16. Fox and Lears, *The Culture of Consumption*, is a wide-ranging exploration of "consumption" values.

17. *Historical Statistics of the United States*, pp. 410, 506; Long, *Wages and Earnings*, pp. 37, 42, 60, 68, 113.

18. See Goody and Watt, "The Consequences of Literacy," and Freire, *Cultural Action for Freedom*.

19. Schudson, *Discovering the News*, p. 39.

20. Norris, "The American Public and 'Popular' Fiction," p. 235.

21. Howells, *Criticism and Fiction*, pp. 9–12. Howells, "The Man of Letters as a Man of Business," p. 30.

22. James, "The Future of the Novel," p. 337.

23. Howells, "Novel-Writing and Novel-Reading," pp. 11–13.

24. *Life in Letters*, 2:34–35.

25. For an important review of the changing nature of reading see Tompkins, "The Reader in History."

26. See the Twain–Pond correspondence in the Major James Pond papers in the Berg Collection of the New York Public Library.

27. Howells, "Novel-Writing and Novel-Reading," p. 8.

28. Radway, *Reading the Romance*; Fisher, *Hard Facts*, chap. 2; Denning, *Mechanic Accents*, pp. 72–73.

29. This contention is the brunt of the work of Wilson, *The Labor of Words*, and is the central difference between the so-called progressive and Gilded Age publishers. See Yard, *The Publisher*; Page, *A Publisher's Confession*; and Doran, *The Chronicles of Barabbas*.

30. See Wilson, "The Rhetoric of Consumption," pp. 44–45.

31. Vanderbilt, *Howells*, pp. 116–26.

32. James, *The American Scene*, p. 85.

33. Ibid. pp. 138–39.

34. Kraft, *No Castles on Main Street*, p. 150.

35. The literature on the connections between gender and culture is voluminous. Among the most important works dealing with the development of nineteenth-century culture are Branch, *The Sentimental Years*; Douglas, *The Feminization of American Culture*; Habegger, *Gender, Fantasy, and Realism*; and May, *The End of American Innocence*, chaps. 3–4.

36. Boyesen, "Why We Have No Great Novelists"; Howells, "The Man of Letters as a Man of Business," p. 21.

37. Howells, *Criticism and Fiction*, p. 160.

38. Douglas, *The Feminization of American Culture*, chaps. 2–3.

39. Tebbel, *Book Publishing*, 2:225–35.

40. Tuchman and Fortin, "Edging Women Out," handles the usurpation of novel writing by men in Victorian England. A similar phenomenon took place in the United States.

41. See Goldman, "The 'Iron Madonna,' " and "Interview with E. P. Roe." This is not to say that nearly a majority of Howells's readers were men. There are a number of plausible reasons that males should be overrepresented in the letters collected in the Howells papers at Houghton Library, Harvard University, on which Goloman based the study. Female reticence about writing such letters and the possibility that they were not saved in the same proportions are two explanations. What is of crucial interest is that Howells did have a significant and interested male contingent among his readers, which suggests that gender also divided the realist readership.

42. Howells, quoted in Ruland, *This Storied Land*, p. 173.

43. Howells, "The Editor's Relations with the Young Contributor," p. 66.

44. See Howells, "Fears Realists Must Wait."

45. Howells, *Criticism and Fiction*, pp. 94–104. Habegger, *Gender, Fantasy, and Realism*, p. 106, also suggests that one of the missions of the realist novel was to undermine the false conventions of romance that prevailed in much of the popular fiction: "The detailed verisimilitude, close social notation, analysis of motives, and unhappy endings were all part of a strategy of argument, and adversary polemic. These techniques were the only way to tell the truth about, to test, to *get at*, the ideal gender types, daydreams, and lies that were poisoning society and the novel. . . . Attempting to break out, and to help their readers break out of a suffocated, half-conscious state, Howells and James had to be circumstantial."

46. Howells, *A Hazard of New Fortunes*, p. 416.

47. Howells, "Novel-Writing and Novel-Reading," p. 24.

48. Norris, "Novelists of the Future," p. 278.

49. See, for instance, the Crane correspondence with Ripley Hitchcock, Hitchcock Papers. Frederic's view of his audience is contained in a letter to Crane, 31 May 1895, in *The Correspondence of Harold Frederic*, p. 344.

50. On the relation of minor naturalists and market signals see Wilson, *The Labor of Words*, pp. 131–276.

51. Rabinowitz, "Assertion and Assumption."

52. *The Nation*, 14 May 1868, 389–90.

53. MacMahon, *Criticism of Fiction*; Thomas Wentworth Higginson, quoted in Roe, *Reminiscences*, p. 54; Henry James, quoted in Rodgers, *The Work Ethic*, p. 132.

54. MacMahon, *Criticism of Fiction*; Shove, *Cheap Book Production*; Tebbel, *Book Publishing*, 2:234–35; Levine, "Shakespeare and the American People: A Study in Cultural Transformation."

55. Ziff, *Literary Democracy*, p. 271; Gilmore, *American Romanticism and the Marketplace*, chaps. 3 and 5, contains a similar but more ironic and pessimistic view of Melville's relationship with the audience and its effect on his writing.

56. *The Scarlet Letter*, pp. 3–4.

57. Norris, "The Responsibilities of the Novelist" and "The American Public and 'Popular' Fiction."

58. Howells, "Novel-Writing and Novel-Reading," p. 25.

59. Howells, "The Man of Letters as a Man of Business," p. 9.

60. Such a trend reached a high point with Norman Mailer, who has frankly embraced the concept of turning one's life into a novel. *Advertisements for Myself*, a collection of his essays, captures the tone perfectly. Mailer's view of the importance of construction of everything, including oneself, stands in contrast with the extreme reticence of Thomas Pynchon, who has steadfastly opposed any public appearances—including the American Book Award ceremonies, to which he sent a comedian to accept for him. In our general context of publicity, it is interesting to note that there is but one known photograph of Pynchon.

61. Book advertising is discussed in Wilson, "Literary Apprenticeship, pp. 38–41; Tebbel, *Book Publishing*, 2:150–60; and Sheehan, *This Was Publishing*, pp. 30–50.

62. Quoted in Potter, *People of Plenty*, p. 183.

63. Bok, *Americanization*, pp. 153–54, 162–63.

64. Quoted in Sheehan, *This Was Publishing*, p. 35.

65. Bacheller, *From Stores of Memory*, pp. 277–78.

66. Tebbel, *Book Publishing*, 2:157.

67. See Wilson, *The Labor of Words*, chap. 1.

68. Although technically a publicity stunt for *The Century*, which was serializing the novel, the calendar had literary value in that part of the plot of the novel rests on the eccentricity of Wilson and the effort that he devoted to his calendar. It was an extension of the novel and included such important lines as "When angry count to a hundred, when very angry, swear."

69. Nye, *The Unembarrassed Muse*, p. 32; Putnam and Putnam, *Authors and Publishers*, p. 85–88.

70. Quoted in Gross, *Publishers on Publishing*, p. 256.

71. Ellsworth, *The Golden Age*, pp. 168–69. So pervasive was literary publicity that one deranged reader actually was moved to assassinate David Graham Phillips.

72. Baran and Sweezy, *Monopoly Capital*, chap. 11; Berger, *Ways of Seeing*, chap. 5; Henry, *Culture against Man*, chap. 1; Potter, *People of Plenty*, chap. 8; Schudson, *Advertising*; and Williams, *Materialism and Culture*, pp. 170–95, are valuable accounts of the uses and functions of advertising. Schudson argues quite persuasively that particular advertising campaigns are not efficacious. In general, sales determine advertising rather than advertising determining sales. In book campaigns effects are especially difficult to trace (p. xv). Schudson goes on to suggest that though advertisements are not uncritically believed by those with other sources of information, many people do not have access to such sources and that the appeal of the ad is the possibility that its claim might not be false. My argument in the present study is not that particular campaigns were effective but that advertising taken as a whole contributed to, but did not create, a climate in which the book was assigned attributes that its author did not intend or that the author worked to create in order to meet expectations for which he or she was not responsible.

Stuart Ewen's *Captains of Consciousness* is a New Left account that suggests that advertising imposed from above constituted a way of viewing life that distracted the working class from organizing by transferring its interests into achieving a good society through relative equality of consumption. Most of the advertising of the period (1890–1920), was, however, clearly directed at the middle classes and, given the income of the working classes at that time, would have been counterproductive. Ewen further suggests at certain points that the wants advertised were invented. In contrast, I have concentrated on the problems for discourse inherent in a system in which stability of wants invariably dissolved. Rather than an imposition, advertising was an adoption to actual wants and desires.

73. Tebbel, *Book Publishing*, 2:161.

74. Schudson, *Discovering the News*, pp. 96–106, discusses the importance of Sunday reading habits, the impact of immigration and urbanization, and the growing importance of female shopping for reading and advertising in the 1880s and 1890s.

75. Interestingly enough, *The Bookman* was edited by Harry Peck, a Columbia University professor with a reputation for exotic behavior and even more exotic tastes. A skeptic of the first order who once argued seriously against the prevailing reputation of Shakespeare, Peck eventually committed suicide after a scandal over homosexuality. Even though the magazine tended to the arty and the avant-garde, it provided a vehicle for authorial promotion and publisher publicity.

76. Sheehan, *This Was Publishing*, pp. 179–80. He concludes that publishers' denials of unethical use of reviews were correct.

77. Among the multitude are Austin, *American Authors' Ancestry*; Bardeen, *Authors' Birthdays*; Barrows, *Acts and Anecdotes*; Bolton, *Famous American Authors*; Howe, *American Bookmen*; Fields, *Authors and Friends*; Gilder and Gilder, *Authors at Home*; Griswold, *Home Life of Great Authors*; Halsey, *American Authors and Their Homes*; Harkins, *Little Pilgrimages*; Laughlin, *Stories of Authors' Loves*; Stoddard, *Poets' Homes*; and Walsh, *Authors and Authorship*. For the mixture of motives for describing literary celebrities at home see Walsh, p. 6, who announces his purpose as to "present to the reader the man that underlies the author, as he appears in the social circle, in the privacy of his domestic hearth, or in public."

78. *PW*, 1 March 1890, 333.

79. For Howells's interviews see *Five Interviews*. Of special interest is Theodore Dreiser's with Howells for the March 1900 *Ainslee's*, entitled "The Real Howells" (*Five*, 137–42). Designed to give the true story—to break beneath the publicity, Dreiser's effort with phrases like "the great Literary Philanthropist" only perpetuated the trend.

In *Melville and Whitman* Van Wyck Brooks uses this venture as proof of Twain's lack of pride in his profession. His case, however, is not convincing. It is based on a misreading of a letter from Twain to Howells about the freedom of river pilots, which Brooks takes to imply a dislike for the profession of authorship. Brooks's argument rests on the questionable belief that promotion and devotion to craft were inconsistent. In the conditions of the late nineteenth century, rather than being contradictory or morally suspect, such actions were part and parcel of what it meant to be an author. Self-promotion or, more precisely, making one's life as much a creation as one's texts was built into the scheme of things.

80. Gilmore, *American Romanticism and the Marketplace*, p. 89

81. *The Writer*, August 1889, 145; Edel, *Henry James*, 5:174–80.

82. Edel, *Henry James*, pp. 240–60.

83. Smith, *Democracy and the Novel*, p. 144.

84. Trachtenberg, *The Incorporation of America*, p. 133.

85. Wilson, *Patriotic Gore*, p. 588; Howells, "Novel-Writing and Novel-Reading," p. 12.

86. MT to J. B. Pond, ALS, 8 July 1884, Pond Papers. "Our" refers to Twain and his partner Cable, whom Twain later regarded as detracting from the show. Writing on 22 December 1884, Twain complained that he would draw better by himself. "His name draws a sixteenth part of the house and he invariably does two-thirds of the reading."

87. *Life in Letters*, 2:115. See as well the correspondence of Howells and James, in which both complained at various times about the popularity and promotion given to inferior writers.

88. Norris, "Salt and Sincerity," pp. 298–99.

89. WDH to HJ, 15 July 1900, in *Life in Letters*, 2:132–34.

90. Howells, "The Art of the Adsmith," p. 265. See also the "Editor's Easy Chair," *Harper's Monthly*, April 1901, February 1906, in which Howells makes advertising as a primary problem of the author and audience. In addition he notes that the false claims of advertising work to strain the relationship of author and publisher. Norris's work on advertising may be seen in "Newspaper Criticisms and American Fiction." He posits a series of stock phrases that he holds a reviewer could apply to each genre and save himself the trouble of actually reading the book.

91. James, *The American Scene*, pp. 9–10.

92. Edel, *Henry James*, 5:241.

93. Stephen Crane to Ripley Hitchcock, ALS, 27 January 1896, Crane papers, Berg Collection.

94. Stephen Crane to Ripley Hitchcock, ALS, 2 February 1896, ibid.

95. Crane, *Letters*, p. 149.

96. See Ziff, *The American 1890s*, chap. 9.

97. Quoted in Turner, *George W. Cable*, p. 282.

98. Howells, "Novel-Writing and Novel-Reading," p. 24.

99. James, "Gustave Flaubert," pp. 337–38.

100. James, "The New Novel," quoted in James, *Theory of Fiction*, p. 157.

101. Howells, *Criticism and Fiction*, p. 15.

102. Howells, *A Hazard of New Fortunes*, pp. 51–52.

103. See Wilson, "The Rhetoric of Consumption," and Lee, "*The Lost Art of Reading*. Roland Barthes's work, particularly the collection of essays in *Image-Music-Text*, was one of the first in the poststructuralist vein to attack the realist conception of language as authoritarian, despite its ostensible democratic sentiments.

104. Howells, *A Hazard of New Fortunes*, p. 23.

105. Ibid., p. 24. Trachtenberg, *The Incorporation of America*, pp. 186–92, makes a similar argument for *The Rise of Silas Lapham*. He sees the narrator as aiming to reform from within the select portion of the reading public. His key evidence for this contention that the novel presents itself as the pedagogy of reading is the dinner conversation at the Corey home. Sewell, the minister, whose

insightful comments on novels match those of Howells's essays, condemns the portrayal of lovemaking in monstrous disproportion to the other relations of life and asserts to the assembled Boston Brahmins and noveau riche Laphams that "novelists might be the greatest help to us if they painted life as it is, and human feelings in the true proportion and relations." As his host responds that Sewell asks too much of the readership, the reader of *Silas Lapham* is left with the strong implication that what the writer should do, so should the reader.

106. Howells, "Novel-Writing and Novel-Reading," p. 22, and *Criticism and Fiction*, pp. 30–40.

107. Howells, *Criticism and Fiction*, pp. 98–99.

108. Norris, "A Problem in Fiction."

109. WDH to Brander Matthews, 9 August 1902, in *Life in Letters*, 2:160–61.

110. Howells, *A Hazard of New Fortunes*, p. 66.

111. James, "The Novels of George Eliot," p. 321.

112. James, "Preface to *The Portrait of a Lady*," p. 54.

113. Preface to *The Wings of the Dove*, reprinted in James, *Theory of Fiction*, pp. 323–34.

114. James, *Notebooks*, pp. 15–18.

115. James, "London Notes," p. 754.

116. Howells, "Novel-Writing and Novel-Reading," p. 13.

Chapter 6

The epigraph is taken from WDH to HJ, 10 October 1888, in *Life in Letters*, 1:417.

1. Brooks, *Washington Irving*, pp. 39–40; Scott, "Early Literary Clubs in New York City," pp. 3–16; "A Succinct Account of the Origin and Progress of the New-York Literary Confederacy by A Member of the Association," Gulian Verplanck Papers.

2. Charvat, *Literary Publishing*, pp. 62–65, documents Barlow's wealth and aristocratic pretensions.

3. Quoted in Simpson, *The Man of Letters in New England and the South*, p. 53.

4. Depeyster, "Notes on Belles-Lettres and Rhetoric," Columbia College (1804) in the Depeyster Papers, contains this summary: Belles-lettres would soothe the mind, gratify fancy, and in some degree weaken violent emotions; its purpose was to refine the taste.

5. Blair, *Lectures*, p. 57.

6. Ibid., pp. 5–7. The title also gives an indication of the Blair's assumption of the closed nature of the writing discourse. He took for granted that one wrote to the same people to whom one spoke. Given the nature of public speaking in the early republican period, the number who listened to the speech generally shared one's background or were those who paid some deference to the speaker.

7. Davidson, *The Revolution and the Word*, chap. 2.

8. Charvat, *Literary Publishing*, pp. 66–68.

9. Brooks, *Washington Irving*, p. 62.

10. Quoted in Simpson, *The Man of Letters in New England and the South*, pp. 57–58.

11. For a representative selection of republican opinion see Wood, *The Rising Glory of America*; Cady, *Literature of the Early Republic*; and Ruland, *The Native Muse*.

12. Jefferson, "Report of the Commissioners," p. 333.

13. Kraft, *No Castles on Main Street*, pp. 32–41.

14. See, for instance, Bartlett, *The American Mind*, pp. 32–72; Miller, *The Life of the Mind in America*, pp. 99–155; and McCormick, *The Second American Party System*, for a discussion of the new professionalization of politics.

15. Mellow, *Nathaniel Hawthorne*, p. 82; Brooks, *Melville and Whitman*, p. 83.

16. Charvat, *Authorship* p. 24.

17. Emerson, "The American Scholar," p. 233.

18. Higginson, *Cheerful Yesterdays*, p. 358.

19. Ibid., pp. 68–70, 90.

20. Ibid., pp. 169–72; Green, *The Problem of Boston*; and Simpson, *The Man of Letters in New England and the South*, discuss the Boston literary clerisy.

21. Higginson, *Cheerful Yesterdays*, pp. 129–31.

22. Eggleston, "The Literary Disadvantages of Being Born Too Late," pp. 214–18.

23. Lathrop, "The Literary Movement in New York," pp. 815–16.

24. See Jaher, "The Boston Brahmins in the Age of Industrial Capitalism."

25. Howells, *Literary Friends and Acquaintances*, pp. 180–81. Howells had deeply ambivalent feelings about the importance of an American literary center. On the one hand, he revered Boston and its support for the ideal of the writer as a transcendental observer. Its dedication to the pursuit of literary greatness, regardless of its success in achieving that aim, struck Howells as exemplary. On the other hand, he was deeply aware of the political history of literary centers, which he connected to prior undemocratic forms of government and social existence. Literary centers, he noted in *Criticism and Fiction*, had historically been located in the capitals of despotic societies. They had relied on an aristocracy of letters, rather than on the diffusion of literary knowledge. For an iconoclastic, but important, view of Boston, see Green, *The Problem of Boston*. Green's book is flawed by his assertion that the Boston literati invited the Irish to participate and that the brooding, illiterate presence of the immigrants did damage to the literary ideal. See also the important essay by Simpson, "The Treason of William Dean Howells," in *The Man of Letters in New England and the South*, pp. 85–128.

26. Parry, *Garrets and Pretenders*, pp. 3–55.

27. Howells, *Literary Friends and Acquaintances*, pp. 70–73.

28. See Jones, *The Age of Energy*, pp. 234, 253, for a discussion of the Genteel Tradition's evaluation of Whitman.

29. Eggleston, *Recollections*, pp. 270–73; Matthews, *These Many Years*, pp. 342–46; Matthews, *Americanisms and Briticisms*, pp. 128–34; Johnson, *Remembered Yesterdays*, pp. 329–34; Osborne, *The Authors Club*, pp. 1–5.

30. On literary centers see Norris, "New York as a Literary Centre."

31. Lathrop, "The Literary Movement in New York," p. 829; Osborne, *The Authors Club*, p. 31.

32. Eggleston, *Recollections*, p. 177.

33. Osborne, *The Authors Club*, p. 41.

34. Ibid., p. 40.

35. *The Bookman* 1, no. 1 (February 1895): 41, captures the tone of the complaint: "The increasing endeavor of the newspaper is to photograph the phantasmagoria of the day and seep it away like the illusion on a screen, with the mirage of the next day. Synthesis, deduction, co-ordination, ultimate purposity, and clear comprehension of the dramatic tendency of events, are less the duty and object of a newspaper than ever before. Opinion, reflection, and public guidance have measurably disappeared before the voracious enterprise of snapping the shutter on every fragment of the passion show with an impartiality that puts the sixteenth marriage of public bawd and the hosiery of the latest gin palace performance from London into the same category as the fate of an empire and the destiny of man."

36. Matthews, *These Many Years*, p. 14; Stedman, "Introduction" to Stoddard, *Recollections*, p. ix.

37. Low and Carnegie were accomplished authors. Carnegie's *Triumphant Democracy* (1886) was at least the equal of a good three quarters of the membership's efforts. He was not, however, a professional author in the sense that the bulk of his income did not come from writing and the majority of his time was not spent in composition. Carnegie's membership had a financial benefit. His donations allowed the club to purchase a home for club activities and to establish a fund to aid indigent authors. Osborne, *The Authors Club*, pp. 30–38. For a clash over a less reputable member see Bassan, "The Poetaster and the Horse Doctors."

38. Johnson, *Remembered Yesterdays*, pp. 200–246; Osborne, *The Authors Club*, pp. 32–33. When Authors Club members spoke of authors, they meant men. Women were excluded from club activities, except when the club honored Harriet Beecher Stowe and on special "Watch Nights." Eggleston (see *Recollections*, p. 175) defended the prohibition on the grounds that the club was envisioned as a place for gentlemanly relaxation.

39. Everett (1835), in Ruland, *The Native Muse*, p. 269.

40. Lynn, *Howells*, p. 253. Garfield was instrumental in obtaining positions abroad for Howells.

41. Hofstadter, *Anti-Intellectualism in American Life*, pp. 233–52, 402–10.

42. Bok, *Americanization*, pp. 69–75.

43. Kirkland, *Dream and Thought*.

44. Carnegie, *The Empire of Business*, p. 113.

45. Howells, "The Man of Letters as a Man of Business." Excerpts in this and the following paragraph are from pp. 33–35.

46. See Lynn, *Howells*, for a view of Howells as a psychologically divided author.

47. For Howells's discussion of the uncoupling of politics and letters in both its aspects—politicians' retreat from literature and scholarship and men of letters' distaste for politics—see "The Politics of American Authors."

48. Garraty, *The New Commonwealth*, p. 135.

49. Howells, *Criticism and Fiction*, p. 128.

50. Howells, "American Literature in Exile." Howells contended that rather than a sign of immaturity in the United States, literary absenteeism was one of growing maturity—an advance wave of American expression: "They may be the vanguard of the great army of adventurers destined to overrun the earth from these shores, and exploit all foreign countries to our advantage. They probably themselves do not know it, but in the act of 'drawing their inspiration' from alien scenes, or taking their own where they find it, are not they simply transporting to Europe 'the struggle for material prosperity' which Sir Lepel supposes to be fatal to them here?"

51. "We have heard it maintained, we will remember, that such things are 'superior to art'; but we understand least of all what *that* may mean, and we will look in vain for the artist, the divine explanatory genius, who will come to our aid and tell us. There is life and life, and as waste is only life sacrificed and thereby prevented from 'counting,' I delight in a deep-breathing economy and an organic form" (James, "Preface to *The Tragic Muse*," p. 84). See also Howells's comments to Stephen Crane in "Fears Realists Must Wait," in which he talks of realism balancing the proportions. See Jameson, *The Political Unconscious*, pp. 192–205, for an extended discussion of the problems posed to late nineteenth-century literary work by class conflict and the threat of revolution.

52. For a neoconservative account of the relationship between authorship and radicalism that argues that intellectuals become ensnared in action and abandon their calling, see Winegarten, *Writers and Revolution*.

53. Pizer, *Garland's Early Work*; Morgan, *American Writers in Rebellion*, pp. 77–92. Both make similar points about Garland's ultimate conservatism. See also Wilson, *The Labor of Words*, for London and Sinclair.

54. FN to Lilla Lewis Parkes, October 1899, in *The Letters of Frank Norris*, p. 44; Stallman, *Stephen Crane*, p. 53–56; Carter, "Mark Twain and the Labor Movement"; Edel, *Henry James*, 4:273–80.

55. WDH to HJ, 15 July 1898, in *Life in Letters*, 2:94–95. To his sister Aurelia, Howells wrote: "After war will come piling up big fortunes again; the craze for wealth will fill all brains, and every good cause will be set back. We shall have an era of blood-bought prosperity and the chains of capitalism will be welded on the nation more firmly than ever" (ibid., 2:90). See also his "Spanish Prisoners of War."

56. WDH to Henry Blake Fuller, 10 November 1901, in *Life in Letters*, 2:149; to HJ, 10 October 1888, ibid., 2:416–18.

57. See Cady, *The Light of Common Day*, chap. 1, for similarities between Howells and James in this regard. Both had Swendenborgian fathers, and both rejected the fundamental principle of earthly facts as signs of another universe.

58. WDH to MT, 31 August, 4 September 1884, in *Twain–Howells Correspondence*, pp. 500–503. See MT to WDH, 17 September 1884, ibid., p. 508, for an admission of Twain's concern that Howells keep himself clean by not voting for the corrupt Blaine. Howells's moral standing, not the electoral outcome, seems to be Twain's fundamental concern.

59. Howells's actions are covered in Cady, *The Realist at War*, pp. 67–80.

60. Ibid., pp. 73–77.

61. The "proper" view is discussed in Smith, *Democracy and the Novel*, chaps. 1 and 5.

62. James, "The Art of Fiction," p. 33.

63. Norris, "Novelists of the Future," pp. 277–78; see also his "Plea for Romantic Fiction."

64. Norris, "The Novel with a 'Purpose,'" p. 206.

65. Howells, *Criticism and Fiction*, p. 9.

66. Norris, "Salt and Sincerity," p. 308.

67. Cady, *The Realist at War*, pp. 108–35.

68. Even Howells, who was more tolerant than most of the realists, had difficulties with Irish political power in Boston and the Jewish presence in European spas. See Vanderbilt, *Howells*, pp. 116–28.

69. Tebbel, *Book Publishing*, 2:139–40; *PW*, 2 March 1895, 160; 15 February 1896, 324; 22 February 1896, 356.

70. Putnam and Putnam, *Authors and Publishers*, pp. 120–21. Note the similarity between Putnam's call and those of some corporate liberals like Mark Hanna, who once opined that any capitalist who did not meet his workers halfway was a fool. The corporate-liberal thesis, which originated with the New Left, can be found in Kolko, *The Triumph of Conservatism*, and Weinstein, *The Corporate Ideal*. As David Montgomery has demonstrated ("Machinists, the Civic Foundation, and the Socialist Party," in *Workers' Control*, pp. 48–90), contrary to the corporate-liberal thesis that firms in monopolizing sectors favored labor conciliation and cooperation, most firms held fast to antilabor policies. On the shop level, class differences remained, and these led to a series of strikes during the first decade of the twentieth century. In a similar way Putnam was almost alone among publishers in his call for a union. Publishers greeted the new authors' organizations as destructive to the personal relationships in writing and shed no tears at their demise.

71. Tebbel, *Book Publishing*, 2:147; Wilson, "Literary Apprenticeship," p. 2; Authors' League of America, *The Authors' League*.

72. Howells, "A Painful Subject," p. 48; "The Editor's Easy Chair," *Harper's Monthly*, February 1906, 472–75.

73. *Harper's Monthly*, pp. 473–74.

74. Cited in *PW*, 13 August 1892, p. 231.

75. Putnam to Marjorie Fulgar, TLS, 4 October 1915, Putnam Papers.

76. Quoted in Ruland, *A Storied Land*, p. 181.

77. Rideout, *The Radical Novel*, chaps. 1–3.

78. Denning, *Mechanic Accents*, pp. 81, 146–47, 200.

79. By the turn of the century, when the House of Morgan bailed out *Harper's*, writers and workers actually had a common enemy.

80. Montgomery, *Beyond Equality*; Foner, *Free Soil, Free Labor, Free Men*.

81. Howells, *Criticism and Fiction*, pp. 129–30. This passage has earned for Howells an undeserved reputation for timidity. Not only did he here and in his novels for the preceding seven years note and examine the class divisions, but his observation of the general mildness of class conflict in the United States was well in line with the realist position of accurate observation. Howells was certainly

correct in noting that wages were higher in the United States than in Europe and that unpopular writers were not sent to winters in Duluth.

82. Ibid., p. 188.

83. Ibid., p. 16.

84. Ibid., p. 139.

85. Norris, "The Responsibilities of the Novelist," p. 195.

86. The recipients of realist scorn were technically anarchist conspirators, rather than revolutionaries. Howells, James, and Norris all slightly displace the central social conflict. Caraher of *The Octopus*, Lindau of *A Hazard of New Fortunes*, and Hoffendahl of *The Princess Casamassima* represent less typical forces within the working class than they do imagined enemies. This important qualification aside, the three political novels do give us in transmuted form the realists' conception of the social problem.

87. Norris, *The Octopus*, p. 436.

88. Ibid., pp. 457–78.

89. *A Hazard of New Fortunes*, p. 393.

90. Ibid., p. 368.

91. WDH to John Hay, 7 January 1884, in *Life in Letters*, 1:357–58. In *The Century* Howells defended Hay's book in similar terms: "We are all workingmen in America, or the sons of workingmen, and few of us are willing to hear them traduced; but, for our own part, they do not seem to us pre-eminent for wisdom or goodness, and we cannot perceive that they derive any virtue whatever from being workingmen."

92. Quoted in Kazin, *On Native Grounds*, p. 21.

93. WDH to T. S. Perry, 14 April 1888, in *Life in Letters*, 1:413–14; to William Cooper Howells, 10 July 1892, ibid., 2:25–26.

94. Howells, "Are We a Plutocracy?" See also "The Editor's Easy Chair," *Harper's Monthly*, May 1901, 968–69. "The splendor of what money can buy is the splendor that dazzles the eye and corrupts the heart, when graced with the literature and art of society journalism." The worship of wealth, Howells concluded, was an infection from which no one is safe.

95. Howells, "Are We a Plutocracy?" p. 191.

96. Ibid., p. 196.

97. Howells, "The Politics of American Authors," p. 293.

98. Howells, *Criticism and Fiction*, pp. 187–88.

99. James, "London Notes."

100. Norris, "The Responsibilities of the Novelist," p. 197.

101. Norris, "The Novel with a 'Purpose,'" pp. 203–5.

102. Ibid., p. 205.

103. HJ to Grace Norton, 24 January 1885, *The Correspondence of Henry James*, 3:64–67.

104. Howells, "The Politics of American Authors," p. 291.

105. James, "Charles Nordhoff's Communistic Societies."

106. Howells, cited in Ruland, *This Storied Land*, pp. 184–88.

107. Howells, *Annie Kilburn*, pp. 149–50.

108. Howells, *The Minister's Charge*, pp. 458–59.

109. Lynn, *Howells*, pp. 293–94.

110. WDH to Hamlin Garland, 6 November 1888, in *Life in Letters*, 1:419.

111. In both *Human Nature and Social Order* (1902) and *Social Organization* (1909) Charles Horton Cooley posed the "social problem" much as Howells had a decade earlier: how can social unity be preserved in a society in which fissaporous forces threatened to destroy social bonds and crush individual worth? Cooley contended that any concept of self existed only in relation to others and was therefore social; furthermore, both self and society were primarily mental phenomena. "The immediate social reality is the personal idea. . . . Society in its immediate aspect, is a relation among personal ideas. In order to have society it is evidently necessary that persons should get together somewhere; and they get together only as personal ideas in the mind" (*Human Nature*, pp. 118–21). These personal images constitute our views of others, the sum of which comprise society.

In Cooley's view what kept society from exploding was sympathy—his version of "complicity." A strong deep understanding of other people—the sign of mental energy and stability—is a prerequisite to social power. "Only in so far as a man understands other people and thus enters into the life around him has he any effective existence; the less he has of this the more he is a mere animal, not truly in contact with human life" (ibid., pp. 140–41). Because social existence is fundamentally an idea, the nature of such ideas is crucial. Rejecting a class consciousness that pressed an allegiance to something other than national unity, Cooley, like the realists before him, argued that in a truly organic society "the struggles and suffering of the poor would arouse the same affectionate and helping solicitude as is felt when one member of a family falls ill." The United States was not such a society and had a deficiency of "we-feeling" (*Social Organization*, pp. 298–300). Many of the institutions of society promoted misunderstandings. "The press, which ought to interpret social classes to each other, is itself divided on class lines, and the papers and magazines which the well-to-do man reads confirm him in his class bias, while the hand-worker feeds his upon labor and socialist publications" (*Human Nature*, p. 73). Suggesting that the ideal of service would dampen class tension, Cooley contended that the central problem was less the vast fortunes of the wealthy than confused ideology. "A real democracy of sentiment and action, a renewed Christianity and a renewed art might make life beautiful and hopeful for those who have little money without diminishing the wholesome operation of the desire for gain. At present the common man is impoverished not merely by an absolute want of money but by a current way of thinking which makes pecuniary success the standard of merit, and so makes him feel that failure to get money is failure of life" (*Social Organization*, p. 304).

112. References in the text are to the Signet editions of *A Hazard of New Fortunes* (1965) and *The Octopus* (1964) and the Apollo edition of *The Princess Casamassima* (1976).

Chapter 7

The epigraph is taken from Norris, "The Responsibilities of the Novelist," p. 194.

1. In an uncharacteristically scathing review, "Professor Barrett Wendell's Notions of American Literature," William Dean Howells complained of Wendell's myopia and termed Wendell's *Literary History of America* (1900) "A Study of New England Authorship in its Rise and Decline, with Some Glances at American Literature."

2. Triggs, "A Century of American Poetry," p. 640.

3. Quoted in Ziff, *The American 1890s*, p. 153. His chapter 7 is particularly good on the apprenticeship function of journalism.

4. Kazin, *On Native Grounds*, pp. 15–16, 33, 35.

5. Howells, "Emile Zola"; James, "Emile Zola."

6. Michaels, *The Gold Standard and the Logic of Naturalism*, pp. 21–28.

7. Sundquist, "Realism and Regionalism," pp. 501, 504.

8. Lukács, *Studies in European Realism*.

9. Chase, *The American Novel and Its Tradition*.

10. The dinner forms the opening scene for May, *The End of American Innocence*, pp. 3–8.

Bibliography

Manuscript Sources

Cambridge, Massachusetts
  Houghton Library, Harvard University
    William Dean Howells Papers
Charlottesville, Virginia
  Clifton Waller Barrett Collection, Alderman Library, University of Virginia
    Stephen Crane Papers
    S. S. McClure Papers
    E. P. Roe Papers
New York, New York
  Berg Collection, New York Public Library
    Irving Bacheller Papers
    Stephen Crane Papers
    J. B. Brisbane Walker Papers
  Butler Library, Columbia University
    Harper and Brothers Papers
    Ripley Hitchcock Papers
    The Home Culture Club Papers
    George Haven Putnam Papers
    Paul Revere Reynolds Papers
  New-York Historical Society
    Authors Club Papers
    Frederick DePeyster Papers
    James Herbert Morse Papers
    Gulian Verplanck Papers
Princeton, New Jersey
  Firestone Library, Princeton University
    Charles Scribner and Sons Papers

Periodicals

Atlantic Monthly, 1876–1900
The Bookman, 1894–1910
The Century, 1885–95
The Chap-Book, 1894–98
The Cosmopolitan, 1890–96
The Critic, 1884–1900
The Dial, 1886–1900
The Editor, 1885–1901
The Forum, 1884–1900
Harper's Monthly, 1885–1906
McClure's, 1893–1902
The Nation, 1880–1900
North American Review, 1816–30, 1872–1902
Pocket Magazine, 1894–95
Publishers Weekly, 1872–1910
Scribner's Magazine, 1875–80
The Writer, 1887–1900

General Bibliography

Abbott, Lyman, ed. *Hints for Home Reading: A Series of Chapters on Books and Their Use*. New York: G. P. Putnam's Sons, 1880.
Adams, John. "Dissertation on the Feudal and the Canon Law." In *The Works of John Adams*, edited by Charles Francis Adams, 3:447–64. Boston: Little, Brown, 1851.
Agnew, Jean-Christophe. "The Consuming Vision of Henry James." In Fox and Lears, *The Culture of Consumption*, pp. 65–100.
Alden, Henry Mills. *Magazine Writing and New Literature*. New York: Harper and Brothers, 1908.
Allen, Frederick Lewis. *American Magazines, 1741–1941*. New York: Harper and Brothers, 1941.
Altick, Richard. *The English Common Reader: A Social History of the Mass Reading Public, 1800–1900*. London: Oxford University Press, 1957.
Anesko, Michael. *"Friction with the Market": Henry James and the Profession of Authorship*. New York: Oxford University Press, 1986.
Arnold, Matthew. *Civilization in the United States*. Boston: Cupples and Hurd, 1888.
Auerbach, Erich. *Mimesis*. Princeton: Princeton University Press, 1943.
Austin, John. *American Authors' Ancestry*. New York: F. L. Freeman, 1915.
Authors Club, The. *The First Book of the Authors Club: Liber Scriptorum*. New York: Authors Club, 1893.
Authors' League of America. *The Authors' League of America*. New York: Authors' League of America, 1912.
Bacheller, Irving. *From Stores of Memory*. New York: Farrar and Rinehart, 1938.

Bailyn, Bernard, et al. *The Great Republic*. Boston: Little, Brown, 1978.

Baker, Houston A., Jr. "Figurations for a New American Literary History." In Bercovitch and Jehlen, *Ideology and Classic American Literature*, pp. 145–71.

————. *The Journey Back: Issues in Black Literature and Criticism*. Chicago: University of Chicago Press, 1980.

Ballard, Harlan. "Succesful Authorship." *The Writer* 2 (October 1887): 111–12.

Ballou, Ellen. *The Building of the House: Houghton Mifflin's Formative Years*. Boston: Houghton Mifflin, 1950.

Baran, Paul. *The Longer View*. New York: Monthly Review Press, 1969.

————, and Paul Sweezy. *Monopoly Capital*. New York: Monthly Review Press, 1966.

Bardeen, Charles W. *Authors' Birthdays*. Syracuse: The author, 1899.

Barrows, Charles Mason. *Acts and Anecdotes of Authors: Facts for Every Reader about Prominent American Books, Authors, and Publishers*. Boston: New England Publishing Company, 1887.

Barthes, Roland. *Image-Music-Text: Roland Barthes*. Edited by Stephen Heath. New York: Hill and Wang, 1977.

Bartlett, Irving. *The American Mind in the Mid-Nineteenth Century*. 2d ed. Arlington Heights, Ill.: Harlan Davidson, 1982.

Bassan, Maurice. *Hawthorne's Son: The Life and Literary Career of Julian Hawthorne*. Columbus: Ohio State University Press, 1970.

————. "The Poetaster and the Horse Doctors." *Midcontinent American Studies Journal* 5 (Spring 1964): 56–59.

Becker, George, ed. *Documents of Modern Literary Realism*. Princeton: Princeton University Press, 1963.

Beer, Thomas. *The Mauve Decade: American Life at the End of the Nineteenth Century*. New York: Alfred A. Knopf, 1926.

Bell, Daniel. *Marxian Socialism in the United States*. Princeton: Princeton University Press, 1952.

Bender, Thomas. "The Cultures of Intellectual Life." In Higham and Conkin, *New Directions in American Intellectual History*, pp. 181–95.

Benjamin, Walter. *Illuminations*. New York: Schocken, 1969.

————. *Reflections*. New York: Harcourt Brace Jovanovich, 1978.

Bennet, Maurice. "A Portrait of the Artist in Eighteenth Century America: Charles Brockden Brown's *Memoirs of Stephen Calvert*." *William and Mary Quarterly* 30, no. 3 (July 1982): 492–507.

Bercovitch, Sacvan. "Afterword." In Bercovitch and Jehlen, *Ideology and Classic American Literature*, pp. 418–42.

————, ed. *Reconstructing American Literary History*. Cambridge: Harvard University Press, 1986.

————, and Myra Jehlen, eds. *Ideology and Classic American Literature*. Cambridge: Cambridge University Press, 1986.

Berelson, Bernard. "Who Reads What Books and Why?" In *Mass Culture: The Popular Arts in America*, edited by Bernard Rosenberg and David M. White, pp. 119–25. New York: The Free Press, 1957.

Berg, Scott. *Maxwell Perkins*. New York: Scribner's, 1979.

Berger, John. *Ways of Seeing*. London: Penguin, 1972.

Berger, Morroe. *Real and Imagined Worlds: The Novel and Social Science*. Cambridge: Harvard University Press, 1977.

Berman, Marshall. *All That Is Solid Melts Into Air: The Experience of Modernity*. New York: Simon and Schuster, 1982.

Berthoff, Warner. *The Ferment of Realism: American Literature, 1884–1919*. Cambridge and New York: Cambridge University Press, 1981.

Besant, Walter. *The Art of Fiction*. Boston: Cupples, Upham and Co., 1884.

Blackmur, R. P., ed. *The Art of the Novel*. New York: Charles Scribner's Sons, 1934.

Blair, Hugh. *Lectures on Rhetoric and Belles-Lettres*. Philadelphia: Matthew Carey, 1793.

Bledstein, Burton. *The Culture of Professionalism*. New York: W. W. Norton, 1976.

Bloor, Ella. *Talks about Authors and Their Work*. Chicago: A. Flanagan, 1899.

Bok, Edward. *The Americanization of Edward Bok*. New York: Charles Scribner's Sons, 1920.

Bolton, Sarah K. *Famous American Authors*. New York: T. Y. Crowell, 1887.

Booth, W. S. *A Practical Guide for Authors in Their Relations with Publishers and Printers*. Boston: Houghton Mifflin, 1907.

Boris, Eileen. *Art and Labor*. Philadelphia: Temple University Press, 1986.

Bosanquet, Theodora. *Henry James at Work*. London: Leonard and Virginia Woolf, 1924.

Bourdieu, Pierre. "La production de la croyance: contribution à une économie des biens symboliques:" *Actes de la recherche en sciences sociales* 13 (February 1977): 18–38.

Boyer, Paul. *Purity in Print—The Vice Society Movement and Book Censorship in America*. New York: Charles Scribner's Sons, 1968.

Boyesen, H. H. "Why We Have No Great Novelists." *Forum* 3 (February 1887): 324–43.

Branch, E. Douglas. *The Sentimental Years*. New York: Appleton, 1934.

Braverman, Harry. *Labor and Monopoly Capital: The Degradation of Work in the Twentieth Century*. New York: Monthly Review Press, 1970.

Brenan, Stephen. "The Publication of *Sister Carrie*: Old and New Fictions." *American Literary Realism, 1870–1910* 18 (Spring and Autumn 1985): 55–68.

Britt, George. *Forty Years, Forty Millions: The Career of Frank A. Munsey*. New York: Farrar and Rinehart, 1935.

Brooks, Van Wyck. *The Confident Years, 1885–1915*. New York: E. P. Dutton, 1952.

————. *The Ordeal of Mark Twain*. New York: E. P. Dutton, 1933.

————. *The Times of Melville and Whitman*. New York: E. P. Dutton, 1947.

————. *The World of Washington Irving*. New York: E. P. Dutton, 1944.

Brown, Herbert Ross. *The Sentimental Novel in America, 1789–1860*. Durham, N.C.: Duke University Press, 1940.

Brownson, Orestes. "Address to the United Brothers of Brown University." In *Collected Works*, 19:220–39.

———. *The Collected Works of Orestes Brownson*. Vol. 19. New York: AMS Press, 1966.

———. "Literature, Love, and Marriage." In *Collected Works*, 19:493–576.

Bryce, James. *The American Commonwealth*. New York: Macmillan, 1888.

Buitenhuis, Peter. *The Grasping Imagination: The American Writings of Henry James*. Toronto: University of Toronto Press, 1970.

Burlingame, Roger. *Of Making Many Books: A Hundred Years of Reading and Writing*. New York: Charles Scribner's Sons, 1946.

Cady, Edwin H. *The Gentleman in America: A Literary Study in American Culture*. Syracuse: Syracuse University Press, 1947.

———. *The Light of Common Day: Realism in American Fiction*. Bloomington: Indiana University Press, 1971.

———. *The Realist at War: The Mature Years of William Dean Howells, 1885–1920*. Syracuse: Syracuse University Press, 1958.

———, ed. *The Literature of the Early Republic*. New York: Rinehart, 1950.

Carnegie, Andrew. *The Empire of Business*. New York: Doubleday and Page, 1902.

Carrier, Esther Jane. *Fiction in the Public Libraries, 1876–1900*. New York: Scarecrow Press, 1965.

Carter, Everett. *William Dean Howells and the Age of Realism*. Philadelphia: J. B. Lippincott, 1954.

Carter, Paul. "Mark Twain and the American Labor Movement." *New England Quarterly* 10 (September 1957): 383–88.

———. *The Spiritual Crisis of the Gilded Age*. Normal: Northern Illinois Press, 1971.

"The Cash Author." *Current Literature* 27 (April 1900): 36–37.

The Century. New York: The Century Association, 1947.

Charvat, William. *Literary Publishing in America, 1790–1850*. Philadelphia: University of Pennsylvania Press, 1959.

———. *The Profession of Authorship in America, 1800–1870*. Edited by Matthew J. Bruccoli. Columbus: Ohio State University Press, 1968.

Chase, Richard. *The American Novel and Its Tradition*. Baltimore: The Johns Hopkins University Press, 1957.

Chevalier, Michael. *Society, Manners, and Politics in the United States*. 1838. Reprinted. New York: Doubleday, 1961.

Chews, Frederick. *Fruit among the Leaves*. New York: Appleton, 1950.

Cole, John, and Carol Gold, eds. *Reading in America, 1978*. Washington, D.C.: Library of Congress, 1979.

Commager, Henry Steele. *The American Mind*. New Haven: Yale University Press, 1949.

Cooley, Charles Horton. *Human Nature and the Social Order*. New York: Charles Scribner's Sons, 1902.

———. *Social Organization*. New York: Charles Scribner's Sons, 1909.

Cooper, James Fenimore. *Notions of the Americans*. Philadelphia: Carey and Lea, 1828.

Cooper, John Milton. *Walter Hines Page: The Southerner as American*. Chapel

Hill: University of North Carolina Press, 1977.

Coser, Lewis, Charles Kadushin, and Walter Powell. *Books: The Commerce and Culture of Publishing*. New York: Basic, 1982.

Cowie, Alexander. *The Rise of the American Novel*. New York: The American Book Company, 1948.

Cowley, Malcolm. *And I Worked at the Writer's Trade: Chapters of Literary History, 1918–1978*. New York: Viking Press, 1978.

———. "A Natural History of American Naturalism." In Becker, *Documents of Modern Literary Realism*, pp. 429–51.

Crane, Stephen. *The Letters of Stephen Crane*. Edited by R. H. Stallman and Lillian Gilkes. New York: New York University Press, 1971.

Crawford, Francis Marion. *The Novel: What It Is*. New York: Macmillan, 1893.

Crèvecoeur, Michel-Guillaume-Jean de. *Letters from an American Farmer*. Philadelphia: Matthew Carey, 1782.

Crothers, Samuel McChord. "The Gentle Reader." *Atlantic Monthly* 86 (November 1900): 654–63.

Croy, Homer. *88 Ways to Make Money by Writing*. New York: The Editor Company, 1917.

Darnton, Robert. "Intellectual and Cultural History." In *The Past before Us*, edited by Michael Kammen, pp. 327–49. Ithaca, N.Y.: Cornell University Press, 1980.

Davidson, Cathy. *The Revolution and the Word: The Rise of the Novel in America*. New York: Oxford University Press, 1988.

Davis, Mike. "Why the U.S. Working Class Is Different." *New Left Review* 123 (September–October 1980): 3–44.

DeForest, John. "The Great American Novel." *The Nation*, January 1868, 27–29.

Denning, Michael. *Mechanic Accents: Dime Novels and Working-Class Culture in America*. London: Verso, 1987.

Derby, James C. *Fifty Years among Authors, Books and Publishers*. Hartford: M. A. Winter and Hatch, 1880.

Dodd, Edward. *The First Hundred Years: A History of the House of Dodd, Mead, 1839–1939*. New York: Dodd, Mead, 1939.

Doran, George. *The Chronicles of Barabbas*. New York: Holt, Rinehart and Winston, 1935.

Dorfman, Joseph. "Joel Barlow: Trafficker in Trade and Letters." *Political Science Quarterly* 59 (March 1944): 83–100.

Douglas, Ann. *The Feminization of American Culture*. New York: Alfred A. Knopf, 1977.

Dreiser, Theodore. "As a Realist Sees It." *New Republic* 5 (25 December 1915): 202–4.

———. *A Book about Myself: Newspaper Days*. New York: Boni and Liveright, 1922.

———. *Dawn*. New York: Boni and Liveright, 1922.

———. *Sister Carrie*. 1900. Reprinted. New York: Signet, 1961.

———. "True Art Speaks Plainly." *Booklover's Magazine* 1 (February 1903): 129.

Duycinck, Everett, ed. *Cyclopedia of American Literature*. New York: Harper and Brothers, 1855.

Eagleton, Terry. *Criticism and Ideology*. London: Verso, 1980.

———. *Literary Theory*. Minneapolis: University of Minnesota Press, 1983.

Edel, Leon. *Henry James*. Vol. 1, *The Untried Years: 1843–1870*. Vol. 2, *The Conquest of London: 1870–1881*. Vol. 3, *The Middle Years: 1882–1895*. Vol. 4, *The Treacherous Years: 1895–1901*. Vol. 5, *The Master: 1901–1916*. New York: Avon, 1953–72.

The Editor: 1001 Places to sell Mss: A Complete and Exhaustive Study of the Market for the Miscellaneous Contributor to the Press. New York: The Editor, 1905.

Eggleston, George Cary. "The Literary Disadvantages of Being Born Too Late." In *Liber Scriptorum*, pp. 214–18. New York: Authors Club, 1893.

———. *Recollections of a Varied Life*. New York: Henry Holt, 1910.

Elliott, Emory, et al., eds. *The Columbia Literary History of the United States*. New York: Columbia University Press, 1988.

Ellsworth, W. W. *The Golden Age of Authors*. New York: Century, 1921.

Emerson, Ralph Waldo. "The American Scholar." In *Selected Writings of Ralph Waldo Emerson*, edited by William H. Gilman, pp. 223–40. New York: Signet, 1965.

———. "Nature." In *Selected Writings*, pp. 186–222.

———. "The Poet." In *Selected Writings*, pp. 306–26.

Ewen, Stuart. *Captains of Consciousness: Advertising and the Social Roots of the Consumer Culture*. New York: McGraw-Hill, 1976.

Exman, Eugene. *The House of Harper*. New York: Harper and Row, 1967.

Febvre, Lucien. *The Coming of the Book*. 1956. Reprinted. London: Verso, 1984.

Ferguson, Robert. " 'We Hold These Truths': Strategies of Control in the Literature of the Founders." In Bercovitch, *Reconstructing American Literary History*, pp. 1–28.

Fields, Annie. *Authors and Friends*. Boston: Houghton Mifflin, 1897.

Fisher, Phillip. "Appearing and Disappearing in Public: Social Space in Late-Nineteenth-Century Literature and Culture." In Bercovitch, *Reconstructing American Literary History*, pp. 155–88.

———. *Hard Facts: Setting and Form in the American Novel*. New York: Oxford University Press, 1985.

Fletcher, William I. *Public Libraries in America*. Boston: Robert Brothers, 1895.

Foner, Eric. *Free Soil, Free Labor, Free Men: The Ideology of the Republican Party before the Civil War*. New York: Oxford University Press, 1970.

Ford, James Lauren. *The Literary Shop and Other Tales*. New York: G. H. Richmond, 1893.

Fortenberry, George, Stanton Garner, and Robert H. Woodward, eds. *The Correspondence of Harold Frederic*. Fort Worth: Texas Christian University Press, 1977.

Fowie, A. A. "How to Get in Print." *The Writer* 1 (April 1887): 9.

Fox, Harold. "William Dean Howells: The Literary Theories in *Criticism and Fiction* and Their Applications of 1886 and 1887." Ph.D. dissertation, University of Southern California, 1969.

Fox, Richard Wightman, and T. J. Jackson Lears, eds. *The Culture of Consumption*. New York: Pantheon, 1983.

Franchere, Hoyt C., and Thomas F. O'Donnell. *Harold Frederic*. New Haven: Twayne, 1961.

Freneau, Philip. "Literary Importation." In *The Poems of Philip Freneau*, edited by Frederic Lewis Pattee, 2:303. Princeton: Princeton University Press, 1907.

Friere, Paulo. *Cultural Action for Freedom*. Harvard Educational Monograph Series. Cambridge: Harvard University Press, 1970.

Furner, Mary. *Advocacy and Objectivity: A Crisis in the Professionalization of American Social Science, 1865–1905*. Lexington: University Press of Kentucky, 1975.

Garland, Hamlin. *Crumbling Idols: Twelve Essays on Art and Literature*. Chicago: Stone and Kimball, 1894.

Garnett, A. "How to Write Short Stories." *The Writer* 3 (April 1888): 86–87.

Garraty, John. *The New Commonwealth*. New York: Harper and Row, 1968.

Garrison, Dee. *The Apostles of Culture: The Public Library and American Society, 1876–1920*. New York: The Free Press, 1979.

Geismar, Maxwell. *Rebels and Ancestors: The American Novel, 1890–1915*. Boston: Houghton Mifflin, 1953.

Gibson, William. "Mark Twain and William Dean Howells: Anti-Imperialists." Ph.D. dissertation, University of Chicago, 1940.

Gilder, Jeanette L. and Joseph B. Gilder. *Authors at Home*. New York: Cassell, 1888.

Gilmore, Michael. *American Romanticism and the Marketplace*. Chicago: University of Chicago Press, 1985.

Ginger, Ray. *The Age of Excess: The United States from 1877 to 1914*. New York: Macmillan, 1965.

Gissing, George. *New Grub Street*. 1891. Reprinted. New York: Penguin Books, 1976.

Goldman, Laurel. "A Different View of the 'Iron Madonna': William Dean Howells and His Magazine Readers." *New England Quarterly* 50, no. 4 (1977): 563–86.

Goldman, Lucien. *Essays on Method of the Sociology of Literature*. St. Louis: Telos Press, 1980.

Goode, John. "The Art of Fiction: Walter Besant and Henry James." In *Tradition and Tolerance in Nineteenth Century Fiction*. London: Routledge and Kegan Paul, 1966.

Goodrich, Samuel G. *Recollections of a Lifetime, or Men and Things I Have Seen in a Series of Familiar Letters to a Friend Historical, Biographical, Anecdotal, and Descriptive*. New York and Auburn: Miller, Orton, and Mulligan, 1856.

Goody, Jack, and Ian Watt. "The Consequences of Literacy." In *Literacy in Traditional Societies*, edited by Jack Goody, pp. 27–68. Cambridge: Cambridge University Press, 1968.

Gosse, Edmund. "The Limits of Realism in Fiction." *The Forum* 4 (June 1890): 391–400.

Gow, Alexander. *Good Morals and Gentle Manners for School and Families*. New York: American Book Company, 1901.

Green, Martin. *The Problem of Boston*. New York: W. W. Norton, 1967.

Green, Samuel Swett. *The Public Library Movement in the United States, 1853–1893*. Boston: The Boston Book Company, 1913.

————. "Sensational Fiction in Public Libraries." *Library Journal* 4 (September–October 1879): 347–49.

Griswold, Hattie. *Home Life of Great Authors*. Chicago: McClurg, 1887.

Gross, Gerald, ed. *Publishers on Publishing*. New York: R. R. Bowker Company and Grosset and Dunlap, 1961.

Habegger, Alfred. *Gender, Fantasy, and Realism in American Literature*. New York: Columbia University Press, 1982.

Hackett, Alice P. *Seventy Years of Best Sellers*. New York: R. R. Bowker, 1968.

Hall, David. "The World of Print and Collective Mentality in Seventeenth-Century New England." In Higham and Conkin, *New Directions in American Intellectual History*, pp. 166–80.

Halsey, Francis Whiting, ed. *American Authors and Their Homes: Personal Descriptions and Interviews*. New York: James Pott, 1901.

Hamilton, Clayton. *Materials and Methods of Fiction*. New York: The Baker and Taylor Company, 1908.

Hamsun, Knut. *The Cultural Life of Modern America*. Cambridge: Harvard University Press, Belknap Press, 1959.

Hanscom, A. L. "Method Needed in Literary Work." *The Writer* 3 (April 1888): 84.

Harkins, E. F. *Little Pilgrimages among the Men Who Have Written Famous Books*. Boston: L. C. Page, 1902.

Harper, Joseph Henry. *The House of Harper*. New York: Harper and Brothers, 1912.

Harris, Neil. *The Artist in American Society: The Formative Years, 1790–1860*. 1959. Reprinted. New York: Simon and Schuster, 1976.

Harris, Richard. "A Young Dramatist's Diary: The Secret Records of R. M. Bird." *University of Pennsylvania Library Chronicle* 25 (Winter 1959): 15–28.

Hart, James. *The Popular Book: A History of American Literary Taste*. New York: Oxford University Press, 1950.

Haskell, Thomas. *The Emergence of Professional Social Science: The American Social Science Association and the Nineteenth Century Crisis of Authority*. Urbana: University of Illinois Press, 1977.

Hauser, Arnold. *The Social History of Art*. New York: Alfred A. Knopf, 1954.

Hawthorne, Nathaniel. *Passages from the American Notebooks*. Boston: Houghton Mifflin, 1909.

————. *The Scarlet Letter*. New York: Bantam Books, 1965.

Hays, Samuel. *The Response to Industrialism, 1885–1914*. Chicago: University of Chicago Press, 1957.

Heiserman, Arthur. *The Novel before the Novel*. Chicago: University of Chicago Press, 1977.

Henry, Jules. *Culture against Men*. New York: Vintage Books, 1965.

Hepburn, James. *The Author's Empty Purse and the Rise of the Literary Agent*.

London: Oxford University Press, 1968.

Hicks, Granville. *The Great Tradition*. New York: Macmillan, 1933.

Higginson, Thomas Wentworth. *Cheerful Yesterdays*. Boston: Houghton Mifflin, 1898.

Higham, John. "Introduction." In Higham and Conkin, *New Directions in American Intellectual History*, pp. xi–xix.

―――. "The Re-Orientation of American Culture in the 1890s." In *Writing American History*, pp. 73–102. Bloomington: Indiana University Press, 1973.

―――, and Paul Conkin, eds. *New Directions in American Intellectual History*. Baltimore: The Johns Hopkins University Press.

Historical Statistics of the United States from Colonial Times to 1957. Washington, D.C., 1960.

Hochman, Barbara. *Frank Norris: Storyteller*. Columbia: University of Missouri Press, 1988.

Hoffman, Frederick. *The Modern Novel in America, 1900–1950*. New York: Regnery, 1951.

Hofstader, Richard. *The Age of Reform*. New York: Alfred A. Knopf, 1955.

―――. *Anti-Intellectualism in American Life*. New York: Vintage, 1964.

Holt, Henry. "The Commercialization of Literature." *Atlantic Monthly* 96 (November 1905): 577–600.

―――. *Garrulities of an Octogenerian Editor*. Boston: Houghton Mifflin, 1923.

Horkheimer, Max. "Art and Mass Culture." *Studies in Philosophy and Social Science* 9 (1941): 290–304.

―――, and Theodor W. Adorno. *The Dialectic of Enlightenment*. New York: Herder and Herder, 1972.

Howe, M. A. Dewolfe. *American Bookmen: Sketches, Chiefly Biographical, of Certain Writers of the Nineteenth Century*. New York: Dodd, Mead, 1898.

Howells, William Dean. "American Literary Centres." In *Literature and Life*, pp. 173–86.

―――. "American Literature in Exile." In *Literature and Life*, pp. 202–5.

―――. *Annie Kilburn*. New York: Harper and Brothers, 1889.

―――. "Are We a Plutocracy?" *North American Review*, February 1894, 185–96.

―――. "The Art of the Adsmith." In *Literature and Life*, pp. 265–72.

―――. *The Coast of Bohemia*. New York: Harper and Brothers, 1894.

―――. *Criticism and Fiction*. 1891. Reprinted. New York: Hill and Wang, 1967.

―――. "The Editor's Relations with the Young Contributor." In *Literature and Life*, pp. 63–77.

―――. "Emile Zola." In *W. D. Howells as Critic*, pp. 386–95.

―――. "Fears Realists Must Wait." Interview with Stephen Crane. *New York Times*, 28 October 1894, 20.

―――. *Five Interviews with William Dean Howells*. Edited by George Arms and William Gibson. New York: New York Public Library Pamphlets, 1950.

―――. *A Foregone Conclusion*. Boston: James Osgood, 1875.

―――. "Frank Norris." In *W. D. Howells as Critic*, pp. 396–405.

_____. *A Hazard of New Fortunes*. 1890. Reprinted. New York: Signet, 1965.
_____. "Henry James, Jr." In *W. D. Howells as Critic*, pp. 59–72.
_____. *Indian Summer*. Boston: Ticknor and Fields, 1886.
_____. *Life in Letters of William Dean Howells*. Edited by Mildred Howells. 2 vols. Garden City, N.Y.: Doubleday, 1928.
_____. *Literary Friends and Acquaintances*. New York: Harper and Brothers, 1900.
_____. *Literature and Life*. New York: Harper and Brothers, 1902.
_____. "The Man of Letters as a Man of Business." In *Literature and Life*, pp. 1–35.
_____. *The Minister's Charge*. Boston: Ticknor and Fields, 1887.
_____. "Mr. Charles W. Chesnutt's Stories." In *W. D. Howells as Critic*, pp. 295–98.
_____. *A Modern Instance*. 1882. Reprinted. New York: Penguin, 1983.
_____. *My Literary Passions*. New York: Harper and Brothers, 1895.
_____. *My Mark Twain*. New York: Harper and Brothers, 1910.
_____. "Neo-romanticism, Imperialism and Taste." In *W. D. Howells as Critic*, pp. 352–60.
_____. "The New Historical Romances." In *W. D. Howells as Critic*, pp. 299–313.
_____. "New York Low Life in Fiction." In *W. D. Howells as Critic*, pp. 256–62.
_____. "Novel-Writing and Novel-Reading." In *Howells and James: A Double Billing*, pp. 7–24. New York: New York Public Library Pamphlets, 1958.
_____. "Of Originality and Imitation." In *W. D. Howells as Critic*, pp. 446–51.
_____. "An Opportunity for American Fiction" [Thorstein Veblen]. In *W. D. Howells as Critic*, pp. 286–91.
_____. "A Painful Subject." *Harper's Weekly*, 9 January 1904, 48.
_____. "The Politics of American Authors." In *Literature and Life*, pp. 290–97.
_____. "Professor Barrett Wendell's Notions of American Literature." In *W. D. Howells as Critic*, pp. 361–78.
_____. *The Rise of Silas Lapham*. 1884. Reprinted. New York: Signet, 1968.
_____. "Spanish Prisoners of War." In *Literature and Life*, pp. 141–53.
_____. *Through the Eye of a Needle*. New York: Harper and Brothers, 1907.
_____. *A Traveller from Altruria*. New York: Harper and Brothers, 1894.
_____. *W. D. Howells as Critic*. Edited by Edwin Cady. London: Routledge and Kegan Paul, 1973.
_____. "The What and the How in Art." In *Literature and Life*, pp. 284–89.
Hubbel, Jay. *Who Are the Major American Writers?* Durham, N.C.: Duke University Press, 1972.
Hughes, H. Stuart. *Consciousness and Society: The Reorientation of European Social Thought, 1890–1930*. New York: Random House, 1958.
Hutton, Laurence. *Talks in a Library*. New York: G. P. Putnam's Sons, 1909.
"Interview with E. P. Roe." *Detroit News*, 23 August 1886.
Iser, Wolfgang. *The Implied Reader*. Baltimore: The Johns Hopkins University Press, 1974.

Jacobsen, Paul. *American Marriage and Divorce*. New York: Holt, Rinehart and Winston, 1959.

Jacobson, Marcia. *Henry James and the Mass Market*. University, Ala.: University of Alabama Press, 1983.

Jacox, Francis. *The Literary Life, or Aspects of Authorship*. New York: Anson, D. F. Randolph, 1913.

Jaher, Frederic. "The Boston Brahmins in the Age of Industrial Capitalism." In Morgan, *The Gilded Age*, pp. 188–262.

James, Henry. "Alphonse Daudet." In *Partial Portraits*, pp. 195–242.

———. *The American*. 1877. Reprinted. Boston: Houghton Mifflin, 1962.

———. *The American Scene*. 1907. Reprinted. Bloomington: Indiana University Press, 1968.

———. "Anthony Trollope." In *Partial Portraits*, pp. 97–136.

———. "The Art of Fiction." In *Theory of Fiction: Henry James*, pp. 27–44.

———. *The Bostonians*. 1886. Reprinted. New York: Penguin Books, 1981.

———. "Charles de Bernard and Gustave Flaubert." *The Galaxy* 21 (February 1876): 219–33.

———. "Charles Nordhoff's Communistic Societies." *The Nation*, 21 June 1874, 259–66.

———. *Daisy Miller*. New York: Harper and Brothers, 1879.

———. "Emile Zola." *Atlantic Monthly* 91 (August 1903): 193–210.

———. "The Future of the Novel." 1899. In *Theory of Fiction: Henry James*, pp. 335–44.

———. "Gustave Flaubert." *Macmillan's Magazine* 67 (March 1893): 332–43.

———. *Henry James Letters*. Edited by Leon Edel. 4 vols. Cambridge: Harvard University Press, Belknap Press, 1974–84.

———. *Henry James: Literary Reviews and Essays*. Edited by Albert Mordell. New York: Grove Press, 1958.

———. "Honoré de Balzac." *The Galaxy* 20 (December 1875): 814–36.

———. "Ivan Turgenieff." In *Partial Portraits*, 291–326.

———. "The Lesson of Balzac." *Atlantic Monthly* 96 (August 1905): 166–80.

———. *The Letters of Henry James*. Edited by Percy Lubbock. 2 vols. New York: Charles Scribner's Sons, 1920.

———. "London Notes." *Harper's Weekly* 41 (31 July 1897): 754.

———. *The Notebooks of Henry James*. Edited by F. O. Matthiessen and K. B. Murdock. New York: Oxford University Press, 1947.

———. *Notes on Novelists*. London: J. M. Dent and Sons, 1914.

———. "The Novels of George Eliot." *Atlantic Monthly* 18 (October 1886): 479–92.

———. *Partial Portraits*. 1888. Reprinted. Ann Arbor: University of Michigan Press, 1970.

———. *The Portrait of a Lady*. 1884. Reprinted as vol. 3 of *The Collected Novels of Henry James*. New York: Charles Scribner's Sons, 1908.

———. "Preface to *The Portrait of a Lady*." In Blackmur, *The Art of the Novel*, pp. 40–58.

———. "Preface to *The Tragic Muse*." In Blackmur, *The Art of the Novel*, pp. 79–97.

_____. *The Princess Casamassima*. 1886. Reprinted. New York: Thomas Y. Crowell, 1976.

_____. *The Spoils of Poynton*. 1897. Reprinted. New York: Penguin Books, 1981.

_____. *Theory of Fiction: Henry James*. Edited by James Miller. Lincoln: University of Nebraska Press, 1972.

_____. "William Dean Howells." *Harper's Weekly* 30 (19 June 1886): 394–95.

James, Louis. *Fiction for the Working Man, 1830–1850*. London: Longmans, 1963.

Jameson, Fredric. *Marxism and Form*. Princeton: Princeton University Press, 1971.

_____. *The Political Unconscious: Narrative as a Socially Symbolic Act*. Ithaca, N.Y.: Cornell University Press, 1981.

_____. "Reification and Utopia in Mass Culture." *Social Text* 1 (1979): 130–48.

Jefferson, Thomas. *Notes on the State of Virginia*. Edited with an introduction and notes by William Peden. Chapel Hill: University of North Carolina Press, 1955.

_____. *The Papers of Thomas Jefferson*. Vol. 1. Edited by Julian Boyd. Princeton: Princeton University Press, 1950.

_____. "Report of the Commissioners for the University of Virginia." In *The Portable Thomas Jefferson*, edited with an introduction by Merril D. Peterson, pp. 332–46. New York: Viking Press, 1975.

_____. *The Writings of Thomas Jefferson*. Vol. 15. Edited by A. A. Lipscomb and A. E. Bergh. Washington, D.C.: Thomas Jefferson Memorial Association, 1903.

Jehlen, Myra. "The Novel and the Middle Class in America." In Bercovitch and Jehlen, *Ideology and Classic American Literature*, pp. 124–44.

Johnson, Robert Underwood. *Remembered Yesterdays*. Boston: Little, Brown, 1927.

Jones, Howard Mumford. *The Age of Energy*. New York: Viking Press, 1971.

_____. *The Theory of American Literature*. Ithaca, N.Y.: Cornell University Press, 1965.

Kaplan, Justin. *Mr. Clemens and Mark Twain*. New York: Simon and Schuster, 1966.

Kaser, David, ed. *Books in America's Past: Essays Honoring Rudolph H. Gjelsness*. Charlottesville: University Press of Virginia, 1966.

Kazin, Alfred. *On Native Grounds*. New York: Harcourt Brace Jovanovich, 1983.

Keller, Morton. *Affairs of State: Public Life in Late Nineteenth Century America*. Cambridge: Harvard University Press, 1971.

Kett, Joseph F. and Patricia A. McClung. "Book Culture in Post-Revolutionary Virginia." *Proceedings of the American Antiquarian Association* 95, part 1 (April 1984): 97–147.

Kilgour, Raymond. *Estes and Lauriat: A History, 1872–1898*. Ann Arbor: University of Michigan Press, 1957.

Kindilien, Carlin T. *American Poetry in the Eighteen-Nineties*. Providence, R.I.: Brown University Press, 1956.

Kipling, Rudyard. *American Notes*. New York: Standard Book Company, 1930.

Kirk, Clara. *William Dean Howells, Traveller From Altruria*. New Brunswick, N.J.: Rutgers University Press, 1962.

Kirkland, Edward. *Dream and Thought in the Business Community, 1860–1900*. Chicago: Quadrangle, 1964.

Kolb, Harold. *The Illusion of Life*. Charlottesville: University Press of Virginia, 1969.

Kolko, Gabriel. *The Triumph of Conservatism: A Reinterpretation of American History*. New York: The Free Press, 1963.

Kraft, Stephanie. *No Castles on Main Street: American Authors and Their Homes*. New York: Rand-McNally, 1979.

Kuklick, Bruce. *The Rise of American Philosophy: Cambridge, Massachusetts, 1860–1930*. New Haven: Yale University Press, 1977.

Kunitz, Stanley Jasspon. *American Authors, 1600–1900*. New York: H. W. Wilson, 1938.

LaCapra, Dominic. *History and Criticism*. Ithaca, N.Y.: Cornell University Press, 1985.

Lasch, Christopher. *The Culture of Narcissism: American Life in an Age of Diminishing Expectations*. New York: W. W. Norton, 1979.

――――. "Mass Culture Reconsidered." *Democracy* 1 (October 1981): 7–22.

Lathrop, George Parsons. "The Literary Movement In New York." *Harper's Monthly* 73 (November 1886): 811–26.

――――. "The Novel and Its Future." *Harper's Monthly* 49 (September 1874): 313–24.

Laughlin, Clara. *Stories of Authors' Loves*. Philadelphia: J. B. Lippincott, 1902.

Lears, T. J. Jackson. *No Place of Grace: Antimodernism and the Transformation of American Culture, 1880–1920*. New York: Pantheon, 1981.

Leavis, F. R. *The Great Tradition: George Eliot, Henry James, Joseph Conrad*. New York: G. W. Stewart, 1948.

Lee, Gerald Stanley. *The Lost Art of Reading*. New York: G. P. Putnam's Sons, 1902.

Leiss, William. *The Limits of Satisfaction*. Toronto: University of Toronto Press, 1976.

Levine, Laurence. "William Shakespeare and the American People: A Study in Cultural Transformation." *American Historical Review* 89 (February 1984): 34–66.

Lichtenstein, Nelson. "Authorial Professionalism and the Literary Marketplace, 1885–1920." *American Studies* 9 (Spring 1978): 35–53.

Lloyd, Henry Demarest. *Wealth against Commonwealth*. Englewood Cliffs, N.J.: Prentice-Hall, 1963.

London, Jack. *Martin Eden*. New York: Macmillan, 1909.

Long, C. L. *Wages and Earnings in the United States: 1860–1890*. Princeton: Princeton University Press, 1960.

Lowenthal, Leo. *Literature, Popular Culture, and Society*. Englewood Cliffs, N.J.: Prentice-Hall, 1961.

Luce, Robert. "Three Pointers for Novices." *The Writer* 1 (May 1887): 31.

Lukács, Georg. *Studies in European Realism*. Cambridge: MIT Press, 1956.

――――. *The Theory of the Novel*. Cambridge: MIT Press, 1971.

Lynn, Kenneth. *William Dean Howells: An American Life*. New York: Harcourt Brace Jovanovich, 1971.

Lyon, Peter. *Success Story: Thē Life and Times of S. S. McClure*. New York: Charles Scribner's Sons, 1963.

Mabie, Hamilton Wright. "A Typical Novel." *Andover Review* 4 (November 1885): 417–29.

McClure, S. S. *The Autobiography of S. S. McClure*. New York: Frederick Stokes, 1914.

McCormick, Richard. *The Second American Party System: Party Formation in the Jacksonian Era*. Chapel Hill: University of North Carolina Press, 1966.

Macdonald, Dwight. *Against the American Grain*. New York: Random House, 1962.

———. "A Theory of Popular Culture." *Politics* 2 (February 1944): 20–23.

McKay, Janet H. *Narration and Discourse in American Realistic Fiction*. Philadelphia: University of Pennsylvania Press, 1982.

McKelvey, Blake. *The Urbanization of America, 1865–1910*. New Brunswick, N.J.: Rutgers University Press, 1963.

McMahon, Helen. *Criticism of Fiction: A Study of Trends in the Atlantic Monthly, 1857–1898*. New York: Bookman Associates, 1952.

Madison, Charles. *Book Publishing in America*. New York: McGraw-Hill, 1968.

———. *From Irving to Irving: Author-Publisher Relations, 1800–1974*. New York: R. R. Bowker, 1974.

———. *The Owl among the Colophons: Henry Holt as Publisher and Editor*. New York: Holt, Rinehart and Winston, 1966.

Mallock, W. H. "The Relation of Art to Truth." *Forum* 9 (March 1890): 36–46.

Manley, Lawrence. *Convention, 1500–1700*. Cambridge: Harvard University Press, 1980.

Martin, Jay. *Harvests of Change: American Literature, 1865–1914*. Englewood Cliffs, N.J.: Prentice-Hall, 1967.

Marx, Karl. *The Grundrisse*. New York: Vintage, 1974.

Marx, Leo. *The Machine in the Garden: Technology and the Pastoral Ideal in America*. New York: Oxford University Press, 1964.

Matthews, Brander. *Americanisms and Briticisms*. New York: Harper and Brothers, 1892.

———. *Aspects of Fiction and Other Ventures in Criticism*. New York: Harper and Brothers, 1896.

———. *These Many Years: Recollections of a New Yorker*. New York: Charles Scribner's Sons, 1917.

May, Henry F. *The End of American Innocence: The First Years of Our Own Time, 1912–1917*. New York: Oxford University Press, 1970.

———. *Protestant Churches and Industrial America*. New York: Harper and Brothers, 1949.

Mead, George. "Cooley's Contribution to American Social Thought." *American Journal of Sociology* 35 (1930): 693–706. Reprinted in Cooley, *Human Nature and Social Order*, pp. iv–xxxi.

Mellow, James R. *Nathaniel Hawthorne in His Times*. Boston: Houghton Mifflin, 1980.

Melville, Herman. *Pierre, Or the Ambiguities*. New York: Signet, 1964.

Michaels, Walter Benn. "Corporate Fiction: Norris, Royce, and Arthur Machen."
In Bercovitch, *Reconstructing American Literary History*, pp. 220–49.
_____. *The Gold Standard and the Logic of Naturalism*. Berkeley and Los An-
geles: University of California Press, 1987.
_____. "The Gold Standard and the Logic of Naturalism." In *The Gold Stan-
dard and the Logic of Naturalism*, pp. 137–80.
_____. "Introduction: The Writer's Mark." In *The Gold Standard and the Logic
of Naturalism*, pp. 1–28.
_____. "Sister Carrie's Popular Economy." In *The Gold Standard and the Logic
of Naturalism*, pp. 29–58.
Miller, Perry, ed. *American Thought: Civil War to World War I*. San Francisco:
Rinehart, 1954.
_____. *The Raven and the Whale*. New York: Harcourt Brace, 1956.
Miller, William. *The American Book Industry*. New York: Columbia University
Press, 1949.
Milowski, Raymond. "William Dean Howells' Golden Age: The Importance of
Art and Middle Class Ideals to the American Republic." Ph.D. dissertation,
University of Minnesota, 1971.
Mitchell, Edward P. *Memories of an Editor: Fifty Years of American Journalism*.
New York: Charles Scribner's Sons, 1924.
Mitchell, Lee. "Naturalism and the Languages of Determinism." In Elliott et al.,
The Columbia Literary History, pp. 524–49.
Mizruchi, Susan. *The Power of Historical Knowledge: Narrating the Past in
Hawthorne, James, and Dreiser*. Princeton: Princeton University Press, 1988.
Montgomery, David. *Beyond Equality: Labor and the Radical Republicans,
1862–1872*. New York: Vintage Books, Alfred A. Knopf, 1968.
_____. *Workers' Control in America: Studies in the History of Work, Tech-
nology, and Labor Struggles*. Cambridge: Cambridge University Press, 1979.
Morgan, H. Wayne. *American Writers in Rebellion*. New York: Hill and Wang,
1965.
_____. *Victorian Culture in America, 1865–1914*. Itasca, Ill.: F. E. Peacock
Publishers, 1973.
_____, ed. *The Gilded Age: A Reappraisal*. Syracuse: Syracuse University
Press, 1963.
Mott, Frank Luther. *Golden Multitudes*. New York: Macmillan, 1947.
_____. *A History of American Magazines*. Cambridge: Harvard University
Press, Belknap Press, 1939.
Neal, John. *American Writers—A Series of Papers Contributed to Blackwood's
Magazine (1824–5)*. Edited with an Introduction by Frederic Lewis Pattee.
Durham, N.C.: Duke University Press, 1937.
Nicolay, Helen. *Sixty Years of the Literary Society*. Washington, D.C.: Privately
printed, 1934.
Noble, David. *The Paradox of Progressive Thought*. Minneapolis: University of
Minnesota Press, 1958.
Nochlin, Linda. *Realism*. New York: Penguin Books, 1972.
Noel, Mary. *Villains Galore*. New York: Harper and Brothers, 1954.
Norris, Frank. "The American Public and 'Popular' Fiction." In *The Responsi-
bilities of the Novelist*, pp. 235–37.

_____. "An American School of Fiction?" In *The Responsibilities of the Novelist*, pp. 270–74.

_____. "Fiction Writing as a Business." In *The Responsibilities of the Novelist*, pp. 255–59.

_____. "The Frontier Gone at Last." In *The Responsibilities of the Novelist*, pp. 221–27.

_____. "The Great American Novelist." In *The Responsibilities of the Novelist*, pp. 228–30.

_____. *The Letters of Frank Norris*. Edited by Franklin Walker. San Francisco: The Book Club of California, 1956.

_____. *McTeague*. 1899. Reprinted. New York: Signet, 1964.

_____. "The Mechanics of Fiction." In *The Responsibilities of the Novelist*, pp. 251–55.

_____. "The Need of a Literary Conscience." In *The Responsibilities of the Novelist*, pp. 213–16.

_____. "Newspaper Criticisms and American Fiction." In *The Responsibilities of the Novelist*, pp. 241–43.

_____. "New York as a Literary Centre." In *The Responsibilities of the Novelist*, pp. 231–34.

_____. "Novelists of the Future." In *The Responsibilities of the Novelist*, pp. 275–78.

_____. "Novelists to Order—While You Wait." In *The Responsibilities of the Novelist*, pp. 244–47.

_____. "The Novel with a 'Purpose.' " In *The Responsibilities of the Novelist*, pp. 203–7.

_____. *The Octopus*. 1901. Reprinted. New York: Signet, 1964.

_____. *The Pit*. 1903. Reprinted. Columbus: Bobbs-Merrill, 1970.

_____. "A Plea for Romantic Fiction." In *The Responsibilities of the Novelist*, pp. 279–82.

_____. "A Problem in Fiction." In *The Responsibilities of the Novelist*, pp. 283–85.

_____. "The Responsibilities of the Novelist." In *The Responsibilities of the Novelist*, pp. 193–97.

_____. *The Responsibilities of the Novelist*. 1903. Reprinted. New York: Hill and Wang, 1967.

_____. "Retail Bookseller: Literary Dictator." In *The Responsibilities of the Novelist*, pp. 266–69.

_____. "Salt and Sincerity." In *The Responsibilities of the Novelist*, pp. 294–320.

_____. "Simplicity in Art." In *The Responsibilities of the Novelist*, pp. 290–93.

_____. "Story-Tellers vs. Novelists." In *The Responsibilities of the Novelist*, pp. 208–12.

_____. "The True Reward of the Novelist." In *The Responsibilities of the Novelist*, pp. 198–202.

_____. "The 'Volunteer Manuscript.' " In *The Responsibilities of the Novelist*, pp. 260–65.

_____. "Why Women Should Write the Best Novels." In *The Responsibilities of the Novelist*, pp. 286–89.

"Novels: Their Meaning and Mission." *Putnam's* 4 (October 1854): 389–96.

Nye, Russel. *Society and Culture in America, 1830–1860*. New York: Harper and Row, 1974.

———. *The Unembarrassed Muse: The Popular Arts in America*. New York: The Dial Press, 1970.

Osborne, Duffield. *The Authors Club: A Historical Sketch*. New York: The Knickerbocker Press, 1913.

Overton, Grant. *The Philosophy of Fiction*. New York: D. Appleton, 1928.

———. *Portrait of a Publisher*. New York: D. Appleton, 1924.

Page, Walter Hines. *A Publisher's Confession*. Garden City, N.Y.: Doubleday and Page, 1905.

———. "The Writer and the University." *Atlantic Monthly* 99 (November 1907): 685–95.

Parrington, Vernon Louis. *The Beginnings of Critical Realism in America*. New York: Harcourt Brace Jovanovich, 1930.

Parry, Albert. *Garrets and Pretenders: A History of Bohemianism in America*. New York: Covici and Friede, 1960.

Pattee, Frederic Lewis. *The Feminine Fifties*. New York: Harper and Brothers, 1924.

———. *A History of American Literature since 1870*. New York: The Century Company, 1917.

Perry, Bliss. "On Reading the *Atlantic* Cheerfully." *Atlantic Monthly* 89 (January 1902): 1–4.

———. *A Study of Prose Fiction*. Boston: Houghton Mifflin, 1902.

Perry, T. S. "American Novels." *North American Review* 115 (October 1872): 366–78.

Petter, Henry. *The Early American Novel*. Columbus: Ohio State University Press, 1971.

Pizer, Donald. *Hamlin Garland's Early Work and Career*. New York: Russell and Russell, 1969.

———. *The Novels of Frank Norris*. Bloomington: Indiana University Press, 1966.

———. *Realism and Naturalism in Nineteenth-Century American Literature*. Carbondale: Southern Illinois University Press, 1966.

Poe, Edgar Allan. *The Complete Poems and Stories with Selections from His Critical Writings*. Vol. 2. New York: Alfred A. Knopf, 1951.

———. *The Literati*. New York: Justin Starr Redfield, 1850.

Porter, Carolyn. "Reification and American Literature." In Bercovitch and Jehlen, *Ideology and Classic American Literature*, pp. 188–217.

Porter, David. *Emerson and Literary Change*. Cambridge: Harvard University Press, 1978.

Porter, Glenn. *The Rise of Big Business, 1860–1910*. Arlington Heights, Ill.: AHM Publishing, 1973.

Porter, Noah. *Books and Reading, or What Books Shall I Read and How Shall I Read Them?* New York: Charles Scribner's Sons, 1871.

Potter, David. *People of Plenty*. Chicago: University of Chicago Press, 1954.

Powers, Lyall. *Henry James and the Naturalist Movement*. East Lansing: Michigan State University Press, 1971.

Putnam, George Haven, and John Bishop Putnam. *Authors and Publishers: A Manual of Suggestions for Beginners in Literature*. New York: G. P. Putnam's Sons, 1897.

Rabinowitz, Peter. "Assertion and Assumption: Fictional Patterns and the External World." *Publications of the Modern Language Association* 96 (1981): 408–19.

Radway, Janice. *Reading the Romance: Woman, Patriarchy, and Popular Literature*. Chapel Hill: University of North Carolina Press, 1984.

Raleigh, John Henry. *Matthew Arnold and American Culture*. Berkeley and Los Angeles: University of California Press, 1957.

Rathburn, John W., and Harry N. Clark. *American Literary Criticism, 1860–1905*. Boston: Twayne, 1979.

Ray, Isaac. *Mental Hygiene*. Boston: Ticknor and Fields, 1862.

Read, Opie. *I Remember*. New York: Richard R. Smith, 1930.

Reynolds, Paul Revere, Jr. *The Middle Man: The Adventures of a Literary Agent*. New York: William Morrow, 1972.

Reynolds, Quentin. *The Fiction Factory*. New York: Grosset and Dunlap, 1955.

Rideout, Walter. *The Radical Novel in the United States, 1900–1954*. New York: Hill and Wang, 1966.

Ridgely, J. F. *William Gilmore Simms*. New Haven: Twayne, 1962.

Rodgers, Daniel T. *The Work Ethic in Industrial America, 1865–1920*. Chicago: University of Chicago Press, 1978.

Roe, E. P. "The Element of Life in Fiction." *The Forum* 5 (April 1888): 229–35.

_____. " 'A Native Author Called Roe.' " *Lippincott's* 42 (October 1888): 479–97.

Roe, Mary. *E. P. Roe: Reminiscences of His Life*. New York: Dodd and Mead, 1889. Reprinted as vol. 18 of *Works of E. P. Roe*. New York: P. F. Collier, 1902.

Ross, Dorothy. "The Development of the Social Sciences." In *The Organization of Knowledge in Modern America, 1860–1920*, edited by Alexandra Oleson and John Voss, pp. 79–138. Baltimore: The Johns Hopkins University Press, 1979.

Ruland, Richard, ed. *The Native Muse: Theories of American Literature from Bradford to Whitman*. New York: E. P. Dutton, 1976.

_____. *A Storied Land: Theories of American Literature from Whitman to Wilson*. New York: E. P. Dutton, 1976.

Schudson, Michael. *Advertising, the Uneasy Persuasion: Its Dubious Impact on American Society*. New York: Basic Books, 1986.

_____. *Discovering the News: A Social History of American Newspapers*. New York: Basic Books, 1978.

Schulte-Sasse, Jochen. "Toward a 'Culture' for the Masses: The Socio-Psychological Function of Popular Literature in Germany and the U.S, 1880–1920." *New German Critique* 29 (Spring–Summer 1983): 85–105.

Scott, Eleanor. "Early Literary Clubs in New York City." *American Literature* 5 (1936): 3–16.

Sears, Lorenzo. *American Literature in Its Colonial and National Periods*. Boston: Little, Brown, 1902.

Seligman, Edwin R. A. *The Economic Interpretation of History*. New York: Columbia University Press, 1907.

Seltzer, Mark. "The Naturalist Machine." In *Sex, Politics, and Science in the Nineteenth-Century Novel: Selected Papers from the English Institute, 1983– 1984*, edited by Ruth Yeazell, pp. 116–47. Baltimore: The Johns Hopkins University Press, 1985.

————. *"The Princess Casamassima*: Realism and the Fantasy of Surveillance." In Sundquist, *American Realism: New Essays*, pp. 95–118.

Seymour-Smith, Martin, ed. *Novels and Novelists*. New York: St. Martin's Press, 1980.

Sheehan, Donald. *This Was Publishing: The Book Trade in the Gilded Age*. Bloomington: Indiana University Press, 1952.

Sherman, Stuart P. *Points of View*. New York: Charles Scribner's Sons, 1924.

Shove, Raymond. *Cheap Book Production in the United States, 1870–1891*. Urbana: University of Illinois Press, 1937.

Silverman, Kenneth. *A Cultural History of the American Revolution*. New York: Thomas Y. Crowell, 1976.

Simpson, Lewis. *The Man of Letters in New England and the South*. Baton Rouge: Louisiana State University Press, 1973.

Smith, Adam. *The Wealth of Nations*. New York: Vintage, 1978.

Smith, Henry Nash. *Democracy and the Novel: Popular Resistance to Classic American Writers*. New York: Oxford University Press, 1979.

————. *Mark Twain*. Cambridge: Harvard University Press, 1962.

————. *Virgin Land*. Cambridge: Harvard University Press, 1950.

————, and William Gibson, eds. *The Mark Twain–William Dean Howells Correspondence*. Cambridge: Harvard University Press, Belknap Press, 1960.

Smith, Herbert F. *Richard Watson Gilder*. New York: Twayne, 1970.

Social Register. New York: Social Register Association, 1890.

Soltow, Lee, and Edward Stevens. *The Rise of Literacy and the Common School in the United States: A Socioeconomic Analysis to 1870*. Chicago: University of Chicago Press, 1981.

Speed, John Gilmer. "Confessions of a Literary Hack." *The Forum* 20 (July 1895): 629–40.

Spiller, Robert, et al., eds. *The Literary History of the United States*. 3d ed. New York: Macmillan, 1963.

Sproat, John G. *"The Best Men": Liberal Reformers in the Gilded Age*. 2d ed. Chicago: University of Chicago Press, 1982.

Stallman, R. W. *Stephen Crane*. New York: George Braziller, 1968.

"The Star System in Literature." *The Dial* 28 (16 May 1900): 389–91.

Steevens, G. W. *The Land of the Dollar*. New York: Dodd, Mead, 1898.

Stepto, Robert. *From behind the Veil: A Study of Afro-American Narrative*. Urbana: University of Illinois Press, 1979.

Stern, Madeline. *Books and Book People in Nineteenth Century America*. New York: R. R. Bowker, 1978.

Stoddard, Richard Henry. *Poets' Homes*. Boston: D. Lothrop, 1877.

————. *Recollections: Personal and Literary*. New York: A. S. Barnes, 1903.

Stowe, William W. *Balzac, James, and the Realistic Novel*. Princeton: Princeton University Press, 1983.

Sundquist, Eric. "In the Country of the Blue." In Sundquist, *American Literary Realism: New Essays*, pp. 3–16.

_____. "Realism and Regionalism." In Elliott et al., *The Columbia Literary History*, pp. 499–523.

_____, ed. *American Literary Realism: New Essays*. Baltimore: Johns Hopkins University Press, 1983.

Swanberg, W. A. *Theodore Dreiser*. New York: Charles Scribner's Sons, 1965.

Sweezy, Paul. *The Theory of Capitalist Development*. New York: Monthly Review Press, 1970.

Taylor, Gordon. *The Passages of Thought: Psychological Representation in the American Novel, 1870–1900*. New York: Oxford University Press, 1969.

Taylor, Walter Fuller. *The Story of American Letters*. Chicago: Henry Regnery, 1956.

Tebbel, John. *A History of Book Publishing in the United States*. Vols. 2–3. New York: R. R. Bowker, 1970, 1974.

Thayer, W. R. "The New Storytellers and the Doom of Realism." *The Forum* 18 (December 1894): 470–80.

Therborn, Goran. *Science, Class, and Society: On the Formation of Sociology and Historical Materialism*. London: Verso, 1976.

Thompson, Daniel Greenleaf. *The Philosophy of Fiction*. London: Longmans, 1890.

Thompson, Maurice. "The Analysts Analyzed." *The Critic* 9 (10 July 1886): 19.

_____. "Materialism and Criticism." *America* 3 (7 November 1889): 183–84.

Ticknor, Caroline. *Glimpses of Authors*. Boston: Houghton Mifflin, 1922.

Tocqueville, Alexis de. *Democracy in America*. 2 vols. New York: Alfred A. Knopf, 1945.

Tompkins, Jane. "The Reader in History." In *Reader-Response Criticism*, edited by Jane Tompkins, pp. 211–32. Baltimore: The Johns Hopkins University Press, 1981.

_____. *Sensational Designs: The Cultural Work of American Fiction, 1790–1860*. New York: Oxford University Press, 1985.

Tomsich, John. *A Genteel Endeavor: American Culture and Politics in the Gilded Age*. Stanford: Stanford University Press, 1971.

Tooker, Lewis Frank. *The Joys and Tribulations of an Editor*. New York: The Century Co., 1923.

Trachtenberg, Alan. *The Incorporation of America*. New York: Hill and Wang, 1982.

Trent, William. *The Cambridge History of American Literature*. Vol. 4. New York: Cambridge University Press, 1923.

_____. *A History of American Literature, 1607–1865*. New York: D. Appleton and Company, 1903.

Triggs, Oscar L. "A Century Of American Poetry." *The Forum* 30 (January 1901): 623–42.

Trilling, Lionel. *The Liberal Imagination: Essays on Literature and Society*. New York: Viking Press, 1950.

_____. "William Dean Howells and the Roots of Modern Taste." In *The Opposing Self*, pp. 67–91. New York: Harcourt Brace Jovanovich, 1979.

Tuchman, Gaye, and Nina Fortin. "Edging Women Out: Some Suggestions about the Structure of Opportunities and the Victorian Novel." *Signs: The Journal of Women in Culture and Society* 6 (Winter 1980): 308–25.

Turner, Arlin. *George W. Cable*. Baton Rouge: Louisiana State University Press, 1966.

Twain, Mark. *Adventures of Huckleberry Finn*. 1885. Reprinted. New York: W. W. Norton, 1962.

————. "Fenimore Cooper's Literary Offenses." *North American Review* 161 (July 1895): 1–12.

————. *Pudd'nhead Wilson*. 1894. Reprinted. New York: Penguin Books, 1981.

Underwood, John Curtis. *Literature and Insurgency; Ten Studies in Racial Revolution*. New York: Mitchell Kennerly, 1904.

Vanderbilt, Kermit. *The Achievement of William Dean Howells*. Princeton: Princeton University Press, 1968.

Veblen, Thorstein. *The Theory of the Leisure Class*. 1899. Reprinted. New York: Viking Press, 1953.

Verplanck, Guilian C. *Discourses and Addresses on Subjects of American History, Arts, and Literature*. New York: J and J. Harper, 1833.

Vidal, Gore. " 'The Peculiar American Stamp,' " *New York Review of Books* 30 (27 October 1983): 45–55.

Walcutt, Charles Child. *American Literary Naturalism: A Divided Stream*. Minneapolis: University of Minnesota Press, 1956.

Walker, Franklin. *Frank Norris*. Garden City, N.Y.: Doubleday, 1932.

Walsh, William S. *Authors and Authorship*. New York: G. P. Putnam's Sons, 1882.

————. "Some Words about E. P. Roe." *Lippincott's* 42 (October 1888): 497–500.

Warhol, Robyn. "Toward a Theory of the Engaging Narrator: Earnest Interventions in Gaskell, Stowe, and Eliot." *Publications of the Modern Language Association* 101 (October 1986): 811–18.

Warner, Sam Bass. *Streetcar Suburbs: The Process of Growth in Boston, 1870–1900*. 1962. Reprinted. New York: Atheneum, 1976.

Watson, Elmo. *A History of Newspaper Syndicates in the United States*. Urbana: University of Illinois Press, 1936.

Watt, Ian. *The Rise of the Novel*. Berkeley and Los Angeles: University of California Press, 1959.

Webster, Noah. *A Collection of Essays and Fugitive Writings on Moral, Historical, Political, and Literary Subjects*. Boston: The author, 1790.

Weinstein, James. *The Corporate Ideal in the Liberal State, 1900–1918*. Boston: Beacon Press, 1968.

Weisberg, Gabriel P., ed. *The European Realist Tradition*. Bloomington: Indiana University Press, 1982.

Weisberger, Bernard. *The New Industrial Society*. New York: John Wiley and Sons, 1969.

Welter, Rush. "On Studying the National Mind." In Higham and Conkin, *New Directions in American Intellectual History*, pp. 64–82.

Wendell, Barrett. *A Literary History of America*. New York: Charles Scribner's Sons, 1900.

Wheeler, Otis B. *The Literary Career of Maurice Thompson*. Baton Rouge: Louisiana State University Press, 1965.

Whipple, Edwin. "Novels and Novelists." In *Literature and Life*, pp. 42–83. Reissue of 1849 Ticknor and Fields edition. Boston: James R. Osgood and Company, 1871.

White, Morton. *Social Thought in America: The Revolt against Formalism*. Boston: Beacon Press, 1957.

———, and Lucia White. *The Intellectual versus the City: From Thomas Jefferson to Frank Lloyd Wright*. 2d ed. New York: Oxford University Press, 1977.

Wiebe, Robert. *The Search for Order, 1877–1920*. New York: Hill and Wang, 1967.

Williams, Ioan. *The Idea of the Novel in Europe, 1600–1800*. London. Macmillan, 1979.

Williams, Raymond. *Culture and Society, 1780–1950*. New York: Oxford University Press, 1958.

———. *Keywords*. New York: Oxford University Press, 1976.

———. *Marxism and Literature*. New York and London: Oxford University Press, 1976.

———. *Problems in Materialism and Culture*. London: Verso, 1980.

———. *Writing in Society*. London: Verso, 1983.

Wilson, Christopher. *The Labor of Words: Literary Professionalism in the Progressive Era*. Athens: University of Georgia Press, 1985.

———. "Literary Apprenticeship and the Progressive Marketplace, 1885–1915." Ph.D. dissertation, Yale University, 1979.

———. "The Rhetoric of Consumption: Mass-Market Magazines and the Demise of the Gentle Reader, 1880–1920." In Fox and Lears, *The Culture of Consumption*, pp. 39–64.

Wilson, Edmund. *Patriotic Gore: Studies in the Literature of the American Civil War*. New York: Farrar, Straus and Giroux, 1962.

———. *The Shock of Recognition: Literature in the United States Recorded by the Men Who Made It*. New York: Farrar, Straus, 1955.

Wilson, Harold. *McClure's Magazine and the Muckrakers*. Princeton: Princeton University Press, 1970.

Wilson, Louis R. *The Geography of Reading: A Study of the Distribution and Status of Libraries in the United States*. Chicago: University of Chicago Press, 1938.

Wilson, Woodrow. *Mere Literature*. Boston: Houghton Mifflin, 1923.

Winegarten, Reneé. *Writers and Revolution: The Fatal Lure of Action*. New York: New Viewpoints, 1974.

Winslip, A. "The Literary Focus." *The Writer* 3 (January 1888): 8–9.

Wolfe, Theodore. *Literary Haunts and Homes*. Philadelphia: J. B. Lippincott, 1901.

Wood, Gordon, ed. *The Rising Glory of America: 1760–1820*. New York: George Braziller, 1971.

Wright, Erik Olin. *Class, Crisis, and the State*. London: Verso, 1978.

Wright, Thomas Goddard. *Literary Culture in Early New England, 1620–1730*. New York: Russell and Russell, 1966.

Wurzbach, Natascha, ed. *The Novel in Letters: Epistolary Fiction in the Early Novel*. London: Routledge and Kegan Paul, 1969.

Yard, Robert Stirling. *The Publisher*. Boston: Houghton Mifflin, 1913.

Ziff, Larzer. *The American 1890s: Life and Times of a Lost Generation*. New York: Viking Press, 1966.

_____. *Literary Democracy: The Declaration of Cultural Independence in America*. New York: Viking Press, 1981.

Index